THE POLITICAL ECONOMY OF POLAND'S TRANSITION

NEW FIRMS AND REFORM GOVERNMENTS

In the time span of a two-term U.S. presidency, Poland changed from being an authoritarian one-party state with a faltering centrally planned economy to become a relatively stable multiparty democracy with a market economy with one of the highest GDP growth rates in Europe. A central feature of these economic and political reforms is a high entry rate for new, domestically owned firms. Using detailed economic and political data, this book examines how these new firms contributed to the Polish transition. The authors test propositions about why some regions have more new firms than others and how the success of these new firms contributed to political constituencies that supported economically liberal parties. The book concludes by contrasting the Polish transition with the experiences of other transitional countries.

John E. Jackson is the M. Kent Jennings Collegiate Professor in Political Science at the University of Michigan, Ann Arbor, where he has been teaching since 1980. He is the recipient of a Guggenheim Fellowship and two J. W. Fulbright Research Fellowships and received his Ph.D. from Harvard University. He is the author of *Constituencies and Leaders in Congress: Their Effects on Senate Voting Behavior* (1974), coauthor of *Statistical Methods for Social Scientists* (1977), and editor of *Institutions in American Society* (1989).

Jacek Klich is Assistant Professor at the Institute of Economics and Management, Jagiellonian University. He received a Ph.D. in Political Science from Jagiellonian University and a Ph.D. in Economics from Krakow University of Economics. He is the recipient of the Alexander Hamilton Fellowship and the ROTARY International Scholarship. He is coeditor of *Managing Health Services in Poland* (2000) and *Privatisation and Restructurisation in East-Central Europe* (1993).

Krystyna Poznańska is Associate Professor at the Warsaw School of Economics. She received her Ph.D.s in Economics and Habilitation from the Warsaw School of Economics. She is the author of *Research and Development Sphere of Enterprises* (2001) and *Source of Competitive Advantage of Enterprises* (2002).

POLITICAL ECONOMY OF INSTITUTIONS AND DECISIONS

Series Editors

Randall Calvert, Washington University, St. Louis
Thráinn Eggertsson, University of Iceland and New York University

Founding Editors

James E. Alt, Harvard University
Douglass C. North, Washington University, St. Louis

Other books in the series

Continued on page following the index

Publication of this book has been supported by the generosity of the William Davidson Institute at the University of Michigan Business School.

THE POLITICAL ECONOMY
OF POLAND'S TRANSITION

New Firms and Reform Governments

JOHN E. JACKSON
University of Michigan, Ann Arbor

JACEK KLICH
Jagiellonian University

KRYSTYNA POZNAŃSKA
Warsaw School of Economics

CAMBRIDGE
UNIVERSITY PRESS

CAMBRIDGE UNIVERSITY PRESS
Cambridge, New York, Melbourne, Madrid, Cape Town, Singapore, São Paulo

Cambridge University Press
40 West 20th Street, New York, NY 10011-4211, USA

www.cambridge.org
Information on this title: www.cambridge.org/9780521838955

First published 2005

Printed in the United States of America

A catalog record for this publication is available from the British Library.

Library of Congress Cataloging in Publication data
Jackson, John Edgar.
The political economy of Poland's transition : new firms and reform governments /
John E. Jackson, Jacek Klich, Krystyna Poznańska.
p.   cm. – (Political economy of institutions and decisions)
Includes bibliographical references and index.
ISBN 0-521-83895-9
1. Poland – Economic conditions – 1990–   2. Poland – Economic policy – 1990–
3. Poland – Politics and government – 1989–   I. Klich, Jacek, 1958–
II. Poznańska, Krystyna, 1954–   III. Title.   IV. Series.
HC340.3.J336 2005
330.9438′057 – dc22   2004058497

ISBN-13   978-0-521-83895-5 hardback
ISBN-10   0-521-83895-9 hardback

Contents

Contents

Tables

Tables

Tables

Figures

Acknowledgments

We want to thank a number of organizations that supported the research and writing in this book. Preparation of the data on new-firm creation and growth was supported financially by a grant from the Charles Stewart Mott Foundation and by funds from the Office of the Vice-President for Research and the Faculty Research Fund of the Rackham School of Graduate Studies at the University of Michigan. The cooperation of the Research Centre for Economic and Statistical Studies, the Polish Central Statistical Office and specifically of Josef Chmiel, the vice-director, was critical in developing the unique longitudinal data that form the basis for the research. The Institute for Social Studies at Warsaw University was very generous in making the data from the Polish General Social Survey available. John Jackson was supported by several organizations during the completion of this project. He received research grants from the Polish–U.S. Fulbright Program in 1993 and in 2003–4 that enabled us to begin and complete the project. Over the course of the project he was a Visiting Professor at the Wallis Center for Political Economy at the University of Rochester in 1994 and 2000; a Fellow at the Center for Advanced Study in the Behavioral Sciences, Palo Alto, California, in 2000–1; and a Visiting Scholar at the William Davidson Institute at the University of Michigan in 2003–4. He also received support from the Faculty Enrichment Fund of the College of Literature, Science and the Arts at the University of Michigan. We gratefully acknowledge the support of these organizations and add the usual disclaimer that the views and conclusions in the book are the authors' and do not reflect the positions of any of these organizations.

Abbreviations

AWS	Akcja Wyborcza Solidarność (Solidarity Electoral Action)
AWSP	Akcja Wyborcza Solidarność-Prawicy (Solidarity Electoral Action of the Right)
BBWR	Bezpartyjny Blok Wspierania Reform (Nonpartisan Bloc for Reform)
EBRD	European Bank for Reconstruction and Development
EU	European Union
GDR	German Democratic Republic
GUS	Główny Urząd Statystyczny (Central Statistical Office)
IMF	International Monetary Fund
KLD	Kongres Liberalno-Demokratyczny (Liberal-Democratic Congress)
KOR	Komitet Obrony Robotników (Worker Defense Committee)
KPN	Konfederacja Polski Niepodległej (Confederation for an Independent Poland)
LPR	Liga Polskich Rodzin (Polish Families League)
MSzP	Magyar Szocialista Párt (Hungary Socialist Party)
OECD	Organization for Economic Cooperation and Development
OPZZ	Ogólnopolskie Porozumienie Związków Zawodowych (All Polish Alliance of Trade Unions)
PC	Porozumienie Centrum (Center Alliance)
PGSS	Polskie Generalne Sondaże Społeczne (Polish General Social Surveys)
PiS	Prawo i Sprawiedliwość (Law and Justice)
PO	Platforma Obywatelska (Civic Platform)
PSL	Polskie Stronnictwo Ludowe (Polish Peasants' Party)
PZPR	Polska Zjednoczona Partia Robotnicza (Polish United Workers Party)

Abbreviations

ROP   Ruch Odbudowy Polski (Movement for the Reconstruction of Poland)

SLD   Sojusz Lewicy Demokratycznej (Democratic Left Alliance)

SLD/UP   Sojusz Lewicy Demokratycznej/Unia Pracy (Democratic Left Alliance/Labor Union)

SOE   state-owned enterprise

SRP   Samoobrona Rzeczypospolitej Polskiej (Self-Defense of the Polish Republic)

UD   Unia Demokratyczna (Democratic Union)

UP   Unia Pracy (Labor Union)

UW   Unia Wolności (Freedom Union)

ZChN   Zjednoczenie Chrzescijańsko-Narodowe (Christian National Alliance)

I

Why Poland?

By most observers' reckoning, Poland during the 1990s was the poster child for a successful transition from a country with a one-party Communist authoritarian government and a centrally planned command economy to one with a relatively stable multiparty democracy with a thriving market economy. In the same time span that the United States measures a two-term presidency, Poland went from a period in which the main economic issue was no longer a shortage of goods but rather a proper distribution of access to the abundance of goods in the stores. The questions about whether a private market could take root and survive had been replaced by concerns that the growth of this private market may have outpaced the public sector's ability to provide the social services deemed to be necessary in a capitalistic society. Muted objections to a one-party state and the minimal likelihood of an alternative developed into open debates about whether there are too many parties. In the bigger picture, these concerns, as real as they are, provide an accurate barometer of the distance Polish economic, political, and social institutions have come since the 1980s. We document these changes in detail, analyze how they have contributed to the Polish success, and make some inferences about what elements contribute to successful and simultaneous economic and political transitions. This chapter places the Polish transition in the context of transitions in a set of Central and Eastern European countries, including the Czech Republic, Hungary, the Baltic states, Russia, and Ukraine.

POLAND'S EXPERIENCE IN A COMPARATIVE CONTEXT

A number of economic and social indicators can be used to assess the direction and speed of transitions, such as GDP, unemployment, personal income, life expectancy, mortality rates, and trust in social and political

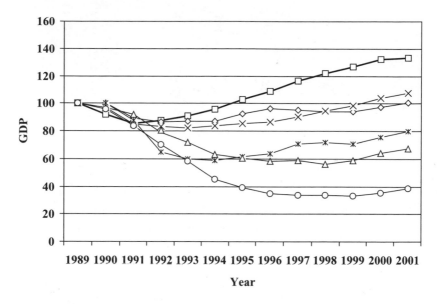

−□− Poland −◇− Czech Rep −✕− Hungary −✳− Estonia −△− Russia −○− Ukraine

Figure 1.1. Real GDP (1989 = 100)

organizations. We present comparative data on GDP, life expectancy, and political confidence in this chapter and present extensive analyses of unemployment and income in Poland in later chapters. Real GDP, a frequently cited indicator, is shown in Figure 1.1 for a number of transition countries, standardized so that 1989 = 100. These data show that Poland had one of the fastest-growing economies in Europe during the 1990s. Despite a recent slowdown, annual real GDP growth averaged more than 4 percent since 1991 and about 6.5 percent since 1994. Per capita income rose about 4 percent annually between 1994 to 1999.

Poland's economy offers an important contrast with some of the other transitional countries. Polish GDP declined more in the early years of the transition than in the other countries, but its recovery was greater and faster. Economic problems in Russia and Ukrainie are well known, although the Russian economy has rebounded since the 1998 crisis, helped considerably by the rise in oil prices. The surprising case may be the Czech Republic. It was offered as the model in the early period, particularly with its successful mass privatization program and low unemployment. As can be seen in Figure 1.1, Czech GDP did not fall as quickly or as much as in Poland and Hungary, but since 1992–93 GDP has been relatively flat. Hungary's GDP growth surpassed that of the Czech

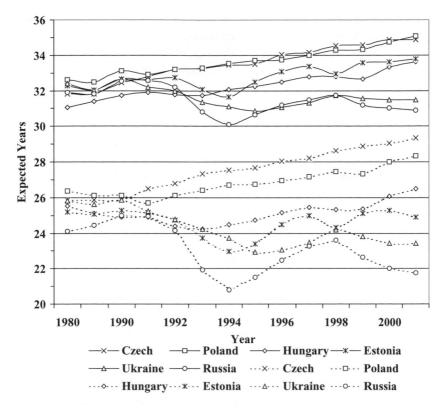

Figure 1.2. Life Expectancy at Age Forty-five for Males (*dotted line*) and Females (*solid line*)

Republic and since 1996 has exhibited a more promising trajectory. These differences in economic performance may be related to differences in the transition strategies in each country.

The indicators of Polish success go beyond the economic, however. A second frequently used set of measures relates to the public health and vital statistics, such as life expectancy among certain age and gender groups, and how they change over time. The decline in life expectancy, particularly among working-age males, in areas such as Russia and some of the states of the former Soviet Union is often cited as an indicator of the stress and social costs brought on by the efforts at economic transformation. Figure 1.2 depicts the life expectancy at age forty-five for males and females for the period 1980 to 2001. This age group, particularly for males, is thought to be the hardest hit by the economic transition. Life expectancy in Poland declined during the 1980s, a period that began with an economic crisis and martial law and is associated with serious economic decline and the continuing struggle to end the Communist government. Life expectancy continued to decline until 1991, when it began an improvement that continued through the rest of the decade. These movements closely correspond to the changes in the economy. What is particularly striking is that the life expectancy for males declined more than for females during the period 1980 to 1990 and then recovered more after 1990.

Life expectancy in the Czech Republic rose the most throughout the transition period, also following a slight decline during the 1980s. The other countries all experienced a significant decline in male life expectancy following the start of the transition. Both Hungary and Estonia, however, have had rising life expectancy after 1993 or 1994, roughly the same time their GDP began to increase, as seen in Figure 1.1. Russia and Ukraine, by contrast, have experienced periods of substantially decreased life expectancy, particularly among males. These declines occurred right after the transition began in 1991 and again after the economic collapse in 1998. These declines are far more pronounced for males than females. As occurred in Poland, in the Czech Republic life expectancy among males increased more than among females between 1990 and 2001. In Hungary and Estonia male life expectancy between 1990 and 2001 did not increase as much as female life expectancy due to a much larger decrease during the first several years of the transition. After reaching a minimum level around 1994, the life expectancy of males in these two countries has increased faster than that of females. These comparisons suggest that it is not the transition to a market economy but the inability to make that transition that is associated with decreased life expectancy. Poland and the Czech Republic, which adapted quickly, saw the most rapid and consistent increases in life expectancy, particularly among males. Hungary and Estonia also experienced increases in life expectancy once their economies began recovering.

A third comparison between changes in Polish and other transitional countries comes from the Central and East European Barometer, a survey of mass opinions in transitional countries. One question asked throughout this period is, "On the whole, are you very satisfied, fairly satisfied, not very satisfied, or not at all satisfied with the way democracy is developing in [your country]?" These responses are coded from 0 to 3, with 3 being very satisfied. Figure 1.3 shows the mean satisfaction among those expressing an opinion for selected transitional countries. Also included are responses from the Polish General Social Survey (PGSS) to a question asking people how much confidence they have in the Sejm, the lower house

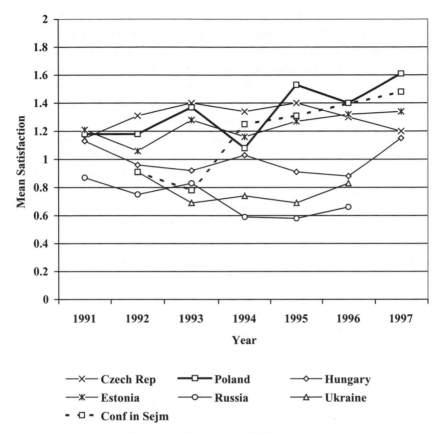

Figure 1.3. Satisfaction with Democracy

in Poland's parliament, coded on a similar 0–3 scale.[1] Overall, despite fluctuations in 1994 and 1995 Poles' satisfaction with democracy increased throughout the 1990s. The data on the Sejm reinforce the observation that Poles are becoming more confident in their political institutions and the emerging democracy during the transition. By 1996 and 1997 Poles expressed more satisfaction with democracy than respondents in the other countries.

Overall, however, respondents are not satisfied with the progress of democracy in their country. Mean satisfaction is consistently about 1,

---

[1] Responses are coded as 3 equals a great deal of confidence, 2 is only some confidence, and 0 is hardly any confidence at all. This is the best match between the PGSS question with three categories of the Euro-Barometer question with four categories. Other coding schemes yielded the same basic plot.

which is not very satisfied, and rises above 1.5 (the midpoint between being satisfied and not satisfied) only for Poland in 1995 and 1997. A comparison of the transition countries shows that levels of satisfaction in the three Central European countries and Estonia are essentially equal in 1991 and generally increased after the mid-1990s except for the Czech Republic, where satisfaction declined in 1996 and 1997. In Hungary and Estonia satisfaction started increasing by the late 1990s after falling during the early stages of the transition. Russia and Ukraine stand in marked contrast to the other four countries. Satisfaction in these two countries was significantly lower and declined over time, although it increased in both places in 1996.[2] On this indicator, Poland again looks like a successful transitional country, although events after 1997 and particularly in 2002–3, as well as recent opinion polls, suggest that Poland's confidence in democracy has declined since these data were collected.

Our last indicator of social health and achievement is the stability and behavior of the governmental system through several different elections. This behavior at the elite level provides insight into the institutional development in Poland and the other transitional countries. Individual government administrations have come and gone, and come back again, but the way this has been done is, to us, a sign of success. Poland experienced repeated major changes in governmental control. In 1991 the reformers first gained a tenuous majority of the seats in the parliament.[3] In 1993 the former Communists won a substantial plurality of the votes and an overwhelming majority of the parliamentary seats. In 1997 a coalition of post-Solidarity parties won a plurality of the votes and seats. Most recently, in 2001, the primary post–Communist Party, the SLD, won nearly a majority of the parliamentary seats. In all four instances the transition from one governing party coalition to the next was far more characteristic of a mature parliamentary system than a country experiencing democratic regime change for the first time in more than half a century. Through different coalition governments each side has moved into and out of control, with an accompanying change in policies but with no threat to the rules of the system and with appropriate respect for the role of the opposition. The whole apparatus seems to have the characteristics of a stable multiparty

---

2 Russia and Ukraine were dropped from the Central and Eastern Euro-Barometer after 1996.

3 The reformers won a majority of the votes in the 1989 elections, but because of the rules in place for that election, they did not have a majority of the seats in the Sejm, the Polish parliament.

Table 1.1. *Vote Divisions for Reform and Opposition Parties (%)*

Country/Year	Reform Parties	Opposition Parties
Poland		
1991	42.3	20.7
1993	31.3	35.8
1997	47.2	39.4
2001	30.9	50.0
Hungary		
1990	55.1	10.9
1994	18.8	52.7
1998	44.9	42.4
2002: 1st round	41.1	42.1
2002: 2nd round	50.0	45.8
Czech Republic		
1990	53.2	13.5
1992	46.5	27.1
1996	44.1	41.6
2002	24.5	48.7
Russian Duma		
1993	58.5	12.4
1995	28.2	22.3
1999	47.3	24.3

parliamentary system in which governments can lose votes of confidence and subsequently lose power but where the basic responsibilities of governing continue.[4]

This pattern had been replicated in many of the transitional countries, with reform governments being replaced by coalitions headed by parties organized by Socialists or former Communist Party officials, often to be replaced by a continuing cycle of reformers or post-Communists. Table 1.1 shows the broad vote divisions between the different countries' reform and opposition parties in elections held during the 1990s and early 2000s.[5]

4 We want to make clear that we are referring to the transitions from one government to another in Poland, not to the stability of the individual parties and their leadership. Other than the post-Communist parties, party structures and leadership have been quite unstable, with a succession of parties and coalitions, particularly on the right.
5 Very broad categorizations are used in defining reform and opposition parties for this discussion. In many instances, the so-called reform parties have quite different views about economic policy, but they have the common orientation to having opposed the previous Communist regimes, hence the title reform. The opposition parties are so defined because they have their origins in the party organizations of the previous regimes.

Hungary's experiences, for example, closely parallel Poland's. The first reform government, the Hungarian Democratic Forum, was replaced by the Hungarian Socialist Party (MSzP) in 1994, which was replaced by an alliance of reformers, the Fidesz, in 1998 which was itself replaced by the Socialists in 2002. As in Poland, despite the recycling of parties, the economic plans remained quite liberal in content and consequences. And, as seen in Figure 1.1, Hungary's economy has performed very well since the mid-1990s.

The Czech Republic followed a different path, but one that led to a similar result. The reform parties easily won the election in 1990 and again in 1992. But, as the economic growth declined, as seen in Figure 1.1, the Socialists won a substantial share of the votes in 1996 and joined the government at that point. An important contrast between the Czech Republic and Poland and Hungary is that here the former Communists remained committed to their previous ideology and did not attempt to become a more centrist party as did the SLD in Poland and the MSzP in Hungary. Nor has the Czech Communist Party had the electoral success of the latter two parties. These patterns in the Central European countries contrast sharply with those in the former Soviet republics. There, the former Communists have remained committed to the communist ideologies and have campaigned actively to replace the reforms with a more traditional set of social, economic, and political policies. Zimmerman (2002) has analyzed the presidential votes in Russia as a contest between these two quite different views of the direction Russia should take.

The patterns in the three Central European countries all reflect well-entrenched and stable democracies, if measured by the ability of the contending parties to manage easily the transfer of authority from one government coalition to the next, and back again. In these three countries the basic direction of the transitional economic policies, even though a major issue in the campaigns, has remained fairly consistent and the commitments to basic democratic principles has been very clear and strong. In the former Soviet states this has not been uniformly true. Actions to promote strong market economies have been weak in many countries, such as Ukraine and Belarus, and many continue to subject the media to continued state control.

POLITICAL AND ECONOMIC REFORM

The overwhelming evidence is that Poland, Hungary, the Czech Republic, and the Baltic states, among others, are succeeding in making the transition simultaneously to a market economy and to an open democratic political structure. Early writers and advisers feared that such simultaneous transitions were unlikely. The basic reasoning is that because economic reforms impose very high costs on existing, politically powerful sectors, such groups will oppose and possibly interfere with the reforms even in stable systems. This process is more fragile if the country is simultaneously trying to create and consolidate legitimate democratic institutions. The democratic dilemma is that the more open the political process, a major aim of democratic reforms, the more susceptible the process is to the claims and demands of those organized sectors that stand to lose economically and possibly politically as a result of the economic reforms. (Elster, 1993, argues that these goals are incompatible, but also see Chan, 1995; Nelson, 1993; and Sachs, 1992.) This pessimistic picture has led some writers to suggest that for economic reforms to be successful there must be either a relatively authoritarian political system or political leaders who occupy offices with a substantial degree of autonomy, such as that found in many central banks (see citations in Hellman, 1998, n. 2). One prescription is to delay political reforms while the economy is being reformed and then democratize, as was done in parts of Asia. Transitional countries, then, are left with the unattractive choice of foregoing or delaying either economic or democratic reforms.

Hellman offers a different but still pessimistic picture of the political economy of transitions. He agrees there are cases where those bearing the costs of the transition have not mobilized to elect parties that will reverse the reforms. But he points to cases where those advantaged in the short run by the reforms mobilize to block or at least slow down a continuation of the reform process. These partial reforms are no more successful at stimulating long-term economic growth and a democratic political system than a policy of very slow or no reforms. According to his argument, the initial stages of the economic transition usually involve the privatization of state-owned enterprises. Given the slowness with which the entire economy can adapt to the transition, these partial reforms create significant rents for the owners of the newly privatized enterprises, who enjoy the monopoly position of the former state enterprises but are not forced to share their rents with the government. In theory, these rents should only be short-term as the economy continues its adjustment and as additional domestic or foreign firms enter and reduce those rents. Hellman's argument is that these short-term winners, most of whom are former managers in the old state enterprises, can use their rents and political access to restrict or even to halt the reforms, thus maintaining both their control and their rents (Hellman, 1998, pp. 221–22, and Sachs and Pistor, 1997). This group of winners does not want to reverse the reform process, as the previous model predicts for the unemployed or others suffering from the initial changes do, but it wants to arrest its progress to maintain what they have gained from the partial reform.

As compelling as these two arguments are, examples where both reforms are succeeding suggest that the logic behind these arguments is too narrow. Obviously, there are forces at work in this process that support the reforms and that, at a minimum, are able to oppose those who wish to stop and even undo the reforms. The core of our analysis is that the creation of new economic entities, not just the restructuring of existing enterprises, is the key to successful economic and political transformations. (On this point, see Kornai, 1990, and Murrell, 1992.) If the reforms are successful, much of the growth in income will come from these previously nonexistent firms, the workers they employ, and their impact on the economies where they are located. This de novo firm creation adds to the constituency for continued reform, counterbalancing opposing forces. In addition to its size, the ability of this constituency to continue the pressure for reforms is then a function of the political institutions that determine the influence of constituencies of different sizes and geographic locations.

Creative Destruction in Poland and East-Central Europe

A brief description of the economic transformation in Poland shows that the creation of new enterprises is critical to the success of the transition. As was expected, employment decreases in state-owned enterprises at the beginning of the transformation were more dramatic than even the most pro-reform advisers had envisioned. In a very short period of time, these enterprises lost close to 3 million jobs. Furthermore, even the firms that were privatized or restructured in some way, which would have included the strongest of these firms, lost between a third and a half their work force. Large, privately owned firms that existed in the previous economic regime did even worse.[6] Although this group represented only about 800 firms, employment in these enterprises declined by

---

6 We define large as firms employing more than 100 workers in 1990, which does not match the Polish definition for large firms, which since 1997 has been firms employing more than 250 persons. Our data also have a category for firms with more than 500 employees. Firms with 101 to 500 employees declined somewhat more than those with more than 500 employees, 76 percent compared with 68 percent.

about 75 percent, or just over 150,000 jobs. (These numbers and proportions are about evenly divided between domestic and foreign-owned private firms.) These dramatic results suggest that it is not ownership per se that determines fitness for the free market but something intrinsic to the enterprise.

The job losses among the large firms existing in 1990 contrast sharply with the growth of the new private sector. The data available from the Polish Central Statistical Office only count enterprises with more than 5 employees, thus omitting a very sizable portion of new and/or small enterprises and the self-employed. But even with this limitation, we estimate that by 1997 (the last year of available data) there were 90,000 new enterprises (i.e., firms that did not exist in 1990) and that these firms employed 2.3 million workers. Separate data presented by the Polish Foundation for the Development and Promotion of Small and Medium-Sized Enterprises (Dzierżanowski, 1999) obtained from a different source estimate that in 1997 there were 1.5 million active enterprises with 5 or fewer workers, which include the self-employed, that employed 2.3 million people. Combining these two data sources places the estimate of jobs created in new private enterprises at more than 4.5 million, or more than a quarter of the total work force.

The picture, then, is far more a replacement of the old economy by a new one than a transformation of the old one. In this sense, one may think of transforming an economy in the macroeconomic sense that the private sector is growing relative to the state sector, but one is much less likely to accomplish this by transforming the existing enterprises than by creating new firms to replace the old ones. As we discuss in subsequent chapters, this process is foreshadowed by the arguments of economic writers such as Josef Schumpeter (1934) and organizational theorists such as Michael Hannan and John Freeman (1977, 1989).

The experiences in some of the other Central European countries undergoing the same transformation contrast with the Polish experience, either by accident or by design, although they all present the same broad picture. Kornai (2000) has proposed two different strategies for transformation. The first, which he used to characterize Poland and Hungary, is a strategy of organic development, where "the main impetus behind the growth of the private sector is mass *de novo* entry" (Kornai, 2000, p. 6). The alternative is labeled a strategy of accelerated privatization, the approach found in the Czech Republic and Russia. We also add the former German Democratic Republic (GDR) to the list of countries following the path of accelerated privatization, although the role of the Federal Republic

Table 1.2. *Privatization in East-Central Europe*

Country	State-Owned Enterprises, 1990			State-Owned Enterprises, 1997		
	Number	% of Jobs	% GDP	Number	% of Jobs	% GDP
Czech Republic[a]	4,900	99	96	200	35	20
Hungary	2,200	85	85	611	29	27
Poland	8,400	60	86	4,080	42	29
Former GDR	8,000			0		

[a] Czechoslovakia in 1990, Czech Republic in 1997.

of Germany and the impact of unification make this a special case. Governments in Russia, the Czech Republic, and the former GDR were more aggressive, and successful, at privatizing the existing state-owned enterprises, following Kornai's second model. Table 1.2 shows the results of the privatization processes, as measured by the number of firms privatized and their shares of employment and GDP in four transitional economies.

The privatization process advanced most rapidly in the GDR and less so in the Czech Republic and Hungary; it lagged the most in Poland. All four countries found it relatively easy to privatize the very small firms, which tended to be concentrated in the trade and service sectors.[7] These privatizations led to a substantial increase in the private sector's share in GDP and employment, especially in the Czech Republic.[8] The privatization of the larger enterprises proved to be more varied among these countries, as each followed different strategies, all requiring considerable changes in legal and managerial structures and administrative regulations.[9] These plans also encountered political opposition of varying depth and effectiveness in each country.

The process in the former GDR, of course, was heavily supported and financed by the German government and enterprises in the former western

---

7 Both Hungary and Poland had already begun the development of private firms in these sectors as part of the efforts during the 1980s to implement versions of market socialism.

8 The size of the private sector before 1990 was the smallest in the former GDR and Czechoslovakia.

9 Post-Communist countries had to develop and then implement whole legal structures for privatization and reprivatization procedures. This in turn meant a considerable workload. For example, the Czechoslovak parliament (until the end of 1992) and then the Czech National Council between 1990 and 1994 approved approximately seventy new privatization acts and decrees (including amendments) (Buchtíková, 1995).

sector. Of the nearly 8,000 state-owned enterprises in the GDR at the beginning of the transition, almost all were fully privatized by 1994. The pattern is similar in the Czech Republic, which was noted for its mass privatization program that distributed shares in the newly privatized firms to the public. Privatization was done in three stages: small enterprises were converted first, in 1991; and large enterprises were privatized later in two steps, a first wave in 1992 and 1993 and a second wave in 1994 and 1995. By the end of 1997, more than 95 percent of state enterprises were privatized. Much of this was accomplished with the cooperation of the managers of these enterprises, who could propose their own restructuring plans.

Poland and, to a lesser extent, Hungary have proceeded more slowly and carefully with privatization. By 1997 only about a half of the firms in Poland and two-thirds of the firms in Hungary had been privatized. In both countries, much of the privatization was done through liquidation, bankruptcy, or outright sales to foreign firms rather than through restructuring the ownership. This form of privatization effectively recycled many of the assets back into the private sector in the form of new firms, although within an organizational structure that differed markedly from their predecessors.

In Poland and Hungary there was more vigorous opposition to the privatizations from managers and workers in the state-owned firms, with the backing of the trade unions. Frydman, Rapaczynski, and Turkewitz (1997) attribute the slow pace of privatization in Hungary relative to the Czech Republic to the increased political influence these groups had as a result of the decentralization during the earlier effort to introduce market socialism and the relative autonomy that had been given to these enterprises. The same argument could apply in Poland, where the unions in particular had acquired considerable independence and political influence during the 1980s. (We discuss Poland's privatization efforts in more detail in the next chapter.)

The important point to note here is that Poland proceeded much more slowly in privatizing the existing state-owned enterprises than did any of the other three countries. As we pointed out, this weakness in privatization was compensated by the development of new private businesses, only some of which resulted from spin-offs from privatized firms. In all the transitional economies for which we have data, the jobs and income created by new firms outstrip the job and income creation of the state-owned and the privatized firms. Although the data are from the early years of the transitions, a study by Frydman et al. (1997) is instructive. In

Table 1.3. *Job Creation and Job Destruction in Transitional Countries (%)*

Country and Time Period	Job Destruction[a]	Gross Job Creation	
		Total[a]	De Novo[b]
Poland: 1990–97	39	48	98
Czech Republic:[c] 1991–96	28	34	97
Estonia:[c] 1989–95	42	33	86
Ukraine:[d] 1991–96	49	5	24
Russia:[d] 1991–96	54	5	35[e]
Michigan, U.S.: 1978–88	51	46	65[f]

[a] As a percentage of initial employment in private and state sectors.
[b] Job creation in de novo firms as a percentage of all job creation.
[c] Jurajda and Terrell, 2001, p. 36
[d] Konings and Walsh, 1999, pp. 10, 11, 13.
[e] Konings and Walsh, 1999, p. 13. Estimated from 1996 data.
[f] Includes job creation in firms with fewer than twenty employees in 1978.

a 1994 survey of 506 mid-sized firms in the Czech Republic, Hungary, and Poland, they compared the job and revenue changes in the state-owned, privatized, and new private firms for the period 1990 to 1993. Eighty-five percent of the new private firms gained employment compared with 43 percent of the privatized and 9 percent of the state-owned firms. Comparisons of revenue change on an annual basis showed the same pattern. The new private firms were much more likely to show an increase in sales than the privatized or state-owned firms. New enterprises were the source of the majority of the jobs created in these transitional economies, as Murrell and Kornai had argued would be the case.

We cannot make as definitive a statement about gross job destruction and creation in the other transitional countries as we have for Poland because we do not have similar data on the total number of jobs created by de novo private firms. For comparison, however, we do have data from employment surveys collected by labor-market specialists for the Czech Republic and Estonia (Jurajda and Terrell, 2001) and from surveys of enterprises in Russia and Ukraine (Konings and Walsh, 1999). Table 1.3 shows the rates of gross job creation and job destruction estimated for available time periods for these four countries and our estimates of these rates for Poland.[10] The job destruction rates varied from about

---

10 Gross job destruction between two time points is defined and measured as the sum of the employment decrease among contracting firms plus the initial employment

30 percent in the Czech Republic to about 55 percent in Russia.[11] These data correspond with the generally accepted view that firms in the Czech Republic underwent the least restructuring, that there were more stringent budget constraints imposed on Polish and Estonian firms, and that firms in Russia and Ukraine were the hardest hit by the transition policies. Data on job destruction and creation in the state of Michigan in the United States are included for further comparison. This state's economy underwent a major restructuring during the 1980s as increased foreign competition forced the large manufacturing firms to become more competitive or to go out of business, which many did. Again, de novo firm creation was the primary basis for the state's economic recovery during the late 1980s and 1990s. (See Jackson, Klich, and Poznańska, 1999, for an explicit comparison of the structures and transitions in the Polish and Michigan economies.) The Schumpeterian process we have been describing in the Eastern and Central European countries is a characteristic of healthy market economies, not a phenomena limited to one time period and region.

Job creation as a proportion of initial employment ranged from 5 percent in Russia and Ukraine to nearly 50 percent in Poland with the Czech Republic and Estonia just over 30 percent. Virtually all the job creation in Poland and the Czech Republic and a large majority of the job creation in Estonia were in de novo firms. By contrast, Russia and Ukraine had very little de novo job creation, which accounts for the low level of overall job creation and undoubtedly accounts for their poor aggregate economic conditions.

The only data we have from the former East Germany are from a longitudinal labor force survey that gives the proportion of respondents in 1995 who report working as entrepreneurs or being self-employed (Diewald and Mach, 1999). Fortunately, they present comparable data from Poland that we have examined for 1993 and 1998 (Jackson and Mach, 2002). We also have similar data from the Czech Republic (Večerník, 1999)

---

of exiting firms. Gross job creation is the mirror image: the sum of the employment increase in all expanding enterprises plus the end-point employment in all enterprises initiated during the time interval.

11 Given the different data used to construct Table 1.3, it is hard to know how to make the denominators in these ratios comparable. We opt to use employment in the sectors undergoing privatization and the entry of new private firms. This corresponds to what Jurajda and Terrell call the old plus new sectors, for Poland it excludes agriculture and public administration and education and for Russia and Ukraine it is the initial employment of the firms in the survey.

Table 1.4. *Entrepreneurs and the Self-Employed (%)*

Year	East Germany	Czech Republic	Poland
1988	2.5		6.9
1995/1993/1993	6.3	9.4	13.1
1997/1998		12.6	19.2

for 1993 and 1997, so from these three sources we can make some comparisons about entrepreneurial behavior. We also show the proportions for 1988 in East Germany and Poland to offer a picture of how things changed in these two countries. These proportions are reported in Table 1.4.

The GDR lags the Czech Republic and Poland in developing entrepreneurs and self-employed individuals. In 1995 in the GDR only 6 percent of the nonfarm respondents reported being so employed. Two years earlier, the figures were 9.4 and 13.1 percent for the Czech Republic and Poland respectively. By 1998 the Czech and Polish proportions are 13 and 19 percent. Poland generates more entrepreneurial activity among its nonfarm population than does the Czech Republic, as seen in Table 1.4, and both do better than the GDR. Germany, unfortunately, does not provide data on job creation or total employment in de novo firms, which would complete the comparisons. The comparisons of the rates of privatization and the proportions of gross job creation in de novo firms in Poland, Estonia, the Czech Republic, the former GDR, Ukraine, and Russia clearly illustrate Kornai's observation about the two different transition strategies. The evidence documents the importance of creative destruction, or replacement, as a key to the Polish success.

Creative destruction is a natural part of any healthy economy. (See Caballero and Hammour, 1994, 2000.) To picture this, think of the economy as a forest rather than as some mechanical entity. A healthy forest requires a continual balance of new, young, and mature trees. Furthermore, it is necessary that there be a regular and constant planting of new trees, some of which will survive and develop into large, mature trees to replace older, decaying ones. In a managed forest, the life of older trees can be extended but only with regular pruning to eliminate deadwood that saps the tree's nutrients. In every case, a healthy forest observed over an extended period of time will not contain the same trees. This health will be dependent upon the rates of birth, survival, growth, and eventual decay. Like life and death in nature, birth, growth, and decline are regular and recurring activities in the economic world. The growth, and even the stability, of an economy will depend on the rate at which new firms come into existence and the rate at which they survive and grow to become mature enterprises. New economies, such as in East-Central Europe, require a rapid and sustained birth process in order to build a market economy. Older, more stable economies, such as in the United States and Western Europe, require a regular process of births and young growth to replenish their economies.[12] This process must, however, be quickened in times of stress that challenge the productivity of the older, mature firms.

The Political Economy of Transitions

The process of replacement as the means for transforming an economy has substantial political and social implications in addition to its economic ones. A static analysis of reform that treats economic and political organizations as given will not foresee the evolution of the new economy and the new political constituencies. When the economic and political reforms are introduced, one very predictable constituency is the people most likely to suffer from the reforms. Inefficient, sheltered enterprises may be subject to new foreign and domestic competition, and government subsidies and transfer payments will probably be reduced. Those interests adversely affected might include organized workers, factory managers, and party members; however, such groups are well organized and likely to have the ability to influence government decisions. By contrast, the constituents for the new economy, as well as the new economy itself, not only may not have existed prior to the beginning of the reforms, but they are virtually impossible to identify and even harder to contemplate organizing.

As the reforms proceed, however, the individuals, organizations, and regions that are successfully adapting and becoming better off economically are an emerging constituency for continuing the reforms. More significantly, this emerging constituency will be associated with the creation of new firms rather than with the transformation and privatization of existing firms and will be most prevalent in areas that can generate higher levels of entrepreneurial activity. This set of economic actors, as well as their political interests, is quite different from the winners that

12 Analyses of the economic changes in the state of Michigan between 1978 and 1988 show exactly this same process. For comparisons of the Polish transition and the changes in Michigan, see Jackson, Klich, and Poznańska, 1999.

Hellman describes. The interests of those associated with de novo firm activity are not tied to the preservation of sheltered oligopolies and government restrictions and regulations, but desire the rapid expansion of their own firms, related markets, and support systems. Thus, reforms that accelerate the movement of all forms of capital from less productive to more competitive uses are in their interests. The rapid reform of financial institutions and the creation of effective credit and equity markets, the development of enforceable property rights, and the ability to buy input goods at competitive prices all further the economic interests of these new enterprises and their owners.[13] Although the owners, management, and workers in the restructured and privatized firms and those founding and working in new firms will likely oppose the reversal of reforms, the participants in this "new" economy will be a constituency for the reforms in place and for their continuation. These two sets are thus likely to support different political agendas and parties.

Poland, because of its success at both economic and political transformations, offers an ideal setting in which to examine these processes, and their interactions, in detail. In the chapters that follow, we first provide a detailed description of the changes and associated events that mark the Polish transformation. Then we present a short model of the evolutionary process that we use to analyze this transformation and a statistical analysis of the regional variations in the transformation of the Polish economy. The statistical results are used to support the conceptual propositions of the model and to estimate quantitatively several of the critical substantive parameters. An important aspect of this regional analysis is to show that the transformation did not proceed evenly across Poland but succeeded in a grand fashion in some areas and failed miserably in others. This contrast, while useful for statistical analysis, points clearly to the costs associated with economic transformations. We analyze some measures of the social costs, such as vital health statistics, to give a picture of how economic success, or its absence, affects aspects of social well-being. These variations in economic performance and in the resulting social consequences contribute strongly to the evolution of political interests that both oppose and that support reform. Subsequent chapters develop measures for these constituencies and analyze how they have played a major role in structuring

---

13 The rent seekers Hellman (1998) describes are also present in historically free-market economies. The efforts by executives and labor leaders in oligopolistic industries to prevent trade agreements and to restrict foreign competition are comparable with the rent-seeking political activities Hellman describes.

electoral competition beginning in 1993 and continuing through subsequent elections. Lastly, we conclude with some observations about the broader implications of these results for combining economic and political transitions. We also then speculate about why Poland may have succeeded at this process where others have met with less to no success, even though following similar macroeconomic policies.

2

The Dynamics of the Polish Political Economy, 1990–1997

The distinguishing feature of the Polish economy during the 1990s is the high rate of job creation among new firms, which provides an important counter to the job destruction among the large state-owned enterprises existing at the start of the transition. As indicated in the previous chapter, Poland was more successful than many other transitional economies in expanding the small and medium-sized enterprise section and in creating jobs in de novo firms. We now want to elaborate on that description; consider the policies of the Polish government, taken both before and after the dramatic changes beginning in 1989, that laid the basis for this creative activity; and discuss some of their social and political implications. This chapter sets the stage for the detailed statistical analyses of the Polish economic and political transformation in subsequent chapters.

INITIAL CONDITIONS AND POLICIES

Two developments during the 1980s had important consequences for Poland's simultaneous development of a market economy and a democratic political system during the 1990s. One is the determined effort throughout the 1980s to reform the economy under the guidelines provided by the concept of market socialism. These efforts at reform left several important positive and negative legacies for the new government taking over in 1989. The other development is the emergence of a strong independent union movement, Solidarność, which became a broad-based resistance movement and eventual political party. The legacy of these developments is that, on the economic side, Poland entered the reform period with rampant inflation and a far larger international debt than other transitional countries but also with a significant private sector. In the political and social sphere, there were strong and legitimate civil organizations and a respected cadre of political and economic leaders.

ECONOMIC REFORM IN THE 1980S

The Polish government undertook a number of economic reforms during the 1980s, following a concept called "market socialism." The theory behind this concept was that countries with planned economies could simulate market outcomes by decentralizing economic decision making, freeing some prices, and increasing the private share of ownership while maintaining a large degree of government participation and control. (For a description of this set of policies as well as a scathing commentary on their inconsistencies and certain failure, see Kornai, 1995.) The contradictions lie largely in the notion that the governments in these countries have the ability and legitimacy to implement the reforms fully. In Poland, at least, neither condition was fulfilled. The bureaucracies in the central ministries quickly reestablished control over the largest enterprises, requiring approval of production plans and prices. For political reasons, the government was never able to free prices to reach some equilibrium between demand and supply. All attempts to increase prices of basic commodities in order to achieve an equilibrium level and to reduce shortages led immediately to increased political organization and opposition and to effective work stoppages. The strikes were followed by wage concessions, thus offsetting any gain in price stability or equilibrium.

In terms of aggregate performance, market socialism did not succeed in Poland. After some improvements in the early 1980s, production and consumption stagnated in the late 1980s, particularly in per capita terms. (See Slay, 1994, for a review based on official statistics.) Inflation averaged about 30 percent annually between 1980 and 1988. The last gasp of the communist economic system began in 1988 when, after a series of highly effective strikes, the incumbent government was replaced by one headed by Mieczyslaw Rakowski. He continued and even increased the economic reforms but never gained control of the foreign debt and inflation. It is estimated that inflation reached almost 250 percent in 1989 while measures of national income and production showed negative growth (Slay, 1994, p. 80). Foreign debt, both in hard currency and in rubles, grew by about 60 percent during the 1980s, reaching U.S. $50 billion. This negative economic legacy was inherited by the reform governments coming to power in 1989.

The most notable success of the reforms was in the areas of foreign ownership and small private enterprises. The government reduced restrictions on foreign and joint ownership to encourage more export production. Planners hoped this would improve the trade balance and help pay for the increased foreign borrowing the regime had undertaken to modernize the capital stock. In macroeconomic terms, both reforms failed. The merchandise trade balance continued to decline and the hard-currency debt increased significantly. The increased foreign ownership, however, increased the size of the private sector, planting an important seed for post-1989 growth.

The second economic legacy of the reforms was a small but vibrant private sector. Many Poles were already taking the initiative to start small enterprises. Slay (1994), using official statistics, estimates the private sector produced close to 20 percent of the national income and employed about 30 percent of the work force in the late 1980s. Our data, also from the Central Statistical Office, suggest these estimates are too generous but still indicate the importance of the private sector prior to the transition. No data on the size or age distribution of the private enterprises are given so we cannot estimate how this private employment was divided between large enterprises with some state ownership, as permitted among foreign trade organizations (FTOs), and totally private enterprises with no state participation. Unlike the private firms, the former enterprises could still be subject to government influence and receive subsidies. The performance of these two different types of firms differed markedly after 1989, and the small private firms formed an important nucleus for the creation of new and growing enterprises after the transition.

SOLIDARNOŚĆ

An unintended consequence of the failed efforts at economic reform was the further growth of a strong, independent labor movement, Solidarność. Some of the economic contradictions of market socialism outlined by Kornai (1995) contributed directly to the growing strength of the labor movement. Put simply, plans to liberalize the economy meant that prices had to be raised. These plans met immediate and strong opposition, further strengthening and legitimizing the union. When the government had to deal with the inevitable strikes, the resulting wage increases put the economy further out of balance. (See Slay, 1994, pp. 65–70.) This is not the place to trace the history and development of Solidarność, both as a trade union and as a broad social and protest movement. For our purposes, it is sufficient to note that the union became one of the critical elements in the broad opposition to the Communist regime.

The Roman Catholic Church was another organization that played a critical role in the development of a formal opposition coalition.[1] Church leaders had opposed the Soviet-imposed regime from the beginning. The continuing confinement of Cardinal Wyszyński under house arrest became a strong and enduring symbol of the church's resistance. The local parishes also supported the opposition movement in far more tangible ways as well. Many priests became outspoken opposition leaders, sometimes paying a high price for their efforts.[2] The churches became places where opposition groups could gather and distribute information. Local churches also paid the bond to get protesters released from jail. The ascension of the Polish Cardinal Karol Wojtyla from archbishop of Kraków to Pope John Paul II gave the church further public recognition, leverage, and immunity as well as a very powerful external figure committed to political reform.[3] In a country that was overwhelmingly and devoutly Catholic, the church was an extremely significant civil organization whose moral and physical resources were a vital part of the growing opposition.[4]

The third important element of the opposition coalition came from the intelligentsia. Representing a wide range of ideological persuasions, it added a powerful voice to the chorus saying that the repressive Communist government had to be removed. Although these individuals did not constitute a formal organization with the presence and resources of the church or a labor movement, they became exceptionally important in developing the ideas and persuasive arguments opposing the regime. Just as important, their arguments, writings, and theories became the basis for the economic and political reforms that replaced the Communist government.

These three elements constituted the umbrella opposition to the Communist government. The roots went back to the 1970s and the formation

---

1 See Weigel, 1992, for a detailed account of the church's resistance to the Communist government, beginning with the imposition of the Communist regime.

2 The most notorious and tragic example being Father Jerzy Popiełuszko who was kidnapped and murdered by police during the martial law period.

3 The pope's tour in 1979 and his subsequent visits drew enormous and enthusiastic crowds throughout Poland and were a direct challenge to the government and are always cited as one of the events that helped legitimize the opposition and delegitimize the Communist regime.

4 In a later chapter we present survey data showing that even in the early and mid-1990s more than 90 percent of the population professed to be religious, of this group, more than 95 percent identified themselves as Roman Catholic, and half said they attended mass at least once a week.

of the Worker Defense Committee (KOR). The Solidarność leaders were a broad representation of Polish society, including trade unionists, such as Lech Wałęsa; academic writers from a variety of ideological persuasions, such as Jacek Kuron, Adam Michnik, and Tadeusz Mazowiecki; and church leaders. These many factions were united by the common goal of ending the Communist regime and reforming the economy and the political system. Their differences over what direction the reforms should take and who should ultimately lead the movement would surface only later. Such differences and disagreements contained the bases for the non-Communist post-transition political parties, though in a splintered form. Despite its ultimate demise as a political party, Solidarność provided transitional Poland with some very important strengths. These include legitimate civil organizations that could hold the society together while the new government and economy were being constructed and a set of strong and tested leaders committed to successful state building and not just to personal aggrandizement.

POLAND'S TRANSITION: SHOCK THERAPY WITHOUT PRIVATIZATION

The consequences of the state policies in the 1980s and particularly those of the Rakowski period, in the form of a large international debt and near hyperinflation, confronted the new government with both crises and constraints. Relative to other Central European countries such as Hungary and what was then Czechoslovakia, Poland had borrowed extensively from international organizations in the 1970s and 1980s in a failed effort to modernize the economy. These large debts and the inflation had two important consequences. First, they constrained how much Poland could borrow to underwrite the transition and thus contributed to the need for stringent macroeconomic policies that would stabilize the economy, begin reducing the balance-of-payments problem, and create a climate for investment. Second, the debt gave international financial institutions greater leverage over Polish policy makers to encourage them to adopt policies consistent with the rapid and stringent transitional strategies favored by these institutions. (See Stone, 2002, for an excellent discussion of this point.)

Two elements of the initial Polish strategy set the conditions for the economic transition and political debates and decisions in the early 1990s. The first was the adoption of the Balcerowicz Plan, the so-called shock therapy, which entailed a rapid shift in macroeconomic policies designed to stabilize the economy quickly and to force a rapid shift to a market economy. The second was the lack of a strong commitment to privatization of the larger state enterprises, despite proposals and legislative initiatives for such a plan.

THE BALCEROWICZ PLAN

The macroeconomic policies initiated in late 1989 and early 1990 were a set of severe measures designed to "get the macroeconomy right." It has been called "shock therapy" for the severity of its jolt to the economy in an attempt to force a rapid rather than a gradual transition to a market economy. This plan (see Balcerowicz, Błaszczyk, and Dąbrowski, 1997, p. 138) had five major components:

- A restrictive monetary policy that reduced the money supply and led to the establishment of interest rates that exceeded inflation in real terms. This part of the plan also introduced interest rate adjustments for loans that were already on the books and that might have been negotiated at a negative real interest rate.
- The elimination of the budget deficit, primarily by reducing subsidies and tax exemptions.
- Extensive price liberalization, including market determination of 90 percent of prices and increases in the remaining administered prices, such as those on fuels and rents.
- Liberalization of foreign trade and convertibility for the złoty. This was initially set at 9,500 per U.S. dollar, devalued in May 1991 and set to a crawling peg formula in October 1991.
- A restrictive income policy, including revocation of the indexing of wages in the state sector and a high tax on wage increases in the state firms – the popiwek.[5]

The macroeconomic policies were accompanied by similarly stringent policies at the microeconomic level designed to force adaptive behavior on the part of state enterprises and the transfer of their resources into privately owned firms. Large enterprises eligible for privatization at the beginning in 1990 totaled 8,441. Table 2.1 shows the different privatization methods and the number of large firms entering and completing

---

5 The popiwek was introduced in 1982 and existed in one form or another under different names throughout the 1980s, but it was raised to severe levels under the transitional policies.

Table 2.1. *Firms in Privatization, 1993 and 1997*

	1993		1997	
Method	Entered	Completed	Entered	Completed
Direct privatization	892	707	1,563	1,424
Liquidation	1,079	186	1,540	677
Capital privatization	527	98	1,254	228
None	5,953		4,084	

each method by 1993 and 1997. In direct privatization, enabled by the Act on the Privatization of State-Owned Enterprises of 1990, any individuals or organizations could buy or lease the enterprise. In liquidation, done under the Act on State-Owned Enterprises of 1981, all or part of the assets of the enterprise was sold at auction. In capital privatization, the firm was restructured as a joint-stock or limited liability company owned by the state treasury with an independent board appointed to run the firm. The intention was that this was a first step to the eventual purchase of the enterprise by domestic or foreign owners.

The most effective strategy by far was liquidation, particularly for small enterprises. The managers or workers in individual stores as well as other private citizens could buy or lease on a lease-to-own plan the assets of the shop being liquidated.[6] This procedure led to the very rapid dissolution of the state-owned enterprises and the reentry of the productive assets into the economy in the form of new fully private enterprises. Balcerowicz et al. estimate that more than 50,000 new private enterprises in the trade, service, and industrial sectors were created in this manner. Liquidation through direct privatization was also the most effective and most frequently used method for privatizing the enterprises classified as large enterprises, though it was mostly applied to the smaller of these firms.

Privatization of the larger state enterprises was, and continues to be, a difficult process. There has been only limited privatization, in contrast to the Czech Republic. Such a plan was proposed in 1991 but defeated in parliament in 1993. There were also few direct sales of enterprises to domestic or foreign buyers, as there were in Hungary. By 1993 fewer than 100 enterprises had been privatized through direct sales (capital privatization). Mostly the approach to these larger firms was to provide incentives for managers and workers to propose privatization plans and

6 The "shop" could have been a branch of a large state-owned enterprise, such as a retail chain, that was being split into individual pieces.

Table 2.2. *Macroeconomic Performance, 1989–1998*

Year	Unemployment (%)	Inflation (%)	Wages (1989 = 100)	GDP (1989 = 100)
1989	0.0	>250.0	100.0	100.0
1990	6.3	140.0	75.8	92.0
1991	11.8	70.3	75.5	85.6
1992	13.6	43.0	73.3	87.8
1993	16.4	35.3	73.0	91.1
1994	16.0	32.3	74.3	95.9
1995	14.9	27.9	76.4	102.6
1996	13.2	19.9	80.7	108.7
1997	10.3	14.9	85.5	116.2
1998	10.4	11.8		121.8

to enforce hard budget constraints. Privatized firms were exempt from the popiwek and dividend taxes.[7] The government also reduced the budget subsidies and tax exemptions for state firms. These changes were part of the effort to reduce the government deficit as well as to force fiscal discipline on the enterprises.

The immediate consequence of these policies was a substantial decline in measured economic activity. Table 2.2 shows four basic measures of macroeconomic performance for the period 1990–97, including the data on GDP shown in Fig. 1.1. GDP dropped about 14 percent between 1989 and 1991 but increased each year after that. Inflation also dropped dramatically after 1990, after being at hyperinflationary levels in 1989 and 1990. Measures of the well-being of workers showed a bleaker pattern. Between 1989 and 1993, registered unemployment, which had been held under 1 percent during the Communist period, climbed dramatically and immediately, reaching a peak of more than 16 percent in 1993, and real wages dropped by 27 percent. Real wage levels in 1989 and 1990, however, are hard to calculate precisely because of the very high levels of inflation.

THE PLAN FOR POLAND

The impact of the stringent economic policies contributed directly to a change in government. The economic strategy for the new government was laid out in a document written primarily by Grzegorz Kołodko, who,

---

7 The so-called dividend tax, dywidendy, was in effect a tax on capital as there were no "dividends" in the sense of a return of profits to owners.

like Balcerowicz, was an excellent technical and academic economist and who became deputy prime minister and finance minister. This plan was less stringent, including such proposals as removing the popiwek, but followed the same basic strategy as its liberal predecessor.

The macroeconomy, which had shown weak signs of improvement in 1993, expanded greatly between 1994 and 1997, as shown in Table 2.2. The broadest indicator of performance, real GDP, was up 16 percent over 1989 and 36 percent over its low point in 1991. Inflation continued to decline, to 15 percent in 1997. The unemployment rate, at 10.3 percent, was still high but considerably below its peak of 16.4 percent, and real wages were still below 1989 levels but were about 13 percent higher than in 1990. At the microlevel the pace of privatization picked up but did not come close to fulfilling expectations. As indicated in Table 2.1, barely more than half the large enterprises had even begun the privatization process and only a quarter had completed it. As in the 1990–93 period, the most successful form of privatization was direct privatization, which means the enterprises were liquidated in whole or in part with the assets going to a completely new firm. The Act on Mass Privatization, first proposed in 1991, was passed in 1996, and at the same time the National Investment Funds established. The road to a market economy, in Poland at least, was built not on the success of the privatization process but on the ability to generate and grow entirely new firms. Some of these, to be sure, were founded on the assets recovered from the liquidated state firms, which returned the assets to the economy as new enterprises. Much of the new economic activity, however, is the result of new, domestically owned and managed enterprises.

THE DYNAMIC CHANGES IN THE POLISH ECONOMY

The success of the Polish economic recovery lay in the ability to generate and grow new enterprises, the process Schumpeter called creative destruction. With the help of a unique database compiled in cooperation with the Polish Central Statistical office and supplemented by other data, we can provide graphic evidence of the process of creative destruction in Poland. (These data are described in more detail in Chapter 3 and its appendix.) The important aspect of these data is that they constitute a longitudinal file in which we can track the changes in employment, payroll, and sales of individual firms over the period 1990 to 1997. These data are also organized by industrial sector, region, and ownership type. The longitudinal structure is required to measure the gross employment and sales changes

Table 2.3. *Employment Change in Existing and New Enterprises, 1990–1997*

Ownership Type	Firms		Employment[a]			Job Creation[b]	
	1990	1997	1990	1997	%	Firms	Jobs
State-owned[c]	8,119	5,527	4,310.5	2,213.1	−48.7		
Continuing[d]	2,251	2,251	2,423.8	1,286.3	−46.9	188	27.5
Restructured	5,800	3,276	1,420.7	926.8	−34.8		
Collective	10,290	9,353	1,460.7	517.9	−64.5		
Continuing[d]	6,325	6,325	1,086.9	451.5	−58.5	518	14.3
Restructured	4,054	3,028	104.4	66.4	−36.4		
Privatized		1,470	1,232.6	723.9	−41.3	159	21.9
Private (<101)	14,365	4,378	259.2	165.3	−36.2	2,698	96.3
Domestic	13,587	4,084	232.0	148.4	−36.0	2,538	87.3
Foreign	778	294	27.2	16.9	−37.9	160	9.0
Private (>100)	803	294	212.2	55.9	−73.7	59	12.5
Domestic	461	181	118.1	36.5	−69.1	37	9.7
Foreign	342	113	94.1	19.4	−79.4	22	2.8
Births						1,582,172	4,655.0
Domestic[e]						83,835	2,045.6
Foreign[e]						5,825	265.5
<Six workers[f]						1,492,509	2,343.9

[a] Employment data in thousands of jobs and percent change.
[b] Number of firms existing in 1990 whose employment increased.
[c] Excludes the count and 1990 employment of subsequently privatized firms.
[d] Firms existing in 1990 and 1997.
[e] Based on firms with more than five employees.
[f] Foundation for the Promotion of Small and Medium-Sized Enterprises (Dzierżanowski, 1999).

among many different classifications of firms. The data also enable us to observe the creation of new firms on an annual basis and to follow the growth or demise of these firms in subsequent years.

Job Creation and Loss among Polish Firms

Table 2.3 shows the net job change and gross job creation among Polish enterprises existing in 1990. There was serious net job loss and very little gross job creation among the currently or previously state-owned enterprises. To quantify the job destruction during the transition, note that state-owned enterprises employed 5.5 million workers in 1990 and collective enterprises employed another 1.5 million.[8] The combined 1997 employment in all possible remnants of these enterprises – those continuing,

---

8 The 5.5 million total includes the 1.2 million employed in firms that were subsequently privatized but that were part of the state sector in 1990.

those restructured but public, and those privatized – was only 3.5 million, meaning that 3.5 million jobs were lost from these enterprises.

In the transition to the market economy after 1990 the fully privatized and restructured firms fared better than those that were not restructured, losing between 35 to 40 percent of their original employment. This should not be construed to mean that privatization or restructuring leads to healthier firms. In the first place, only the most potentially profitable state-owned enterprises were privatized or restructured, so we should expect these enterprises to do better based on initial attributes. Second, we do not have estimates for how much employment was lost among the restructured firms between 1990 and the year they were restructured. We only measure the employment change after restructuring. The state-owned and former state-owned enterprises remaining in the state sector lost between a half and two-thirds of their 1990 employment.

In the private sector, as it existed in 1990, the small domestic firms fared best. (We arbitrarily define small as have 100 or fewer employees.) There were more than 13,000 such firms and in the aggregate they lost 36 percent of their 1990 employment. Small foreign-owned firms did about the same, losing 38 percent of their jobs. The large domestic and foreign-owned firms fared the worst, losing over two-thirds and three-quarters of their total employment, respectively. The clear implication here is that these enterprises, begun in a totally different economic environment, were very poorly suited to compete during the transition.

The new and small private sector was by far the greatest source of new jobs – the creative aspect of creative destruction. Domestically owned firms begun after 1990 were by far the biggest job producer. Nearly 84,000 of these firms with more than 5 employees existed in 1997, and they employed 2 million workers. In addition, among small domestic private firms existing in 1990, 17 percent of them grew and added 87,300 jobs. This latter group was by far the largest source of gross job creation among all firms existing in 1990. Nearly 6,000 foreign-owned firms were started after 1990, employing nearly 265,000 workers in 1997.

It is very important to remember that these data grossly understate the employment in new and/or small enterprises because of the regulations excluding firms with 5 or fewer employees from having to file data with the Central Statistical Office. We can partially overcome these limitations using data developed by the Foundation for the Promotion of Small and Medium-Sized Enterprises (Dzierżanowski, 1999). Using a different data source based on registrations of firms, the foundation estimates that in 1997 there were nearly 1.5 million firms with 0 to 5 employees and these enterprises employed 2.3 million workers. (These figures include self-employed individuals.) Combining the estimates from the two data sources suggests that 4.6 million jobs were created in firms begun after the transition began.

The Appendix Table 2A.1 shows this same information for the manufacturing and the trade and retail sectors. The important point here is that the job destruction and creation shown for the whole economy describes the pattern within more specialized sectors. The dominant source of gross job creation is the new firms entering the economy, followed by the set of small domestic and foreign firms existing in 1990. The former state-owned firms and the large private firms existing in 1990 suffered the largest job destruction, measured in proportional terms.

Changes in Sales

Sales are an important indicator of the growth or decline of firms, particularly for sectors where the transition is supposedly forcing them to be more efficient. In the Central and East European planned economies it was widely held that because state-owned enterprises employed too many people for the level of output, they had to reduce their employment and become more efficient in order to be competitive. In this case, the employment loss shown in Table 2.3 might actually indicate improvement, not decline. The 1990 and 1997 sales for each of the categories of firms in Table 2.3 are shown in Table 2.4. Comparisons of sales changes from 1990 to 1997 for each category of firm could indicate whether the former state-owned firms were indeed becoming more efficient and competitive and actually growing despite the job loss.

The sales data in Table 2.4 show the same relative picture as the employment data. (The data are in millions of real 1990 złotys.) The most dramatic story portrayed here is the consistent decline in sales in real terms for all types of state-owned and formerly state-owned enterprises. These declines were generally on the order of 10 percent to 20 percent for the seven-year period. This was true for the privatized firms (−13 percent), the restructured but not fully privatized collective firms (−45 percent), and the state-owned firms that stayed in business throughout the period (−13 percent). The notable exception was the restructured state-owned firms, where sales declined by 0.7 percent. It is also the case that the larger private firms did not perform well. Including the firms that went out of business, sales declined by 26 and 55 percent for these large domestic and foreign firms.

Table 2.4. *Sales in All Existing and New Enterprises, 1990–1997*

Ownership Type	Firms		Sales[a]			Growing[b]	
	1990	1997	1990	1997	%	%	S_{97}/S_{90}
State-owned[c]	8,119	5,527	470.1	381.5	−18.8		
Continuing[d]	2,251	2,251	293.0	256.0	−12.6	21.0	1.75
Restructured	5,800	3,276	126.4	125.5	−.7		
Collective	10,290	9,353	81.2	64.0	−21.2		
Continuing[d]	6,325	6,325	59.9	57.4	−4.2	22.2	2.36
Restructured	4,054	3,028	12.0	6.6	−45.0		
Privatized		1,470	178.0	154.6	−13.1	20.8	1.65
Private (<101)	14,365	4,378	32.2	36.4	+13.1	53.8	7.13
Domestic	13,587	4,084	26.9	32.1	+19.3	55.1	7.48
Foreign	778	294	5.3	4.3	−18.9	48.9	5.20
Private (>100)	803	294	23.2	14.3	−38.4	29.3	3.28
Domestic	461	181	13.3	9.8	−26.3	30.4	3.07
Foreign	342	113	9.9	4.5	−54.5	27.4	3.78
Births		1,582,172		837.6			
Domestic[e]		83,835		500.9			
Foreign[e]		5,825		136.6			
<Six workers[f]		1,492,509		200.1			

[a] Sales data in millions of 1990 złotys and percent change.
[b] Percent of firms existing in 1997 whose sales share increased from 1990 to 1997.
[c] Excludes the count and 1990 sales of subsequently privatized firms.
[d] Firms existing in 1990 and 1997.
[e] Based on firms with more than five employees.
[f] Estimates from Foundation for Small and Medium-Sized Enterprises.

The second significant result shown in Table 2.4 is the substantial sales gain among the small domestic private firms existing in 1990. Even if we include in the 1990 base the enterprises that did not survive until 1997, there is a 19 percent sales growth. These firms seem much better adapted to function in the new economy, in contrast to any set of the other firms existing in 1990. Lastly, and not surprisingly, sales by the new firms dominate the total, accounting for over 800 million złotys in sales, or more than half the total volume.

Firms existing in 1990 and 1997 are stratified on the basis of whether their share of sales within their sector increased during this period. The two columns to the right in Table 2.4 show the proportion of these continuing firms whose shares increased and the ratio of 1997 to 1990 aggregate sales for each of the ownership types. Two differences are immediately apparent. A much larger proportion of the small private firms increased their shares than is observed among any other type. More than half the firms in this category increased their share, compared with about a fifth of the state-managed and privatized firms and about 30 percent of the large private firms. Second, the aggregate growth rates in sales among the types of firms followed the same pattern, with the small private firms showing the largest growth and the state-managed and privatized enterprises showing the smallest growth rates.

Again, the economic changes displayed in Table 2.4 are for the whole economy, but the picture they present about the growth and decline within ownership and size categories is fairly indicative of what happened within specific sectors. Appendix Table 2A.2 shows the same sales changes for the manufacturing and trade sectors.[9] The only substantial difference among the manufacturing firms is that the restructured state-owned firms had aggregate sales growth of about 14 percent rather than the decline shown in the data for all sectors. The trade sector showed different patterns, beginning with the fact that this sector was dominated in terms of numbers of firms by collective enterprises and new and small private firms. The number of state managed firms was quite small, though a small proportion of these exhibited a large growth rate, as shown in the right-hand columns. The former collective enterprises all faired poorly, exhibiting declining sales in real terms. Only a small proportion increased their sales share, and the growth rate was quite modest even for these firms. The small private firms did much better, with aggregate sales growing substantially despite the loss of two-thirds of the firms, though this growth was on a small base in 1990. Nearly half the small private firms increased their market share and those who did grew at a very high rate.

The implication conveyed by the sales data is that a very small proportion of the present and former state-owned and privatized firms was able to adapt to the new economy. The vast majority declined both in employment and sales, indicating they were not functioning well in a market economy and that the loss of employment was not simply a part of the process of becoming more fit and a possible prelude to future growth. Significantly, the same observations apply to the large private enterprises existing in 1990. They exhibited the same pattern of employment and sales decline. It may be that it is not the type of ownership per se that

---

9 The Foundation for the Promotion of Small and Medium-Sized Enterprises does not report sales by sector for firms with five and fewer employees. This omission means we grossly understate the sales attributable to new and small firms, which is likely to be a significant deficiency in the trade sectors, where firms are smaller than in manufacturing.

Table 2.5. *Regional Variations in De Novo Firm Creation*

	1991	1992	1993	1994	1995	1996	1997
Domestic firms							
Mean	1.05	1,36	1.65	1,82	2.51	3.98	4.15
Standard deviation	0.43	0.53	0.63	0.72	0.96	2.07	1.98
Max. − min.	1.64	2.04	2.57	3.08	4,06	8.26	8.38
Foreign firms							
Mean	0.03	0.06	0.07	0.08	0.15	0.21	0.23
Standard deviation	0.03	0.07	0.09	0.10	0.18	0.26	0.30
Max. − min.	0.20	0.40	0.51	0.58	0.98	1.50	1.73
Foreign firms excluding Warsaw							
Mean	0.03	0.05	0.06	0.07	0.14	0.18	0.20
Standard deviation	0.02	0.05	0.06	0.08	0.13	0.19	0.20
Max. − min.	0.12	0.20	0.24	0.27	0.52	0.77	0.83

Note: New firms per 1,000 members of the work force.

plays a large role in a firm's success, but the "technology" in the broadest sense and how well suited that technology is for the current economic environment. In this case, that technology must include organizational structures and incentives as well as products and production methods.

These data describe a pattern of decline and growth that strongly reinforces Schumpeter's proposition about creative destruction as the process of economic development and Kornai's description of a private economy that is indigenous rather than a managed creation. Poland's economy, and society broadly, would be suffering immense hardship if there had not been the level of entrepreneurial activity, both to take over the small and medium-sized pieces of the state-owned enterprises and to start new ones.

Regional Variations

An important aspect of the de novo job creation in the Polish economy is that it was very unevenly distributed across the country. Table 2.5 shows the distribution of de novo domestic and foreign firms (plus the small 1990 firms) in 1997 per 1,000 members of the work force among the forty-nine voivodships. (The data for firms and employment in each voivodship are presented in the Appendix as Table 2A.3.) The density of domestic firms ranged from over seven per 1,000 workers in the urban areas such as Warsaw, Lublin, Poznań, Gdańsk, and Kraków to less than two in Zamość and Tarnobrzeg. Data on the number of new jobs as a proportion of the work force follow the same patterns, with the same voivodships at the top and the bottom. If we had data at lower levels of aggregations, we would see even more variations. Many of the urban voivodships, such as Kraków and Gdańsk with their large steel mills and shipyards, respectively, had areas where job destruction was enormous and also had areas with high rates of firm creation. The standard deviation in the rate of de novo firm creation and the gap between the most and least successful voivodships increased during the transition. These data demonstrate that the ability to adapt to the new rules and incentives created by the transition to a market economy varied widely. The relatively small role played by foreign firms in de novo economic activity noted in earlier tables is also evident in these data. Even including Warsaw, where foreign firms ultimately accounted for 10 percent of all new firms, the average density of new foreign firms peaked at 0.30 per 1,000 workers in 1997. Excluding Warsaw the average was about 0.25. The entry of new firms that is at the core of the Polish transition is an indigenous process, built on the entrepreneurial activity of Poles.

The magnitude of the variation in how well regions were adapting to the new economic rules and regime is also evident in data comparing the distributions of unemployment and real wages over time. Table 2.6 shows the ratio of highest to lowest levels and the standard deviation and skewness in these rates among the voivodships. Two different trends appear in these data. In unemployment, the ratio has increased substantially while the standard deviation and skewness peaked about 1993 or 1994 and have declined since. These results indicate a widening of the differences during the early stages of the transition but then a narrowing as it proceeded. The increase in the ratio occurred because the areas with low unemployment in 1993 had larger proportional, though smaller absolute, decreases in unemployment.[10] The differences in average wages, excluding Warsaw, increased during the early years but then remained fairly stable, with the skewness decreasing sharply after 1995. Including Warsaw changes this picture so that wage differences by all three measures continued to increase throughout the entire period. This picture might also change, however, if we had regional price indices because the inflation rate has likely been higher in Warsaw than in other regions.

Table 2.6 shows the yearly correlations between the rate of new domestic-firm creation relative to the size of the work force in each voivodship and the unemployment rate and average salary in each location.

10 The maximum value dropped from a high in 1993 of 30.3 to 21.2 percent while the minimum value dropped from a high of 7.6 to 2.7 percent.

Table 2.6. *Variations in Regional Economic Performance*

	1991	1992	1993	1994	1995	1996	1997
Unemployment							
Difference[a]	14.4	18.2	22.7	23.3	23.0	21.6	18.5
Standard deviation	3.58	4.41	5.62	5.34	5.10	4.85	4.21
Skewness	−0.34	0.31	0.44	0.45	0.33	0.28	0.09
Correlation with							
new firms[b]	−0.46	−0.44	−0.43	−0.43	−0.45	−0.60	−0.66
Real wages with Warsaw							
Ratio[c]	1.41	1.45	1.52	1.56	1.59	1.62	1.70
Standard deviation	7.68	9.57	10.69	12.41	12.65	13.10	14.29
Skewness	1.92	2.06	1.86	1.91	1.96	2.02	2.23
Correlation with							
new firms[b]	0.37	0.50	0.51	0.43	0.46	0.67	0.70
Real wages excluding Warsaw							
Ratio[a]	1.41	1.45	1.48	1.56	1.56	1.52	1.49
Standard deviation	6.90	8.22	9.24	11.00	11.04	11.01	11.23
Skewness	2.00	1.95	1.67	1.90	1.89	1.71	1.39
Correlation with							
new firms[b]	0.27	0.34	0.33	0.28	0.30	0.49	0.50

[a] Difference between the highest and lowest unemployment rate among voivodships.
[b] Correlation with new domestic firms per 1,000 members of the work force, weighted by the size of the nonfarm work force.
[c] Ratio of highest level to lowest level among voivodships.

These correlations show that over the course of the transition, with increasing amounts of new-firm creation, there is an increasing negative relationship between de novo firm creation and unemployment and an increasing positive correlation with wages. It is not just the sign of these correlations that is important, but the fact that their magnitudes are increasing, suggesting that new-firm creation is more strongly associated with low unemployment and higher wages as the amount of this activity increases. These correlations are consistent with the findings of Berkowitz and DeJong (2001), who find a positive correlation between new-firm creation and income growth in Russia. The correlations among Polish regions anticipate our more detailed discussions in Chapters 3 and 4, where we rigorously analyze the processes of de novo firm and job creation and their relationship with economic and social conditions.

The picture, then, is one of an economic transition that is unevenly distributed among Poland's regions, with some areas adapting to the new regime and creating new firms and jobs at a much faster pace than others. The regional variations in job destruction, de novo job creation, and the associated measures of economic success and distress have important economic, social, and political consequences, as the statistical analyses in later chapters will show.

THE SPEED OF TRANSITION

This tale of creative destruction, with its significant economics gains in some sectors, regions, and types of enterprises and its devastating losses in others has significant social and political implications. Not surprisingly, sectors and individuals experiencing the destructive side of the process are not supportive of the reform policies and look for ways to alter them and their results. Less certain, however, is whether the areas and individuals adapting to the new rules and economic structure constitute a constituency for continuing the reforms. This is where the economics and politics of transition become joined.

Analysis and discussion of the political economy of transition from a planned to a market economy, as just depicted for Poland, have spawned important theoretical work focused on the speed of transition (Aghion and Blanchard, 1994; Castanheira and Roland, 2000; Dewatripont and Roland, 1992; Fidrmuc, 1998, 2000a, and 2000b; Jackson, 2003; Rodrik, 1995; and Roland 1994 and 2000). The key part of these models is the balance between how fast the private sector expands relative to how fast the state sector contracts. If private-sector job creation is too slow or state-sector job destruction too fast the success of the transition is jeopardized. The Polish data just presented elaborate the features of these models in important ways. Because virtually all the job creation is in the de novo sector, the success of the Polish transition did not depend much on the performance of the restructured and privatized firms, whose employment and sales declined nearly as much and as rapidly as the remaining state-owned firms. The rates of de novo firm creation, survival, and growth, analyzed in much more detail in Chapter 3, determined the speed and success of the Polish transition.

Most of the models of the speed of transition contain an implicit political sector whose policies affect the success or failure of the transition. The government's policies, in turn, are functions of the size and behavior of different worker groups. In the Aghion and Blanchard model (1994) the unemployment level stimulates demands for increased unemployment benefits. These benefits must be financed by taxes levied on the private

37

sector, which reduces its growth, thus limiting the speed and possible success of the transition. Rodrik (1995) has a similar model but includes the state-sector workers in the political section. These voters demand continued state subsidies as they become threatened with layoffs. As with the Aghion and Blanchard model, the private-sector taxes that finance these subsidies restrict, and possibly doom, the transition. Fidrmuc (1998), by contrast, argues that state-sector workers will support reform policies so long as they expect to get jobs in the private sector. As, or when, that expectation disappears, these workers support parties offering greater subsidies for the old sector.

Jackson (2003) adds an endogenous electoral component to these models where the size and growth of various constituencies is based on the job creation and job destruction process. This model incorporates the evidence that job creation is done by de novo firms by basing the electoral support for the liberal economic parties on the size of this de novo sector. This electoral support then translates into seats in the parliament where the party can influence the setting of subsidy and tax policies. These policies affect the rates of decline of the state sector and the growth of the de novo sector and thus the speed and success of the reforms. Results from this model indicate that the likelihood of successful economic and political reforms increases with the rate of de novo job creation, with the propensity of workers in the de novo jobs to vote for the liberal party, and with the way in which vote shares translate into seat shares and thus into the ability to influence economic policy.

Although not part of the formal model, Jackson's model offers an important proposition that further connects the growth of the de novo sector to increased pressure on the government to pursue policies that support the economic reforms. The growth of employment in new firms, as distinguished from employment in restructured firms, creates both an economic middle class and a political center. If parties take winning elections seriously, the larger this center, the more constrained competing parties are in their ability to advocate and adopt policies that restrict the economic changes.[11] Or, to put this in a more positive context, the faster and larger this centrist constituency grows, the more likely parties are to support pro-reform policies, even if the party originated as an antireform party. It is not just the share of the votes that goes to the economically liberal party

---

11 See Cox, 1990, and Merrill and Adams, 2002, for models that predict that as the density of voters in the center increases, parties will move toward this center, even in multiparty elections.

but the pressure the de novo sector puts on the whole electoral system that leads to the greater likelihood of liberal economic policies.

The model in Jackson's paper was motivated by the question of how, and under what conditions, economic and political reforms are mutually supportive. It was strongly influenced by the empirical evidence from the Polish case (Jackson, Klich, and Poznańska, 2003a and 2003b). The model shows that if the rate of expansion of the de novo sector is sufficiently fast, political support for the liberal economic parties will grow, leading to the pursuit of policies that promote and continue the reforms. Otherwise, political opposition to the reforms becomes sufficiently large so as to continue subsidies for the state sector and for the unemployed and to choke the growth of the new private sector. In this case, the economic reforms are likely to fail. This model provides a structure within which to organize the analysis of the Polish economic and political reforms and their interconnections.

THE POLITICS OF THE POLISH TRANSITION

The sequence of Polish elections during the 1990s follows the broad outlines of the political economy models of transition in the beginning, but then deviates from that model in important ways. The broad coalition of union leaders and workers, church leaders and parishioners, and intellectuals and students that constituted Solidarność won an overwhelming and dramatic victory over the ruling Communist Party (PZPR) in the first elections held in June 1989. Despite retaining the presidency and holding a guaranteed majority in the new parliament, the Communists asked the reformers to take control of the government. This ushered in the reform era, and the stringent economic policies associated with Leszek Balcerowicz, setting the stage for the subsequent debates about the pace, direction, and consequences of the economic reforms and for the series of elections recounted briefly in Chapter 1.

Table 2.7 shows for the national elections held during the 1990s the major parties and candidates for the parliamentary and presidential elections by their political grouping, their shares of the vote nationally, and their share of the seats in the succeeding parliament. The dominant, contending parties constitute three broad groupings: the centrist, liberal parties that began and championed the economic reforms; two post-Communist parties, so-named because their leaders were active in the Communist Party before the reforms; and the off-again, on-again coalition of church- and trade-union-based parties, whose association began with

Table 2.7. *Major Parties, Candidates, Votes, and Seat Shares*

Party/1995 Candidate	Votes				Seats		
	1991	1993	1995[a]	1997	1991	1993	1997
Economic liberals	28.5	20.0	9.2	13.4	143	90	60
UD/Kuroń	12.3	10.6	9.2		62	74	
KLD	7.5	4.0	–		37		
UW(UD + KLD)				13.4			60
PC/BBWR	8.7	5.4			44	16	
Post-Communist	20.7	35.8	39.4	34.4	108	303	191
SLD/Kwaśniewski	12.0	20.4	35.1	27.1	60	171	164
PSL/Pawlak	8.7	15.4	4.3	7.3	48	132	27
Catholic + trade union	13.8	11.3	33.1	33.8	85		201
Catholic	8.7	6.4	–		58		
Solidarity trade union	5.1	4.9	–		27		
Wałęsa/AWS			33.1	33.8			201
Economic left						41	
UP/Zieliński	2.1	7.3	3.5	4.7	4	41	
Far right, nationalist						22	6
KPN/Olszewski/ROP	7.5	5.8	6.9	5.6	46	22	6
Other	27.4	19.8	7.9	8.1	74		
Correlations with de novo employment/work force							
Economic liberals		0.79	0.73	0.84			
Post-Communists		−0.59	−0.20	−0.11			
Catholic + trade union		−0.16	0.02	−0.19			
Economic left		0.61	0.69	0.15			
Far right		0.07	−0.47	−0.33			

[a] Presidential election, first round.

Solidarność.[12] There were important and significant differences between the parties' economic platforms, though the magnitudes of these differences varied over time and at times there were differences within these groups, and even within the parties and coalitions themselves. We discuss each election in more detail in Chapters 5 and 6.

The Democratic Union (UD), under the leadership of Prime Minister Tadeusz Mazowiecki, and its junior partner, the Liberal Democratic

---

12 For the purpose of Table 2.7 we have grouped two independent blocs, the Centrum Alliance (PC) in 1991 and the Nonpartisam Bloc for Reform (BBWR) in 1993, with the economic liberals. These blocs, though independent, ran with Wałęsa's encouragement and tacit support. Their economic policies and political constituency place them closer to the liberals than to any other party cluster.

Congress (KLD), took the lead in the first reform government and in promoting the liberal economic agenda, the Balcerowicz Plan. The politics that followed would seem to confirm the predictions, and concerns, of those who said that simultaneous economic and political reform were perilous. As shown in Table 2.2, there was an immediate drop in output and wages and an increase in unemployment. With parliamentary elections scheduled for 1991, there was no lack of opposition to the liberals. The strongest opposition parties were the post-Communist Democratic Left Alliance (SLD) and the Polish Peasant Party (PSL). The SLD was urban-based and contained the remains of the Communist trade union, the OPZZ. In 1991 it campaigned strongly against the economic reforms and in favor of state intervention to protect Poland's heavy industry (see Tworzecki, 1996, p. 59). As its name implies, the PSL was rurally and agriculturally based. It strongly favored continued subsidies for farmers, either directly or in the form of high tariffs on imported foodstuffs, and for other state sectors. On the right, the Solidarność trade-union party opposed the economic policies and dramatically escalated the amount of strike activity, although it remained a nominal part of the government. On the far right, the liberal economic policies were opposed by the very nationalistic Confederation for an Independent Poland (KPN). The SLD made a very strong, and to some surprising, showing in the 1991 election. It won almost as many seats (sixty) as the UD (sixty-two). This clearly marked SLD as the leading opponent of the liberal economic reforms, only two years after the Communist's embarrassing showing in the 1989 election.

The very democratic political reforms further reinforced the concerns of those pessimistic about simultaneous reforms. An unlikely coalition of post-Communists and UD members adopted electoral rules allowing parties receiving very small fractions of the vote to nonetheless obtain seats in the parliament. The SLD-PSL-UD coalition that passed these rules is strange not just because of the unlikelihood of these three parties agreeing on anything, but this plan was not in the UD's interests. As one of the larger parties, it would have benefited from a less proportional votes-to-seats rule. With these electoral rules, the proliferation of parties, and the debates about Poland's direction, it is not surprising that twenty-nine parties won seats in the new parliament. Equally predictable, with this many parties and personalities, was the inability of any party to form a stable coalition. There were two governments and one failed attempt at forming a government between 1991 and 1993. These governments adhered fairly closely to the liberal economic agenda laid out in the Balcerowicz Plan.

By spring 1993 the deleterious effects of the shock therapy reached their peak, with high unemployment and falling personal income. It is also the point at which a sustained recovery was beginning, though that was not perceptible at the time. The last liberal government, headed by Hanna Suchocka and whose cabinet included Leszek Balcerowicz, was brought down in June 1993 on the initiative of a Solidarność trade-union member who was joined by the combined opposition of the SLD, PSL, KPN, and UP (Labor Union), a new left-wing but anti-Communist labor party. This action precipitated the 1993 elections.

The 1993 election was the outcome predicted and feared by reformers. It was held at the time that unemployment was highest and wages the lowest during the transition. The election was seen by many as a referendum on the liberal economic reforms, though there were other significant political issues as well, with the opposition SLD and PSL expected to do very well. The SLD had moderated somewhat its antireform platform from the 1991 election in an effort to attract voters. Aleksander Kwaśniewski, the SLD leader, increasingly tried to model the party's positions and strategies in the image of Tony Blair's Labour Party in Great Britain and Gerhard Schroeder's Social Democrats in Germany. The SLD did not, however, completely retreat from its antireform positions and strongly opposed the high tax on wage increases in the state sector (the popiwek), wanted to slow the already crawling pace of privatizations, and said it was willing to increase the budget deficit. The PSL, on the other hand, did not moderate its platform and continued advocating subsidies for farmers and for the state-owned enterprises, import restrictions, and larger budget deficits to finance social services. The KPN and the Solidarność trade-union party also strongly opposed the reforms, though from the right. They would, for example, support some amount and forms of privatization but not the elimination of various subsidies for large state-owned enterprises.

As the pessimists predicted, the two post-Communist parties won an overwhelming plurality of the votes, finishing first and second in the national vote, with the UD a distant third. New electoral rules adopted before the 1993 election gave the SLD and the PSL a dominant position in the new parliament, with nearly two-thirds of the seats, even though together they got just over one-third of the vote. As we discuss in detail in Chapter 6, these new electoral rules, pushed by the UD, provide an excellent illustration of how easy it is to walk backward off cliffs. After experiencing the difficulty in governing with twenty-nine parties in parliament, the UD leadership pushed through a series of reforms to limit the representation of smaller parties and to enhance the advantage of larger parties in future elections. What would have been an astute move in 1991 when the UD held more of a majority turned out to be a self-defeating position by 1993 when its support was eroding.

In the fall of 1993 the concerns of those who doubted the likelihood of simultaneous reforms and the pessimistic predictions of the political economy models of transition seemed quite accurate. The SLD and the PSL formed a coalition government that held office for a full term from 1993 and 1997. In 1995 Aleksander Kwaśniewski, the SLD leader, defeated Lech Wałęsa, the incumbent Solidarność icon, for the presidency by a margin of only 3.4 percent, establishing the SLD as the dominant party in Polish politics. But, alas or fortunately, reformers' and observers' concerns and predictions were misplaced. The SLD-led government altered the pace and direction of the economic reforms but did not alter the basic commitment to a market economy and a liberal political regime. Further, as seen in Table 2.2, the economic recovery that was beginning by the time of the 1993 election proceeded at a vigorous pace. The rate of creation, survival, and growth of de novo firms rose substantially, as we will see in the next chapter, and as evidenced in Table 2.3.

A major surprise occurred in 1997 when Solidarność Election Action (AWS), a right-wing coalition of the Solidarność trade union and the Catholic parties led by Marian Krzaklewski, the trade-union leader, defeated the SLD and became the leading coalition party in a new government. Coming after four years of increasing prosperity and decreasing unemployment, this result was contrary to the retrospective voting models that presume incumbent administrations are rewarded or punished for the state of the economy and how it has changed during their administration. Probably as surprising as the AWS victory was the return of Leszek Balcerowicz, the leader of the Union of Freedom (UW), which is the successor party to the UD and the KLD after their merger, as the deputy prime minister and finance minister. Their victory and the Balcerowicz appointment were particularly surprising as the AWS had campaigned on an economic platform that was decidedly less liberal than that of the SLD and promised to aid the badly lagging coal and steel sectors that had yet to be privatized or restructured. As we recount in Chapter 8, it was a very short-lived victory and coalition, and one that did not continue the economic success. Also as a surprise during this period, the SLD continued its evolution to a neoliberal economic platform. By the 2001 election it was openly advocating support for new and small businesses and calling one part of its platform "Entrepreneurism Above All."

The Polish transition began much as the political economy models and observers expected. Stringent economic reforms and dramatic political reforms were begun simultaneously. These were followed by the predictable economic distress and for some the equally predictable electoral success of parties claiming to be opposed to the reforms. The full story of the transition, however, plays out quite differently. The dominant post-Communist party, built on the foundation of the Communist-sponsored labor union, continued the reforms, stimulated the creation of de novo enterprises, and led a dramatic economic recovery with an impressive growth rate. This party was then defeated by a right-wing coalition based heavily in the politics and economics of the past.

To anticipate our arguments in Chapters 5 and 6 about the evolution of electoral support for parties likely to pursue liberal economic policies, Table 2.7 shows the simple correlations between the rate of new-job creation relative to the size of the work force in each voivodship and the proportion of the votes in the 1993, 1995, and 1997 elections won by the various party groups or their presidential candidates. In each of these elections, de novo job creation is strongly and positively correlated with votes for the liberal parties. Results show an initially strong but then decreasing negative correlation between new job creation and votes for the post-Communists and a consistent but moderate negative correlation between the jobs variable and votes for the trade-union-led coalition. There is an increasing negative correlation between job creation and votes for the far-right parties. The only unexpected correlation, given our simple predictions here, is the strong positive association between job creation and votes for the UP, whose platform was to the left of the SLD. In part this correlation reflects the difficulties with simple ecological correlations, as UP is a very small and decidedly urban party whose support was concentrated in areas with strong job creation that also voted for the liberal parties. It also reflects the limitations of simple correlations of any sort, as there are other factors at work in these elections that affect the patterns of support for all parties. Subsequent chapters examine these relationships in detail with several types of data and methods in order to test the proposition rigorously that de novo economic activity creates a liberal political constituency that supports reform parties and that pressures potentially nonreform parties.

SUMMARY

The summary of the Polish economic and political transition serves two purposes. For readers not familiar with the Polish case, it should familiarize them with facts, circumstances, and events that occurred between 1990 and 1997 and which are the focus of the analytical work in the succeeding chapters. More important, this material provides a descriptive outline for the main themes of the book. The economic transition was driven by job destruction in the older and larger state and private enterprises and by job creation in new firms. Some of these new firms started phoenix-like from the ashes of former state firms created by the different privatization schemes but many of them are start-ups in the purest sense of the term. This process, accomplished over a relatively short period of time, corresponds closely to the creative destruction metaphor that Schumpeter (1934) used to describe the generic process of economic development. As seen here and in Chapter 1, it is the rate of de novo creation that highlights the Polish transformation.

The political transition was affected substantially by both aspects of the economic transition. As expected, the consequences of the stringent reforms and the resulting job destruction fueled significant political opposition, seen in the early SLD, the PSL, and the AWS opposition to the reforms and to the political parties pursuing those reforms. Less expected was the ability of the reform parties, such as the UD and then the UW, to maintain a political base and to continue to play a significant role in influencing economic policy. This political base contained a large proportion of people who were committed to the reforms because they believed that in the long run an open, market economy would produce a higher standard of living and a healthier society. This base also contained a significant number of people committed to the liberal policies because they were part of this de novo economy. Our analysis shows that these people are quite different and have very different policy preferences from the employees and managers in the restructured and privatized firms. Hellman (1998) pictures this group as ultimately more committed to partial reforms and to maintaining their monopolistic positions than to a fully open and competitive market. We argue that the employees in the de novo sector and residents in regions where these firms are succeeding continue to support liberal policies and parties.

An even less expected outcome is the transformation of the SLD from being adamantly opposed to reforms and strongly promoting continued state subsidies to large enterprises to proposing a neoliberal economic policy. By 1997, and subsequent to that time as we note in Chapter 8, the SLD increasingly abandoned these views in favor of policies and programs that would stimulate the formation of new enterprises and continue the reforms, though with less vigor than desired by the liberals in the UW (or the KLD). Part of this transformation can be attributable to its learning the lessons provided by the evidence on job creation. Part can be attributed to pressure from international financial institutions, particularly in the early period after the 1993 election. But this information and pressure existed in other transitional countries. What is important here, as Jackson's model suggests, is the political pressure on the SLD created by this growing middle-class, centrist, and liberal constituency associated with the de novo firm creation. In the remaining chapters we tell the statistical story of where and why this de novo firm creation became so important and how it contributed to a strong political constituency that continued to support liberal economic parties that could keep the reform process moving forward. These statistical stories provide the empirical details underlying Jackson's model of the political economy of transitions.

Appendix 2A: Firm Dynamics and Creation

This appendix presents disaggregated data on firm dynamics, defined by the numbers of firms, their employment, and their sales and on firm creation to complement the data presented in this chapter. The data on firm dynamics in Tables 2A.1 and 2A.2 are the same data shown in Tables 2.3 and 2.4 disaggregated into two major sectoral components – manufacturing and trade and services. Table 2A.3 reports the number of new domestic and foreign firms per 1,000 workers and their employment as a share of the work force in 1997 for each voivodship. As such, it presents more detailed information than is summarized in Table 2.5.

Table 2A.1. *Firm and Employment Dynamics by Sector, 1990–1997*

Ownership Type	Firms 1990	Firms 1997	Employment[a] 1990	Employment[a] 1997	%	Job Creation[b] Firms	Job Creation[b] Jobs
Manufacturing							
State-owned[c]	3,355	1,086	1,800.7	717.9	−60.1		
Continuing[d]	1,086	1,086	1,347.8	484.2	−53.2	90	16.4
Restructured	1,159	769	297.3	233.7	−21.4		
Collective	3,052	1,469	510.5	176.4	−65.4		
Continuing[d]	1,469	1,469	301.6	169.4	−43.8	152	8.1
Restructured	369	184	16.2	7.0	−56.8		
Privatized		858	867.4	537.8	−38.0	97	16.2
Private (<101)	8,361	2,183	150.4	82.3	−45.3	1,358	47.0
Domestic	7,745	1,972	127.8	70.2	−45.1	1,251	41.0
Foreign	616	211	22.6	12.1	−46.5	107	6.0
Private (>100)	570	187	160.6	45.0	−72.0	47	10.6
Domestic	278	90	79.9	27.6	−65.5	25	7.8
Foreign	292	97	80.7	17.4	−78.4	22	2.8
Births						313,035	1,467.6
Domestic[e]						30,433	907.0
Foreign[e]						2,276	144.7
<Six workers[f]						280,326	415.9
Trade							
State-owned[c]	464	257	207.0	65.2	−68.5		
Continuing[d]	257	257	147.9	46.9	−68.3	18	1.2
Restructured	439	289	33.3	18.3	−45.1		
Collective	3,090	2,521	583.3	175.4	−69.9		
Continuing[d]	2,521	2,521	527.8	167.2	−68.3	93	2.7
Restructured	304	204	20.1	8.2	−59.2		
Privatized		158	39.6	18.3	−53.8	25	1.7
Private (<101)	1,574	615	27.0	21.3	−21.1	376	12.9
Domestic	1,523	582	25.8	20.0	−22.5	356	12.1
Foreign	51	33	1.2	1.3	+8.3	20	.8
Private (>100)	53	27	11.0	2.9	−73.6	5	.7
Domestic	47	23	10.1	2.7	−73.3	5	.7
Foreign	6	4	.9	.2	−77.8	0	.0
Births						1,025,123	622.0
Domestic[e]						26,108	444.0
Foreign[e]						1,957	70.8
<Six workers[f]						997,058	107.2

[a] Employment data in thousands of jobs and percent change.
[b] Number of firms existing in 1990 whose employment increased.
[c] Excludes the count and 1990 employment of subsequently privatized firms.
[d] Firms existing in 1990 and 1997.
[e] Based on firms with more than five employees.
[f] Estimates from Foundation for Small and Medium-Sized Enterprises.

Table 2A.2. *Sales Dynamics by Sector, 1990–1997*

	Firms		Sales[a]			Growing[b]	
Ownership Type	1990	1997	1990	1997	%	%	S_{97}/S_{90}
Manufacturing							
State-owned[c]	4,213	1,086	258.7	149.5	−42.2		
Continuing[d]	1,086	1,086	162.9	97.3	−40.3	16.0	1.18
Restructured	1,159	769	46.0	52.2	+13.5		
Collective	3,052	1,469	35.1	18.7	−46.7		
Continuing[d]	1,469	1,469	21.4	18.0	−15.9	15.5	2.01
Restructured	369	184	1.5	.7	−52.3		
Privatized		858	128.9	110.6	−14.2	24.1	1.62
Private (<101)	8,361	2,183	18.1	14.3	−21.0	57.0	5.28
Domestic	7,745	1,972	14.1	11.8	−16.3	58.4	5.55
Foreign	616	211	4.0	2.5	−37.5	44.1	4.24
Private (<100)	570	187	16.6	10.9	−34.3	37.4	3.29
Domestic	278	90	8.3	6.8	−18.1	43.3	3.08
Foreign	292	97	8.3	4.1	−50.6	32.0	3.78
Births		32,709		203.3			
Domestic[e]		30,433		153.3			
Foreign[e]		2,276		50.0			
Trade							
State-owned[c]	622	257	37.5	45.4	+21.1		
Continuing[d]	257	257	24.5	32.1	+31.0	8.6	11.97
Restructured	439	289	16.7	13.3	−20.4		
Collective	3,090	2,521	31.8	27.3	−14.2		
Continuing[d]	2,521	2,521	28.6	25.4	−11.2	7.4	3.77
Restructured	304	204	5.2	1.9	−63.5		
Privatized		158	7.5	15.7	+109.3	14.6	6.65
Private (<101)	1,574	615	6.3	12.6	+100.0	47.8	15.22
Domestic	1,523	582	5.7	11.6	+103.5	48.5	15.70
Foreign	51	33	.6	1.0	+66.7	36.4	10.93
Private (>100)	53	27	3.0	2.3	−23.3	3.7	−
Domestic	47	23	2.8	2.2	−21.4	4.3	−
Foreign	6	4	.2	.1	−50.0	0	−
Births		28,065		324.7			
Domestic[e]		26,108		255.3			
Foreign[e]		1,957		69.4			

[a] Sales data in millions of 1990 złotys and percent change.
[b] Percent of firms existing in 1997 whose share of sales increased between 1990 and 1997.
[c] Excludes the 1990 employment of subsequently privatized firms.
[d] Firms existing in 1990 and 1997.
[e] Based on firms with more than five employees.

Table 2A.3. *De Novo Firm and Job Creation in 1997 by Voivodship*

Voivodship	Domestic Firms[a]		Foreign Firms[a]	
	Number	Jobs	Number	Jobs
Warsaw	9.8	24.2	1.74	8.0
Biała Podlaska	2.0	5.3	0.04	0.12
Białystok	3.5	9.1	0.07	0.37
Bielsko-Biała	5.3	15.1	0.27	2.05
Bydgaszcz	6.0	14.8	0.22	1.12
Chelm	2.2	5.4	0.01	0.08
Ciechanów	2.6	7.4	0.07	0.60
Czestochowa	5.0	12.1	0.11	0.43
Elblag	5.3	13.3	0.15	1.94
Gdańsk	7.8	17.9	0.61	2.24
Gorzów Wielkopolski	4.8	12.6	0.48	3.23
Jelenia Góra	3.5	7.4	0.37	1.33
Kalisz	4.5	11.2	0.14	0.71
Katowice	6.3	15.7	0.24	1.01
Kielce	3.2	8.0	0.06	0.33
Konin	2.7	6.5	0.11	0.85
Koszalin	5.2	12.8	0.32	1.38
Kraków	6.7	17.2	0.39	1.12
Krasno	2.1	6.2	0.03	0.15
Legnica	4.5	11.8	0.16	0.52
Leszno	4.2	11.4	0.21	1.08
Lublin	9.5	18.6	0.51	2.00
Łódz	3.0	9.2	0.06	0.32
Łomża	2.3	5.0	0.02	0.06
Nowy Sacz	3.0	6.7	0.06	0.25
Olsztyn	4.5	12.0	0.16	0.82
Opole	4.0	9.0	0.26	0.89
Ostrołęka	2.0	8.1	0.06	0.37
Piła	5.0	14.6	0.16	1.48
Piotrków Tryb	3.1	9.8	0.07	0.78
Płock	3.3	8.5	0.09	0.76
Poznań	9.0	19.9	0.84	3.24
Przemysl	2.3	5.0	0.01	0.02
Radom	2.8	6.4	0.09	0.91
Rzeszów	2.9	7.5	0.09	0.50
Siedice	2.3	6.1	0.07	0.23
Sieradz	3.6	8.7	0.06	0.28
Skierniewice	3.2	7.3	0.17	2.07
Słupsk	4.6	13.1	0.28	1.74
Suwalki	2.7	7.7	0.06	0.39

(continued)

Table 2A.3 *(continued)*

Voivodship	Domestic Firms[a]		Foreign Firms[a]	
	Number	Jobs	Number	Jobs
Szczecin	6.2	14.1	0.70	2.37
Tarnobrzeg	1.4	3.6	0.03	0.08
Tarnów	2.4	7.9	0.04	0.40
Toruń	4.3	12.9	0.15	0.65
Wałbrzych	3.8	9.7	0.21	0.57
Włocławek	2.8	8.0	0.07	1.05
Wrocław	5.7	14.9	0.63	2.64
Zamość	1.7	4.6	0.01	0.16
Zielona Góra	4.4	11.6	0.47	2.41

[a] De novo firms in 1997 per 1,000 work force and jobs per work force in percent.

3

Creative Destruction and Economic Transition

This chapter develops and analyzes statistically a model of economic development that is consistent with the description of the changes in the Polish economy presented in the previous chapter. This model draws heavily on the arguments of Joseph Schumpeter ([1911] 1934) and later works of organizational theorists in sociology and economists in industrial organizations. Schumpeter's proposition is that economic growth is the "new combination" of materials and processes to create new products, production methods, markets, raw materials, or organizations: he also says these "new combinations are, as a rule, embodied, as it were, in new firms which generally do not arise out of the old ones but start producing beside them" (Schumpeter, 1934, pp. 65–66). The emphasis is on new firm creation, survival, and growth as a means for transforming and expanding economic activity rather than on the transformation and growth of existing enterprises. In fact, the new economic organizations displace and replace the older, outmoded ones – what Schumpeter and others refer to as creative destruction. The key variables of birth, survival, and growth of new firms constitute the entrepreneurial process.

MODELING NEW-FIRM CREATION, SURVIVAL, AND GROWTH

In our simple model of economic evolution, there are three central variables: the creation of new firms, the survival rates of these firms, and the growth rates of the surviving firms. This emphasis on these variables as a means for transforming and expanding economic activity is the focus of work in organizational ecology. (The early work in this area was by Hannan and Freeman, 1977 and 1989. See Amburgey and Hayagreeva, 1996; Carroll, 1988; Singh, 1990; and Singh and Lumsden, 1990, for review articles.) The essence of this work is that economic development and transformations are comparable to biological processes where birth and survival are critical to the continuation of a species. The analogy is that the long-term growth and adaptability of an economy depend on the creation, survival, and growth of new firms.

Consideration of the dynamics within industries has also captured the attention of economists modeling industrial organizations. Caballero and Hammour (1994) make claims similar to those of Schumpeter and Hannan and Freeman about the importance of new firms as a source of growth during and after recessions and then apply this argument specifically to the transitional economies (Caballero and Hammour, 2000). Earlier work on selection, entry, and the growth of industrial sectors by Jovanovic (1982) and Geroski (1991) has now been extended by Pakes and Erikson (1995) to a formal model of firm growth and size, suggesting that important differences follow from the type of innovations that dominate an industry. Audretsch (1995) also couples discussions of technological innovation with questions of growth and survival. Following Birch (1981), there has been a lively debate about the role of small firms in creating jobs. This debate, though marked by some questionable statistical work and exaggerated claims, frames important policy issues of firm survival and mobility and their implications for economies in a broad set of international contexts. (See Davis, Haltiwanger, and Schuh, 1996, and Jackson, 1998, for critiques of this debate, and Caves, 1998, for an excellent summary of this literature.)

Our simple model of economic dynamics emphasizes firm creation, survival, and growth, and defines the variables characterizing a cohort of firms as follows:[1]

F_s^T total number of firms at time s

F_{os} number of firms created in year s

$\overline{S}_{os}$ average initial size of the firm in the cohort created in year s

F_{ts} number of firms in cohort s remaining in year t

$\overline{S}_{ts}$ average firm size in the remaining firms in cohort s in year t

a_{ts} proportion of the firms in cohort s that survive from year $t - 1$ to year t

---

[1] Cohorts can be defined as homogeneously as one wants, such as for specific industry classifications, ownership types, or initial size. For simplicity we ignore such disaggregations here and only refer to cohorts by year of birth.

b_{ts} growth rate among the surviving firms in cohort s from year $t - 1$ to year t

S_{ts} aggregate size of the cohort s in year t, for example, total employment or total sales

Firm size can be measured in any number of ways. We use both employment and sales revenue.

From these terms we can express the number of firms created at time s to make a cohort, the number surviving in successive years, and their total size (employment or sales revenue) as,

$$F_{0s} = \gamma_s(F_s^T) \tag{3.1}$$

$$F_{1s} = a_{1s} F_{0s}$$

$$F_{ts} = a_{ts} F_{t-1,s} = a_{1s} \cdots a_{ts} F_{0s} \tag{3.2}$$

$$\overline{S}_{1s} = b_{1s} \overline{S}_{0s}$$

$$\overline{S}_{ts} = b_{ts} \overline{S}_{t-1,s} = b_{1s} \cdots b_{ts} \overline{S}_{0s} \tag{3.3}$$

$$S_{0s} = \overline{S}_{0s} F_{0s}$$

$$S_{1s} = \overline{S}_{1s} F_{1s} = b_{1s} \overline{S}_{0s} a_{1s} F_{0s} = b_{1s} a_{1s} S_{0s}$$

$$S_{ts} = \overline{S}_{ts} F_{ts} = b_{ts} \overline{S}_{t-1,s} a_{ts} F_{t-1,s} = b_{ts} a_{ts} S_{t-1,s} = (b_{1s} a_{1s}) \cdots (b_{ts} a_{ts}) S_{0s}. \tag{3.4}$$

These are simply accounting expressions showing the relationships among the variables. Subsequent work will add behavioral and economic content to these expressions to represent propositions about how birth, survival, and growth rates vary over time, region, and sector. We model γ_s, a_{ts}, and b_{ts} as functions of variables that differ over time, location, and industry.

An important implication of these equations is that the total employment or sales revenue in any year t for the cohort of firms born in year s depends on the number of firms and their average size in the birth year and the survival and growth rates in the following years. Changes in any of these terms alter the aggregate employment in all subsequent years. The total size of a cohort increases in each year when the growth rate in average firm size exceeds the reciprocal of the survival rate, $b_{ts} > 1/a_{ts}$. The total number of firms in an economy at year T is the sum of F_{ts} for every previous year's cohort, $s = 1, 2, \ldots, T$, and the aggregate size is a similar sum for S_{ts}:

$$F^T = \sum_{s=1}^{T} F_{Ts} \quad \text{and} \quad S^T = \sum_{s=1}^{T} S_{Ts}. \tag{3.5}$$

Equation 3.1 proposes that the number of births in cohort s is related to the total number of firms of that type existing at the time the cohort is formed. Arthur, Ermoliev, and Kaniovski (1987) and Arthur (1990) develop and illustrate a model with increasing returns to scale, or agglomeration effects, for a given sector in a particular region. These effects suggest that the probability of a new firm in a region is proportional to the number of firms of that type already in the region. This process leads to an increasing concentration of firms of particular types in certain areas. Krugman (1991) shows that for the United States and Western Europe most manufacturing industries are concentrated in only a few locales, and these locations are derived from either advantages or accidents in place when the industry first developed. Jackson and Thomas (1995) found similar effects for the emergence of manufacturing enterprises at the two-digit industry level in the United States during the early 1970s. The specification of Equation 3.1 captures the potential for these agglomeration effects. Further, variations in regional comparative advantages in generating firms of a given type are reflected in different values for γ_{ts}. Regions with more natural endowments, better physical infrastructure, cost advantages, and the like will have a higher values for γ_{ts}.

Equations 3.2 to 3.4 record the number of firms remaining in a cohort in subsequent years; the average size of the remaining firms in such terms as employees per firm or sales per firm; and the aggregate size of the cohort, such as total employment or total sales in year t. The coefficients denoted as a_{ts} record the survival rate for firms in cohort s in year t, whereas the coefficients denoted by b_{ts} record the growth rate for these remaining firms. As expressed here, these coefficients have no behavioral or economic content and are merely descriptions of what has occurred to a cohort over some period of time. Our interest is first in examining whether these descriptive terms follow any regular pattern over the life of different cohorts, as suggested by the organizational ecologists, which would suggest that this set of equations is a useful way to model the dynamics of economic growth and change. If such regularity is present, we then want to test propositions about how these coefficients vary over time and region as functions of the various factors that might give a region a competitive advantage. This latter effort adds economic and policy meanings to these expressions. Before we can undertake such examinations, however, we must first develop data that allow us to define birth cohorts and to then follow them over time.

MEASURING CREATIVE DESTRUCTION IN THE
POLISH ECONOMY

Obtaining data to describe this evolutionary process, to permit us to estimate the relevant birth, survival, and growth rates, and to enable statistical analysis of regional variations is a daunting task. Data on small and medium-sized enterprises are problematic in most settings. Our needs are even more demanding. Firm-level longitudinal data that define birth cohorts and that follow these cohorts over time are essential. A unique dataset created in collaboration with the Polish Central Statistical Office (GUS) provided a solution. From its records based on data that individual firms submit on an annual basis, we built a longitudinal file. Creating the dataset requires linking these individual records for every firm for each year it reported. The data now cover all firms reporting during the period from 1990 to 1997 and include statistics on employment, payroll, sales, sector, region, and the type of ownership, including state-owned, cooperative, domestic private, foreign private, and privatized.

Several limitations to these data need to be kept in mind as we describe and analyze the transformation of the Polish economy. The obvious limitation is the data do not include information on firms that do not report, thus understating the amount of economic activity. There are two sources of nonreporting. One is the firms in the gray economy. The presence and magnitude of this segment is a concern in all economies, but particularly in the former Communist countries where the government had so little legitimacy. The second source of nonreporting is official, in that firms with five or fewer employees are not required to file reports with the GUS. This problem is more serious because it means the data systematically omit the very smallest firms so that we do not observe firm births in the literal sense. We only observe firms that have been successful enough to pass this threshold.

We make one correction to errors introduced by this threshold. Firms may surpass this threshold in one year, fall below it in subsequent years, and reappear afterward. Counting such a history as a birth, a death, and yet another birth would overstate birth and failure rates and understate the economic activity generated by the firm in the interim years. GUS prepared a computer subroutine to check for the reentry of firms and, in such cases, to create records for the missing years. In these records we interpolate their employment, payroll, and sales data so that we can treat these firms as continuing members of their respective cohort. This procedure should provide a more accurate measure of survival and growth among our cohorts.

From the standpoint of documenting the amount of entrepreneurial activity in Poland and its contribution to the emerging private sector, these omissions mean we seriously underestimate the phenomena. From the standpoint of the creative destruction metaphor and the model in Equations 3.1 to 3.4 as descriptions of the Polish economy, these omissions are much less of a problem. In the long run, the ability of firm creation to be an engine for economic transformation requires that a portion of the new firms grow into large, relatively stable enterprises. In essence, we are interested in the upper tail of the size distribution of any cohort. The omissions in the GUS data truncate the distribution at the small end but leave the upper tail relatively intact. In our analysis of factors that are correlated with birth, survival, and growth rates, the ability to obtain accurate statistical results depends on the degree to which the omitted activity is uniformly proportional to the amount of activity we do measure. If we are consistently observing a given proportion of all creative activity, then our results will accurately reflect the statistical associations between various factors and the level of entrepreneurial activity. Only our prediction of the total level will be biased, but that is not the main purpose of this study.

Appendix A presents a statistical comparison of the GUS data with data on the number of firms developed from a different data source. These alternative data include estimates of the number of firms with five or fewer employees. These data are inferior to the GUS data as measures of the dynamic aspects of an economy and thus as measures with which to estimate the variations in the parameters in the evolutionary model.[2] They are useful, however, to assess the extent of measurement biases in the GUS data. The conclusion of this comparison is that the GUS data will function as an accurate proxy for the size of the new-firm sector, including the very small firms. Further, the GUS data provide more reliable measures, despite the absence of the data on very small firms.

A second set of errors is more troubling. There is clear evidence of gaps in the record keeping and handling, as happens with all administrative data of this magnitude. The most glaring evidence of this problem was the discovery in the 1997 data of a large number of firms that appeared

---

2 These alternative data are based on the registration of new firms. Their major limitation is that they do not record firm exits, making analysis of survival and growth rates impossible.

to have made their initial filing in 1996. For a small number of firms these filings constituted a reentry of a firm that had previously been in the data, which is accounted for in our methodology. For most firms, however, these were "new" firms in the sense of being new to the data. As discussed in a subsequent section, these data overstate births in 1996 and make the 1996 cohort particularly large.

Despite these omissions and problems, these data offer the best available measures of the creative destruction process that is at the heart of Poland's economic transformation since 1990. They are also the best available measures in any of the transitional economies that can document the amount, importance, and dynamics of de novo enterprises. These data also offer the best measures with which to test propositions about the evolutionary process and about factors that are associated with it.

Birth of New Enterprises

As shown in Chapter 2, the birth of new firms and, to a lesser extent, the success of small private firms existing in 1990 were the source of employment growth for Poles. We begin with the raw numbers on firm creation each year. Table 3.1 shows the number of new domestic and foreign firms started each year. For purposes of comparison, we treat small firms existing in 1990 as a cohort of new firms. This surely overstates the number of firms begun in 1990, as some existed in previous years, but it provides one more cohort for discussing the process of birth, survival, and growth.

The creation of domestically owned firms was very robust in the early years of the transition, then fell noticeably in 1993 and 1994. The high birthrate in 1991 and 1992 very likely reflects the effects of the small-enterprise privatization described in Chapter 2. This process liquidated many state enterprises, with the assets being used to start new, private firms. Births then rebounded dramatically in 1995 and subsequent years. The likely explanation for the very large number of births recorded for 1996 is related to the data problems described previously. The large number of births in 1996 and the low number in 1993 and 1994 suggest the data may understate the birthrates for 1993 and 1994 and then overstate them for 1996.

The average initial firm size decreased after 1994 among both domestic and foreign cohorts, although the foreign cohorts start with larger firms. The decrease in average firm size is particularly apparent in the 1996 cohort. Because the GUS data measure firms with more than five

Table 3.1. *Births and Size of Cohorts*

Birth Year	Domestic			Foreign		
	Firms	Mean Size	Jobs[a]	Firms	Mean Size	Jobs[a]
All sectors						
1990[b]	13,587	17.1	232.0	778	34.9	27.2
1991	11,739	26.2	307.2	183	40.2	7.4
1992	11,281	22.7	256.6	774	32.9	25.5
1993	9,663	21.1	204.3	504	33.1	16.7
1994	7,671	22.1	169.9	534	32.3	17.3
1995	17,239	16.5	284.9	1,858	22.7	42.3
1996[c]	41,389	13.2	544.6	1,984	18.2	36.1
1997	20,020	14.3	287.2	1,398	19.4	27.2
Manufacturing and construction						
1990[b]	9,775	17.1	172.0	640	37.3	23.9
1991	7,735	27.3	211.3	139	44.6	6.2
1992	6,271	26.2	164.5	398	40.5	16.1
1993	5,302	24.6	130.2	251	43.4	10.9
1994	4,121	25.8	106.3	295	38.0	11.2
1995	8,151	19.2	156.5	831	27.8	23.1
1996[c]	20,727	13.4	278.7	819	21.0	17.2
1997	9,226	16.5	152.3	509	24.2	12.3

[a] Total jobs in thousands.
[b] Based on small firms (employment ≤ 100) existing in 1990.
[c] See text for explanation for extraordinarily large number of births in 1996.

employees, these results reveal a rapidly increasing movement of very small firms across this threshold, producing the increased number of new entrants and their decreased average initial size. The year with the smallest average size is 1996, the year with a very large number of new firms, suggesting that at least some of the increase may be very small firms passing the five-employee threshold and not just an administrative problem.

The entry of new firms was not limited to the trade and service sector, where entry is easier and there was more small-scale privatization. The lower half of Table 3.1 shows the number, average size, and total employment of new manufacturing and construction firms each year. Roughly half the new firms each year, both domestic and foreign-owned, were in this group, indicating that the de novo firms were spread throughout the economy. The manufacturing and construction firms were larger than the average size for all sectors, particularly among the foreign-owned firms.

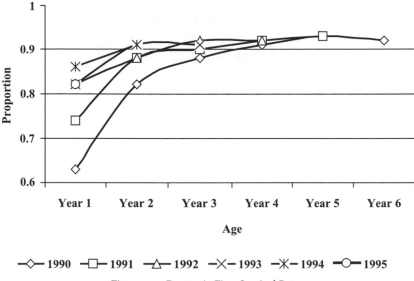

Figure 3.1. Domestic-Firm Survival Rates

Survival of New Enterprises

The second critical factor in creating a new economy is the survival rates among these cohorts of new firms. Low survival rates have two serious implications. One is that there must continue to be a very high birthrate in order to maintain any given employment level. More seriously, a high failure rate means that workers and physical and financial capital are being continually recycled from one enterprise to another. The significant costs to such a process place a high burden on an emerging economy. A high failure rate may also serve to discourage other possible entrepreneurs, if one assumes a likely, and negative, demonstration effect.

Figures 3.1 and 3.2 show the aggregate year-to-year survival rates for each cohort of domestic and foreign firms reported in Table 3.1.[3] Survival rates among the domestic firms exhibit a fairly uniform and monotonic pattern increasing with age. The survival rates among cohorts of foreign firms also increase with the age of the cohort, but the pattern is not as smooth or monotonic. Part of this more erratic pattern can be attributed

---

3 The criteria for inclusion in the database combined with our methodology indicate that our survival rates for the last year of any cohort will significantly understate the true rate. Some firms counted as exits will reemerge in later years and be counted as survivors at that time. For this reason, we have omitted the last year for each cohort.

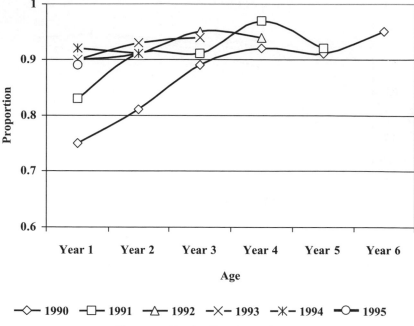

—◇— 1990   —□— 1991   —△— 1992   —✕— 1993   —✳— 1994   —○— 1995

Figure 3.2. Foreign-Firm Survival Rates

to the relatively smaller size of the foreign-owned cohorts, as seen in Table 3.1. As expected, the foreign firms have a higher survival rate than domestic firms. As noted earlier, they start with a larger average size, which helps survival. They are also likely to have more abundant and more secure financial capital and more experienced management. What is surprising, however, is that the magnitude of this difference is large only in the first year and represents only a few percentage points difference in subsequent years.

The second important aspect of Figure 3.1 is the increase in the survival rate among domestic firms in succeeding cohorts. There are several likely explanations for these improvements. One is that in the beginning many of the new private firms were likely the result of the liquidation of small state enterprises and, even though they were now under new, private management, they might not have been well suited to adapt to the private market. A second possibility is that Polish entrepreneurs became more skillful at knowing what businesses to start and what is required to start and to sustain a new business. A related possibility is that new firms are beginning with better endowments, in the form of financial capital, management, or products that make them more viable. It is important for the development of the Polish economy that this improvement in first-year survival rates continue. The multiyear survival rate is the product of each annual rate, so that a low survival rate for the first year means a low long-term survival rate for the cohort. For example, survival rates of 0.7, 0.85, and 0.9 for the first three years implies only 53.5 percent of the firms survive past year three. Increasing just the first year survival rate to 0.85 increases that rate to 65 percent.

Growth in Firm Size

The last element in the evolutionary model is the change in average firm size. We measure size by employment, although sales revenues can also be used. We choose employment because of the broader social and political implications associated with employment and unemployment. Related to this measure is the annual change in total employment in the cohort, which is the number of firms times the average employment per firm. This latter measure takes into account both the survival rate and the growth rate in surviving enterprises. As seen in Equation 3.4, if the annual growth in firm size exceeds the reciprocal of the survival rate, the total employment of the cohort increases.

Figures 3.3 and 3.4 show the annual growth rates for all surviving firms in each cohort. The pattern for domestic firms has several interesting aspects. Growth decreases precipitously after the first year but then, after a flat period, increases slightly. It is hard to identify from these figures whether this is a characteristic of cohort aging or a response to an improving economy. Some observers might explain this result by pointing out that the whole economy is growing, which will clearly aid all firms. But this explanation is not fully satisfactory. As shown in Table 2.3, the creation and growth of new enterprises are major contributors to the success of the macroeconomy. The figures also suggest that growth rates are increasing with each successive cohort, just as we saw with survival rates. This may be further evidence that Polish entrepreneurs are becoming better skilled at knowing what firms to start and how to manage them once started.

Foreign firms generally had higher growth rates than domestic firms. This is not totally unexpected, as these firms are likely to have a higher level of capital, both financial and human. With financial capital, foreign-owned firms will have greater access to capital pools, either internally if the Polish firm is a subsidiary of a foreign firm or externally if the

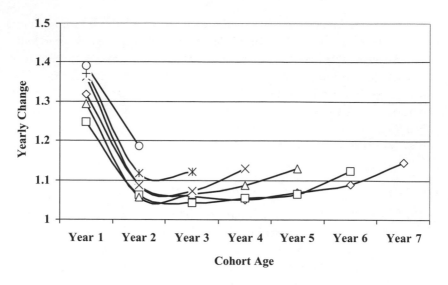

─◇─ 1990 ─□─ 1991 ─△─ 1992 ─✕─ 1993 ─✳─ 1994 ─○─ 1995 ─+─ 1996

Figure 3.3. Yearly Domestic-Firm Employment Growth

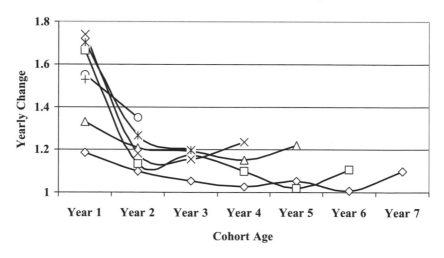

─◇─ 1990 ─□─ 1991 ─△─ 1992 ─✕─ 1993 ─✳─ 1994 ─○─ 1995 ─+─ 1996

Figure 3.4. Yearly Foreign-Firm Employment Growth

Table 3.2. *Total Employment Growth in Domestic and Foreign Cohorts*

Cohort	Year						
	1	2	3	4	5	6	7
Domestic							
1990	0.83	0.89	0.93	0.95	0.99	1.01	0.98
1991	0.92	0.94	0.94	0.97	0.99	0.97	
1992	1.06	0.93	0.98	1.00	0.98		
1993	1.12	0.99	0.98	0.98			
1994	1.19	1.02	0.98				
1995	1.14	1.02					
1996	0.98						
Foreign							
1990	0.89	0.88	0.93	0.94	0.96	0.95	0.99
1991	1.38	1.03	1.06	1.06	0.94	1.02	
1992	1.20	1.11	1.14	1.08	1.10		
1993	1.56	1.09	1.09	1.07			
1994	1.57	1.15	1.08				
1995	1.38	1.22					
1996	1.21						

foreign owners are using their own financing or their access to financial institutions. The question of human capital may be less obvious but is no less important. In the years for which we have data, foreign-owned firms are much more likely to include, or at least to have access to, managers with experience in private markets. This expertise includes everything from marketing, to finance, to product development, to human resource skills. The hope is that, as Poles gain experience and education, this human capital difference will shrink.

Equation 3.4 shows that the total employment in a cohort will be increasing if the product of the growth rate and the reciprocal of the survival rate exceeds one. This relationship is important because it indicates whether a cohort is continuing to add jobs to the economy and is thus a source of long-term growth. Table 3.2 shows the rate of total job growth for each cohort, defined as the ratio of total jobs in year t to those in year $t - 1$ for each cohort. Foreign-owned firms, except for the 1990 cohort, are more successful at adding to aggregate employment than are domestic firms. The domestic firms only add to total employment in year 1 for the four youngest cohorts and year 2 for only two cohorts, whereas for foreign firms this is true for all but the first cohort. Given the patterns

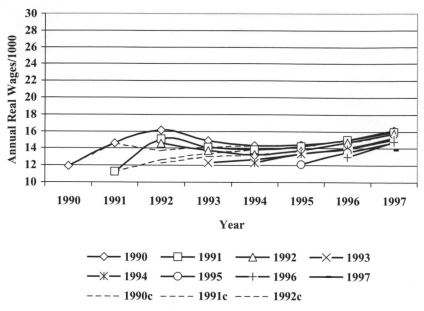

Figure 3.5. Wages in New Domestic Firms

in Figures 3.1 and 3.3, one objective for economic development policy in Poland needs to be to help entrepreneurs increase their likelihood of surviving for the first several years.

Payroll per Worker

A measure of the success of these new firms in building an economy with highly valued jobs is the wages they pay. Job growth is important, but it is also important that these jobs pay well and offer the opportunity for an increasing wage as the firm becomes more successful. From the data on total payroll and the data on employment, we can calculate the average wage per worker per year. We want to compare these data over the age of each cohort for the domestic and foreign-owned new firms, between domestic and foreign-owned firms of the same age, and between these new, fully private firms and the privatized, restructured, and remaining state-owned firms. The latter comparisons will indicate how resources are being allocated, and reallocated, between the old sectors and the new private sectors.

Figures 3.5 and 3.6 plot the average payroll per worker per year (in thousands of new Polish złotys, adjusted for inflation) for each domestic

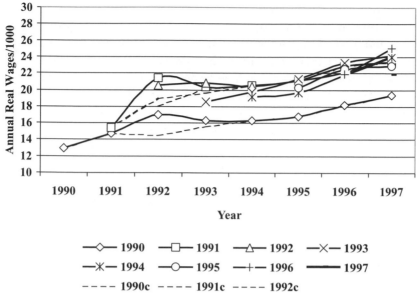

Figure 3.6. Wages in New Foreign Firms

and foreign cohort.[4] The most obvious fact is that foreign-owned firms pay substantially higher wages than do the domestic firms. Wages in foreign firms also increased faster than wages in domestic firms. This raises the interesting question, which we address later, of whether these higher wages enable foreign firms to dominate and crowd out domestic firms. These wage differences may also reflect productivity differences, with foreign-owned firms having a higher amount of capital per worker, which our data do not measure.

One encouraging aspect of these figures is that, for both types of firms, real wages increase as the cohort ages, despite the slump in 1993 and 1994.[5] This pattern is particularly noticeable for cohorts beginning in 1993. In the domestic sector, real wages in a cohort's initial year stayed fairly constant over the seven years. They then rise as the cohort ages. One obvious implication here, but not the only one, is that as a cohort ages the

4 We used the consumer price index (CPI) to deflate wages. Using the general GDP deflator would have raised estimated real wages by about 10 percent in 1991 and 21 percent for the years 1994 to 1997.

5 It may be the case that real wages for 1992 are overstated, such as would happen if the CPI understates the real level of inflation for that year. The particularly large wage increases for all cohorts, both domestic and foreign, suggest the data may be overstating real wages.

"best" firms are the survivors and presumably, as they succeed, they are able to offer higher wages to their employees. These results provide evidence about why longitudinal data on firms are important. The successful firms in a cohort are both paying higher wages and increasing in size. Any cross-sectional examination of how wages vary with firm size will reach the conclusion that larger firms offer better, higher-paying jobs. Too often observers then conclude that the new jobs being created in an economy are not as "good" as existing jobs because they are in new, small firms that pay less. An accurate assessment of the quality of a new job, however, should be what its wages become as the firm prospers and grows.

An important comparison is between payroll per worker in both types of private firms and wages in firms remaining in the state sector. This latter sector comprises firms going through restructuring but still state-owned and those that were not restructured at all. A critical dimension to this contrast is that wages in the private sector are market-driven based on the competition for and the need to retain labor. In the state sector, by contrast, firm decisions are much more susceptible to political concerns of various sorts. The more politically organized the workers are, the more likely their wages are to reflect political as well as economic concerns. These propositions are particularly important in the Polish case because the most successful parties in the 1993 election campaigned on a platform of slowing down some of the economic reforms, of softening the harshness of the consequences of the Balcerowicz Plan for economic reform, and specifically of relaxing the tax on wage increases in the state-managed sector, the so-called popiwek.

Figure 3.7 shows the average payroll per worker for enterprises that remained in the state sector from 1990 through 1997. One group, the 1990 cohort, was state-owned and state-managed the entire period. The others went through some form of restructuring, presumably in preparation for privatization. The changes with time are much more dramatic among these firms than among the private firms, and their largest increases coincide with the change in control of the government in late 1993. The increase in 1993 is far more dramatic if we adjust 1992 wages as we did for private firms. In the 1990–92 period the wage level in state firms is comparable with those in the private domestic sector. After 1993, however, they take a dramatic jump upward and continue to increase in subsequent years. A comparison of the ratio of wages in enterprises remaining in the state sector to wages in private firms shows they are about even through 1992, about 22 percent higher in 1993, and 35 percent higher in 1994–97 for a given cohort and age. Comparisons with wages in

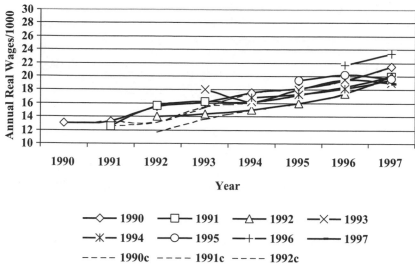

Figure 3.7. Wages in State-Sector Firms

foreign-owned firms give similar results. The ratio of wages in state-controlled firms to wages in foreign-owned firms shows significant increases from 1993 to 1997. These comparisons offer fairly strong evidence that wages increased substantially in state enterprises, relative to private domestic and foreign-owned enterprises at the time the post-Communist parties assumed control of the parliament.

Sales per Worker

Our final set of comparisons concerns the sales per worker in each type of firm. Albeit rough, this comparison permits a modest assessment of the level and changes in productivity. Figures 3.8 to 3.10 show the ratio of sales per worker per year for each cohort and type of firm. (The data are in real terms, based on the price index for GDP.) In the long run, sales per employee is another important test for the shift to a private economy. In order to be successful, wage growth must be matched with productivity growth. We have already observed that wages increased with age within cohorts for domestic firms and, over time, independent of cohort age for state-controlled firms. In addition, wages in state-controlled firms increased markedly after the change in control of parliament. If these wage increases are not accompanied by productivity increases, it indicates that scarce resources are still flowing to inefficient parts of the economy.

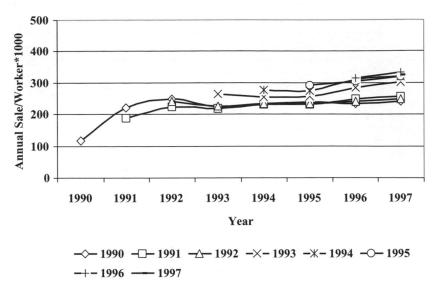

Figure 3.8. Sales per Worker, Domestic Firms

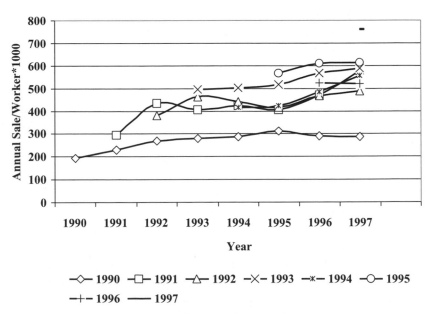

Figure 3.9. Sales per Worker, Foreign Firms

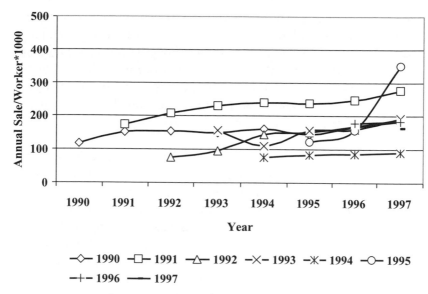

Figure 3.10. Sales per Worker, State-Sector Firms

Comparisons across parts of these figures are interesting. It is obvious that the foreign-owned firms have a much higher ratio of sales to employment than either private or state-sector domestic firms. The sales-to-employment ratios for private domestic firms show a similar pattern to that for foreign-owned firms, only at a lower level and at a slower rate of growth. These comparisons suggest a much higher level of capital use in foreign firms, which is not surprising. The most significant patterns for private firms, both domestic and foreign, is the rapidly increasing productivity of each successive cohort.

The contrast between the private firms and the state-owned firms is also revealing. We have already noted that payroll per worker increased dramatically in the state firms beginning in 1993 and in subsequent years. There is no evidence, with the exception of the 1991 and 1992 cohorts, that these wage increases are accompanied by comparable increases in output per worker. The implication from these results is that more resources are being used to support workers in these firms but without a corresponding increase in output, as measured by sales.

REGIONAL ANALYSIS AND STATISTICAL MODELS

Tables 2.4 and 2.5 in Chapter 2 show there are great variations in how well regions adapted to the new economic rules and in their subsequent economic performance. The remainder of this chapter adds some behavioral content to the evolutionary model in Equations 3.1 to 3.4 and uses these regional variations to test the propositions. There is a twofold objective here. One is to test the applicability of our model as well as the specific propositions added to the model. The second is derived from the first, as we want to be able to add to the discussion about regional and national economic policies that might stimulate new firm creation and growth.

Converting Equations 3.1 to 3.4 to a model of economic development and transition is done by specifying factors that are associated with systematic variations among regions, over time, and within cohorts in the key parameters in these equations, γ_s, a_{st}, and b_{st}. One important set of propositions estimates the relative size of any agglomeration and congestion effects. Agglomeration effects may arise because of demonstration effects whereby people begin to emulate successful entrepreneurs, from the development of local resources such as a specialized labor force or a set of business service firms that stimulate the creation of new firms, or some other form of economies of scale in the region. (See Krugman, 1991, for a good discussion of some of the reasons for these agglomeration effects.) Nowak, Urbaniak, and Zienkowski (1994) argue that such effects have been very substantial in Poland.

An important set of propositions related to agglomeration concerns the spillover effects from foreign-owned to domestic firms. An important debate is whether increasing the number of foreign firms stimulates the efficiency and growth of domestic firms (Aitken and Harrison, 1999). The addition of foreign firms may provide an economic stimulus in a region through their employment and wages. They also may create a demand for locally produced intermediate goods and underwrite local firms to supply that demand. Finally, foreign firms may also introduce new technologies, both the hard and soft kinds, as they demonstrate better management practices and organizational forms.

The other side of the agglomeration propositions is congestion effects, whereby an increased number, size, and/or growth of firms, both domestic and foreign, raises the level of competition in any given sized economy. The foreign firms in particular may depress the development of local firms because of direct competition for markets and through indirect competition for factors of production. The foreign firms are likely to be larger and have better access to financial, human, and physical capital, all of which gives them an advantage over local enterprises. We have already seen that foreign firms pay substantially higher wages than domestic firms, which should allow them to hire the best local workers. The deeper financial pockets will enable foreign firms to survive any fluctuations in demand and to engage in various types of predatory behavior, if they choose. One of the objectives in our study is to estimate how γ_s, a_{st}, and b_{st} vary with variations in the density of foreign firms.

A second set of propositions, taken from the organizational ecology literature, argues that survival and growth rates vary systematically with the age and characteristics of the cohort. Survival rates in particular should increase with the age of the cohort as the weaker and less economically fit firms exit. The figures graphing growth rates suggest that growth rates initially decline with age but then begin to increase as the cohort stabilizes. We include an age-squared term in the growth equations to represent this possibility. Cohorts with larger firms will have higher survival rates but lower growth rates, and cohorts with higher productivity levels will have higher survival and growth rates. Lastly, the graphs of survival and growth rates suggest that both rates are higher among the later cohorts, hence our inclusion of a variable measuring the sequence of cohorts. We also include a dummy variable for the initial cohort, as it includes firms started before 1990. These early firms may represent a different ecology than the later entrants.

We extend the basic arguments about cohort characteristics to propose that the parameters relating to the birth, survival, and growth of any cohort will vary with regional and temporal conditions. These variables are roughly grouped in categories representing institutional, human, and physical capital. Physical capital is measured by the kilometers of roads per square kilometer in the voivodship and the number of telephones per capita. Human capital is measured by the average years of schooling in the voivodship.

The institutional capital category is the most interesting as these factors are the most susceptible to policy interventions during a transition. One set of institutions that is critical to a de novo economy comprises its banks and other financial organizations (Pissarides, Singer, and Svejnar, 2003). Both theoretical and empirical arguments suggest that the development of new enterprises is aided by the presence of local and moderately concentrated banking institutions (see Bonaccorsi di Patti and Dell'Ariccia, 2003; Jackson and Thomas, 1995; and Kwast, Starr-McCluer, and Wolken, 1997). The private banking system evolved during the transition, with the number of banks and the degree of decentralization expanding during the period of our data.[6] We measure access to local financial services by the number of commercial banks and the number of cooperative banks in the voivodship. The presence of commercial banks should stimulate the development of the de novo economy. The number of cooperative banks should have the opposite effect as their loans went predominately to agriculture, thus reducing the local capital available for business ventures.[7] We do not have data on bank concentration so we cannot test the further proposition about firm creation and bank concentration reported by Bonaccorsi di Patti and Dell'Ariccia (2003).

An additional institutional variable is the number of local economic development agencies. Some regions were far more aggressive in their efforts to stimulate business, which should be reflected in higher birth and growth rates. The number of agencies working to support development is a measure of this activity. It may also act as a proxy for a broader set of attitudes and approaches that characterize some local governments as more "pro-business" than others.

Local conditions that affect the competitiveness of a region, such as access to Western markets, population density, proportion of the work force in farming, and the concentration of large state-owned enterprises (SOEs) are also included in the models. The state-enterprise variable is particularly significant because it measures whether the presence of and possible domination of the regional economy by the large, least-entrepreneurial and market-oriented enterprises and their work force inhibit the creation and growth of new firms.

The statistical analyses examine for both domestic and foreign-owned firms the annual birthrates and the number of small firms existing in 1990 and the survival and employment growth rates of the firms born each year. We then model the annual wage growth in the surviving new firms and compare their patterns of wage growth to the wage growth of the existing and former state-owned firms. These last models are a way to test systematically the argument presented in the graphs that wage growth

---

6 Both the decentralization and localness of the Polish banking industry reversed itself after the period of our study, as banks were consolidated and acquired by foreign owners.

7 Jackson and Thomas (1995) present a similar argument and empirical results from U.S. data from the early 1970s. They show that the proportion of deposits in savings and loans and credit unions, as opposed to commercial banks, is negatively related to the growth of employment in new enterprises. At that time S&Ls and credit unions were restricted to mortgages and consumer loans, respectively.

is more related to productivity and firm growth in the private firms than in the state firms.

Birthrates

The specific equation modeling births is:

$$Log\left(\frac{B_t^{d/f}}{Wrkfrc}\right) = X_t C + Year_t D + A_1 Log(Pop) + A_2 Log(TF_{t-1}^d)$$

$$+ A_3 Log(TF_{t-1}^f) + A_4 Log\left(\frac{B_{t-1}^{d/f}}{Wrkfrc}\right), \qquad (3.6)$$

where

B_t^d and B_t^f	number of domestic and foreign births in a voivodship in year t
Wrkfrc	size of the work force in the voivodship divided by 1,000
X_t	set of economic, demographic, and infrastructure variables describing each voivodship
C	vector of coefficients measuring the relationship between the log of births per capita and each of these descriptor variables
$Year_t$	set of dummy variables for each year, with 1997 being the base year
D	coefficients to measure how birthrate in year t differs from the birthrate in 1997
Log(Pop)	log of population
$TF_{t-1}^{d/f}$	total number of domestic or foreign firms in year $t - 1$ per capita
$B_{t-1}^{d/f}$	births in new private domestic or foreign firms in the previous year

The lagged birthrate is included to proxy the effects of any omitted factors that might give a voivodship a competitive advantage in supporting new private firms. Inclusion of this variable should help our variables measuring the total number of firms capture any agglomeration effects and not itself proxy omitted competitive factors. The estimator used is the negative binomial for event counts. Robust standard errors and clustering within voivodships are used for all estimations so that our estimates of the coefficient standard errors should be accurate. Estimation is done separately for manufacturing and construction, for trade and services, and for all other sectors. The statistical results are shown in Tables 3A.1 and 3A.2.

The birth of new domestic firms is related to several forms of human, physical, and institutional capital. Most important from a policy perspective, the measures of local organizational infrastructure, as captured by the number of local commercial banks and the number of local development agencies, are strongly and positively related to birthrates in all sectors, although the relationship between manufacturing births and banks is small and not statistically significant. The number of cooperative banks is negatively related to birthrates, as expected. Variations in telephones per capita are positively and significantly related to births, but roads are not. Education levels were related to the birthrates of trade and service and other firms but not to the birth of manufacturing firms. Among the other regional variables, regions with a large proportion of farmers and employment in large state enterprises in 1990 had lower birthrates, as did the Warsaw voivodship. The birthrates of foreign-owned firms show a somewhat but not completely similar pattern. (Estimates for the "other sector" category are somewhat unreliable in that outside of Warsaw there are many voivodships in which there were no foreign births.) The similarities are with the farming, state enterprise, cooperative bank, and telephone variables. The important differences are that foreign births are higher along the western border and in Warsaw and unrelated to the number of local commercial banks and development agencies. The only surprise here is the negative relationship with cooperative banks, which one would expect to be zero. These results suggest that the cooperative bank variable may be proxying some other factor that retards or stimulates firm creation.

The estimation of agglomeration effects provide some potentially provocative results. The birthrates for domestic and foreign firms in a region, and particularly domestic manufacturing firms, are strongly related to the presence of other firms of that ownership type in that sector in that region, as expected by the agglomeration hypothesis. The two surprises were the strong associations between the number of domestic firms and the entry of new foreign-owned firms in the manufacturing and trade and service sectors. Conversely, the associations between the total number of foreign-owned firms and the birthrate of domestic firms is quite small, though the coefficients are statistically significant. The implication here is that the location of new foreign-owned firms may follow the expansion of the domestic de novo economy but has relatively little stimulus on the creation of new domestic firms.

One further variation of the agglomeration hypothesis was examined. In some of the early regional development literature, the manufacturing sector was treated as the engine for local development. This assumption is being challenged as more types of services are marketed on a broad and global scale, but this does not diminish the argument about manufacturing being an important part of the economic base. We included the total number of domestic and foreign-owned manufacturing firms in each voivodship in the equations for the births of trade and service and other firms. There was no association between the density of either type of manufacturing firms and the birth of domestic firms in either sector. The only significant results were associations between the births of foreign-owned trade and other firms and the location of foreign-owned manufacturing firms. This suggests a possibility that these other firms were being developed as part and in support of a larger foreign activity.

The importance of agglomeration effects raises the question of why certain regions had a good head start in 1990, defined as a relatively large number of small private firms per capita. To help unravel this question, we estimated an equation for the number of small private domestic and foreign-owned firms in each sector in each voivodship in 1990 using the exogenous variables relevant for 1990, which excludes the bank, development agency, and unemployment variables but includes a variable measuring the proportion of the work force employed in large state-owned enterprises. The expectation is that areas with high concentrations of their economy in these enterprises will have difficulty encouraging new enterprises, particularly at the beginning of the transition. Table 3A.3 reports these results.

The variables related to the initial conditions complement the results modeling birthrates. For example, SOE employment in 1990 is negatively related to the number of manufacturing firms in 1990 but not to the birthrate of manufacturing firms, while it is negatively related to the birthrates in the other two sectors. Similarly, education levels are positively related to the number of domestic manufacturing firms in 1990 and to the birthrates for trade and service and other firms but not to birthrates in manufacturing. Given the very large agglomeration effect estimated for manufacturing these variations in initial conditions will persist throughout the transition. If the equation for domestic births is estimated without the two variables for total domestic and foreign firms, there is a large and statistically significant coefficient on the education variable. Areas with higher schooling levels were advantaged in the firm-creation process, but the effect is largely observed through the effects of the initial conditions and the agglomeration effects in that sector. The other important results are that areas with larger populations, more telephones per capita, and in the western rim all started with more private and particularly more foreign-owned private firms. Interestingly, voivodships with a large farming sector were not initially disadvantaged, except for having smaller total populations, but then lagged considerably in the creation of new firms in all sectors, both domestic and foreign. Regions began the transition with different initial endowments of private firms, which are related to some of the region's locational and structural characteristics, and the agglomeration effects perpetuate these advantages.

Survival

The second part of the model examines the survival rate of new firms and how that rate varies with the age and attributes of the cohort and with local factors. The equation used to model survival rates is

$$
Log\left(\frac{P_t}{1 - P_t}\right) = X_t B + Year_t D + A_1 Log(Cohort) + A_2 Cohort_1
$$

$$
+ A_3 \frac{1}{Age} + A_4 Log\left(\frac{E_{t-1}}{F_{t-1}}\right) + A_5 Log\left(\frac{S_{t-1}}{E_{t-1}}\right)
$$

$$
+ A_6 Log(F_0) + A_7 Log\left(TF^d_{t-1}\right) + A_8 Log\left(TF^f_{t-1}\right)
$$

$$
+ A_9 Log(Pop), \tag{3.7}
$$

where

$P_t = F_t/F_{t-1}$	proportion of firms surviving from year $t - 1$ to t, the dependent variable being the log of the odds of this probability of surviving
X_t	set of economic, demographic, and infrastructure variables describing each voivodship
B	vector of coefficients measuring the relationship between the log of survival and each of these descriptor variables
$Year_t$	set of dummy variables for each year, with 1997 being the base year
D	coefficients for year t that measure how births in that year differ from the birthrate in 1997

Cohort	sequence number of the cohorts, with the 1990 small firms being cohort 1, the 1991 births being cohort 2, and so on
$Cohort_I$	dummy variable to indicate if the cohort is the cohort of firms existing in 1990
Age	age of cohort in years
E_{t-1}/F_{t-1}	average firm size in the previous year
S_{t-1}/E_{t-1}	average sales per employee, or average productivity, in the previous year
F_0	number of firms in the cohort's initial year
$TF_{t-1}^{d/f}$	total number of domestic or foreign-owned firms in previous year for all cohorts
Log(Pop)	log of population

Two of the specifications in the survival equation follow from the graphical information on survival shown in Figures 3.1 and 3.2. The reciprocal of the age of the cohort is included to test the proposition that survival rates improve as the cohort ages, which presumably means as the weaker firms leave the cohort. Three different functional forms were tested, log, a negative exponential, and the reciprocal, with the reciprocal providing the best fit in all instances. Figures 3.1 and 3.2 suggest that survival rates improved with each successive cohort. To test this observation, each cohort is numbered starting with the 1990 cohort of existing small firms as cohort one. The log of this cohort number is included to test the proposition suggested by these figures that survival rates increased with successive cohorts. Again, the three functional forms were tested, with the log form having the best fit in all but the equation for domestic firms in the other sector. The variables measuring the initial size of the cohort and the total number of domestic and foreign firms are included to assess whether there are agglomeration effects in survivability or competition effects that reduce survival rates.

The statistical results are presented in Tables 3A.4 and 3A.5. Caution needs to be taken with the estimates for foreign-owned firms in the trade and services and other sectors as there are many regions and years where there were no births, and where there were births, the cohort is often very small. Survival rates are most strongly associated with the characteristics of each cohort. For all cohorts except foreign manufacturing, survival rates increased as the cohort aged, and the rate of increase is close to being the same for all the cohorts where age mattered. Among domestic firms, survival rates were higher in each successive cohort with the largest improvements occurring between the 1991 and the 1992 cohorts. Foreign trade and service firms followed a similar pattern, while among foreign manufacturing firms survivability decreased among successive cohorts, except for the initial cohort where the survival rate was low.

Average productivity and firm size are generally strong, positive predictors of the annual survival rate within cohorts, although the relationship between survival and productivity is small and statistically insignificant for domestic trade and service firms and for foreign manufacturing firms. The association between sales per employee and survival suggests a clear ecological process whereby the more efficient firms survive. The relationship between size and survival is no surprise, as larger firms can persist longer than smaller firms, although among cohorts of new firms size may also indicate a higher-quality firm.

With one interesting exception, there is no evidence that increasing the number of firms decreases the survival rates. For domestic and foreign-owned firms there is only one negative coefficient relating survival rates to the number of initial firms in a cohort, and for foreign trade and service firms the positive relationship is statistically significant. This last result may be a statistical aberration, but we can certainly say there is no evidence that larger cohorts have lower survival rates. For domestic firms there is only one statistically significant negative relationship between the total number of firms and the survival rate, which is for trade and service firms and the number of domestic firms. What is particularly important about this set of results is the absence of evidence that increasing the number of foreign-owned firms decreases the survival of domestic firms. The one set of consistent statistically significant results indicates that increasing the total number of foreign-owned firms decreases the survival of foreign-owned firms, and this was evident in all three sectors. One caveat about the lack of evidence for competitive effects is in order, however. Our industrial categories are very broad, and the competitive effects might be evident within narrowly defined clusters of homogeneous firms where competition may be more direct.

The relationships between survival rates and the variables describing local economic and institutional characteristics are neither very statistically significant nor consistent in their sign and magnitude. The only exceptions are that the survival rates of domestic firms are higher in Warsaw and in more densely populated areas. The lack of strong associations suggests that survival is more a function of the characteristics of each cohort and possibly of the individual firms in a cohort than of the environment in which the cohort exists.

Size of Firm

The growth in average employment per firm in each cohort is the third equation in the model. The equation used to model the changes in average size is

$$Log\left(\frac{E_t/F_t}{E_{t-1}/F_{t-1}}\right) = X_t B + Year_t D + A_1 Log(Cohort) + A_2(Age = 1)$$

$$+ A_3 Age_t + A_4 Age_t^2 + A_5 Log\left(\frac{E_{t-1}}{F_{t-1}}\right)$$

$$+ A_6 Log\left(\frac{S_{t-1}}{E_{t-1}}\right) + A_7 Log(F_0) + A_8 Log(TF_{t-1}^d)$$

$$+ A_9 Log(TF_{t-1}^f) + A_{10} Log(Pop). \qquad (3.8)$$

The left-hand side variable is the log of the change in the average employment per firm from year $t - 1$ to year t. The explanatory variables are as defined in the survival equation, with the exception of the age variables. A dummy variable for the cohort's first year and a quadratic form for the relationship between the cohort's age and employment growth are included. These specifications were selected to test the patterns in Figures 3.3 and 3.4, where it appears that firm growth is very large in the first year, declines in subsequent years, and then increases in the later years. The included year dummies will account for whether the observed increase in growth rates is a year effect.

Tables 3A.6 and 3A.7 show the statistical models for growth. As with survival, there is very little association between changes in firm size and the variables describing each voivodship. And as with survival, it is the variables describing the characteristics of each cohort that are strongly related to changes in firm size. With the exception of domestic firms in the trade and services sector, growth was strongly, positively, and significantly related to sales per worker. These results parallel those in the survival equation and together suggest that among private firms resources are moving to the more efficient firms. The larger the average firm size for domestic firms, the smaller the growth rate, suggesting there may be an optimal size for a given sector and that growth slows as this level is approached. For foreign-owned firms the relations were negative but not statistically significant, except among the small number of firms in the other sector.

The relationships with age followed what is observed in Figures 3.3 and 3.4. Employment among the surviving firms increased substantially in the cohort's first year among both domestic and foreign-owned firms. Growth continued but at a decreasing rate as the cohort aged. For the two largest domestic cohorts and for the foreign manufacturing cohort the growth rate began increasing again. (It is important to keep in mind that we are discussing changes in the growth rate, not whether average size is increasing or declining.) For the domestic firms the turnaround in growth rates appears to occur around the fifth year, whereas for foreign manufacturing firms it is about year 3. It is hard to know at this point whether this result is spurious, is characteristic of this time period and cohorts, or reflects a systematic long-term dynamic whereby only the most successful firms survive for as long as five years, at which point the rate of growth in average firm size begins increasing because only the most efficient and fit firms remain.

There is no systematic relationship between the number of firms, either initially in a cohort or in total, and growth rates. There are as many positive as negative associations, and only one coefficient of the eighteen in this set is statistically significant, raising the possibility that this is a chance occurrence. These results mirror those in the survival equations and offer more evidence that, for at least the early years of the transition, increasing the number of firms in a sector and region does not restrict the survivability or growth within a cohort. It will require a much longer set of panel data to know if this result is characteristic only of the early years of a transition, where the likely market is far from being saturated, or represents a longer-term phenomenon.

These results, including the lack of systematic associations with local economic and demographic characteristics, suggest that growth is much more dependent on the characteristics of individual firms, such as their level of productivity, size, and age than upon local factors, including the number of other firms, that are common to all firms in a cohort.

Wage Growth and Productivity

There are two important factors to examine in analyzing wage growth. The first is whether and how fast wages grow among cohorts of successful new firms. As suggested earlier, this is a good indicator of the quality of the jobs being created and whether the surviving firms create well-paying jobs in the long run. Figures 3.5 and 3.6 show that the jobs created in new firms pay less than jobs in larger firms, but that, over time, real wages increase in the successful firms. The second question is how wage growth compares among the different classes of firms. The evidence in Figures 3.5 to 3.7 is that wage growth followed quite different patterns in domestic private and state-managed firms. Furthermore, Figures 3.8 and

3.10 suggest that wage growth does not necessarily match productivity growth in the state-managed firms. The statistical analysis examines both questions. The statistical model for wage changes is

$$
Log\left(\frac{W_t}{W_{t-1}}\right) = (X_t - \overline{X}_t)B + Year_t D + A_1(Age = 1) + A_2 Age
$$

$$
+ A_3(Cohort = 1) + A_4 Log\left(\frac{E_{t-1}}{F_{t-1}}\right) + A_5 Log\left(\frac{S_{t-1}}{E_{t-1}}\right)
$$

$$
+ A_6 Log\left[\frac{(S/F)_t}{(S/F)_{t-1}}\right] + A_7 Log\left(\frac{W_{t-1}}{\overline{W}}\right) + A_8 Log(Pop),
$$

$$
(3.9)
$$

where

$\dfrac{W_t}{W_{t-1}}$	average wages, defined as payroll per worker, at time t, divided by wages at time $t - 1$
X_t	set of economic, demographic, and infrastructure variables describing each voivodship (these variables are expressed as deviations about the mean values for all voivodships in year t, $\overline{X}_t$, so the equation represents the wage changes expected in an average voivodship)
C	vector of coefficients measuring the relationship between wage changes and each of these descriptor variables
$Year_t$	set of dummy variables for each year, with 1997 being the base year
D	coefficients for year t that measure how wage changes in that year differ from those in 1997
$(Age = 1)$	dummy variable for the first year of the cohort's existence
Age	age of cohort in years, included
$(Cohort = 1)$	dummy variable for the 1990 cohort of firms
E_{t-1}/F_{t-1}	average firm size in the previous year
S_{t-1}/E_{t-1}	average sales per employee, or average productivity, in the previous year
$\dfrac{(S/F)_t}{(S/F)_{t-1}}$	ratio of sales per firm year t to sales per firm in year $t - 1$
$\dfrac{W_{t-1}}{\overline{W}_v}$	ratio of wages, defined as average payroll per worker, in year $t - 1$ to the average wage in the voivodship for the period 1991–97

The model parallels the ones used to examine survival and growth with several additions. In addition to the lagged level of productivity, the equation also includes the change in average sales per firm, with the expectation that the faster the sales growth in a cohort, the more firms will increase wages, both because they have the resources and because they will need to attract workers in order to expand further.[8] The annual wage growth is also related to wages at time $t - 1$ divided by the average payroll per worker in the cohort's voivodship over the period 1990 to 1997 for firms of each ownership type.[9] The proposition here is that the more wages exceed this average in one year, the smaller the expected increase during the following year, and vice versa if wages are too low. Presumably the smaller this adjustment process, the less wages reflect market conditions. A dummy variable measuring whether the cohort is the set of firms existing in 1990 is included to test whether this set of firms behaved differently with respect to wage changes. This difference may be particularly evident among the state firms, as this cohort did not experience any type of restructuring, whereas the later cohorts went through some restructuring and were shifted to the treasury in anticipation of privatization.

Variables measuring the yearly unemployment rate and the proportion of de novo jobs created in the local economy are added to the set of regional characteristic variables. These are intended to assess the tightness of the local labor market. The expectation is that higher unemployment will put downward pressure on wages, whereas higher rates of new job creation will have the opposite effect. This labor dynamic is increasingly seen as an important aspect of successful transitions (see Jackson, 2003, and Tichit, 2003). Unemployment depresses wages, which contributes to the success of new firms, which in turn eventually bids up wages, which then attract workers from state enterprises to move directly to the new sector.

The statistical results are presented in Tables 3A.8–10. For most cohorts in all sectors and ownership categories wages increase significantly during the first year of the cohort's life. In only a few sectors do wages continue to increase over the life of the cohort independently of other factors such as local conditions, size, and productivity. There is also no pattern of relationships between firm size and wage increases, other factors held

---

8 Sales data are in real terms using the national GDP deflator, and wages are adjusted using the CPI index. Both indices are published by the Polish Central Statistical Office.
9 This average wage was computed using the payroll and employment data aggregated for all ownership types and all sectors.

constant. This result suggests that size, per se, is not a factor affecting wages. There is also no systematic evidence that wages changed differently in the 1990 cohort than in other cohorts.[10]

The next question is whether annual wage changes are related to differences in productivity and sales growth or to differences between a cohort's wage levels and average local wages. The short answer is yes, but more so for the private firms than for the state-managed firms. The coefficients on lagged sales per employee and on the change in sales variables indicate that variations in both these variables are more strongly associated with differences in wage growth among the private firms than among the state-managed enterprises. Manufacturing wages were the most sensitive to productivity differences, and the coefficients for domestic and foreign-owned firms are about twice the magnitude of the coefficient for state firms and the difference is well beyond twice the size of the standard errors of the coefficients. For the service and trade sector the coefficients and the differences by ownership type are all small and statistically insignificant. For the other category the relationship between productivity and wage growth is significant for both groups of private firms and effectively zero for state firms. Other than the trade and service sector, where productivity is unrelated to wages, wage setting in private firms differed substantially from that in state firms, with wages in the former group much more related to productivity.

Wage growth is strongly related to sales growth for all types of firms and sectors. In all sectors, the coefficients for domestic and foreign firms are equal or nearly so and the coefficients for state firms are smaller by about 0.02, although this difference is not much larger than the estimated standard errors. Lastly, wages in all sectors and firm types are responsive to deviations from average wage levels in the region. The further they deviated in one year, the larger the correction the next year. The only difference between domestic and state firms in the magnitude of this adjustment is in the trade and service sector, where the cohorts of domestic firms appear to be particularly responsive to market deviations. The results here suggest that all types of firms react similarly to sales growth and local wage levels in setting their own wages.

The two variables designed to assess conditions in the local labor market, unemployment and de novo job creation, showed mixed and

---

10 There were two statistically significant coefficients, among foreign-owned trade and service firms and state-managed Other firms, but neither is strong enough to warrant an inference of systematic differences between this and the other cohorts.

inconclusive results. The relationships between wage changes and the amount of new-job creation are positive (except for the cohorts of foreign-owned trade and service firms) but only statistically significant in about half the equations. These results suggest that firms in areas with more de novo job creation pay higher wages, as expected, but we must acknowledge the uncertainty of this conclusion. There is no pattern to the relative magnitude of the coefficients in the different sectors, suggesting that if firms are forced to pay higher wages in areas with more new-job creation, it is true for all types of firms. There is no consistency in the relationships between unemployment and wage changes. Only about half the coefficients were negative, as predicted, and only one of these is statistically significant. The safest conclusion is that wages are unrelated to local unemployment rates. Local labor market conditions, as influenced by the amount of new-job creation, may affect wages, and if they do, they do so for all firms equally.

Comparisons of yearly wage growth, independent of other variables, in the domestic relative to the state-managed sectors are revealing. The year variables in Tables 3A.8–10 show the expected wage increase for that year for a cohort with average values for all the variables, including lagged size and sales per employee, for that type firm and sector and with no change in sales and a lagged wage equal to the voivodship average. In 1991 real wage increases in such average domestic firms greatly exceeded increases in state-managed cohorts. In 1992 the changes were about equal. But by the end of 1993 and in 1994, real wages dropped in cohorts of domestic firms but increased substantially in cohorts of state-managed firms. Then between 1995 and 1997 real wages increased in both sectors but at a faster rate in the state sector. The wage increases in these base cases for foreign-owned cohorts were continually higher than in domestic cohorts and consistently exceeded those in the state-managed sector except among manufacturing cohorts from 1993 on. The higher wage increases in the state-managed relative to private domestic firms coincide with the period when the government was controlled by the coalition of post-Communist parties, who campaigned on a promise to lift or reduce the popiwek. The large wage increases in foreign-owned firms indicate the considerable pressure these firms place on the local labor markets, where domestic firms must compete for workers but cannot match the wages.

Annual wage increases for private firms tended on average to be higher in Warsaw than in other regions, other things being equal. Cohorts of domestic trade and service firms are the only exception here. For state firms, wage increases in Warsaw equaled or were less than increases in other regions. This is the only regional variable that exhibited a consistent pattern of associations with wage increases. The other variables included had both statistically insignificant and inconsistent coefficients. These results suggest that except for being located in Warsaw, where prices were rising faster than in other parts of Poland, the factors determining wage increases are largely those associated with the sales and productivity of the firms.

CONCLUSION

Our conclusion falls into three categories: the Schumpeterian view of economic growth and transition as a process of creative destruction where "new" economies replace older, outmoded ones; the transition of the Polish economy per se; and the implications of the estimated models of wage growth and what they indicate about how wages are set in firms under state control relative to firms under market control.

The evidence about Poland's continuing successful effort to build a market economy strongly reinforces Schumpeter's views on economic development and the creative destruction metaphor. The decline of the older, state-owned enterprises, even those that were restructured or privatized, fits the first part of this description. These establishments may not have disappeared, and some may prove to be economically successful in the long run, but they are not a vibrant and growing aspect of the Polish economy.

The entirely new firms, most of which are domestically owned, are the source of both job and sales growth in the Polish economy – the creative part of creative destruction. The figures and the statistical analyses are very consistent with our model of the creative destruction process. This model places the focus on the birth, survival, and growth rates of new firms. Efforts to increase the rate of economic growth require a focus on factors that increase these rates. The statistical analysis of these rates among voivodships suggests that birthrates may be the most susceptible to public-policy efforts. Variations in birthrates are strongly correlated with a number of local factors that can be altered through public actions. These factors were the years of schooling, the extent of the local development effort, and possibly the size and structure of the local banking industry.

The results also suggest important agglomeration effects whereby the birth of new firms is higher in areas that already have a concentration of such firms, particularly in the domestic manufacturing sector. This suggests that efforts to stimulate development in areas with a low density of new enterprises will be particularly difficult and slow. The results also suggest that once the process is initiated it will continue to gain momentum. The agglomeration results imply that the process of new-firm creation is likely to expand in areas geographically close to areas that already have a successful new economy. One area for further research is on factors that explain these agglomeration effects. Our results strongly suggest their existence, but we have no evidence about why they exist. It may be a demonstration effect, where the visibility of new enterprises stimulates others to start firms. Or it may be as complex as the presence of a set of attitudes among the local population that encourages entrepreneurial activity. (On this possibility, see Jackson and Marcinkowski, 1996.) Other possibilities include the attributes and training of the local labor force and the presence of local organizations and policies, such as legal and accounting firms or tax laws, that are more oriented toward new enterprises.

The contrasts between domestic and foreign-owned enterprises are particularly important as Poland, and possibly other countries, consider ways to stimulate or transform their economies. Foreign-owned firms constitute a very small fraction of the total number of new firms and of the jobs created by these firms. Furthermore, there is no statistical evidence that increasing numbers of foreign firms is a significant stimulus to the creation, survival, or growth of the domestic firms. In broad terms, these findings are consistent with those of Aitken and Harrison (1999), who find very few externalities to direct foreign investment when they examined Venezuelan firms. The foreign firms' advantage, for Poland at least, is that they have higher survival and growth rates and pay higher wages than domestic firms. Even considering these differences, national and local governments should be conservative in the concessions they make to attract foreign firms and concentrate their efforts on factors that stimulate local enterprises. Conversely, there is no evidence that increasing the number of foreign firms inhibits the development of domestic firms, meaning there is no justification for efforts to restrict the activities of foreign firms.

The broad lesson here is that a healthy economy continually needs to create and develop new firms. In periods of dramatic change and transition, this ecological process becomes a necessity. This general conclusion applies to mature market economies facing serious challenges as well as to transitional economies. (See Jackson et al., 1999, for comparisons of the transformation of the Michigan and Polish economies that make this point.) The efforts to continue the economic transition in Eastern Europe must develop policies and institutions that will stimulate and sustain the entrepreneurial process.

In terms of the results specific to the Polish economy, the most important result is the continual increase in the survival and growth rates among domestic firms during the 1990s. This is significant because that is one aspect of the Polish economy that may have been retarding long-run job creation. Long-run growth within any cohort depends on both the survival rate of these firms and the growth rate of the average surviving firm. A low survival rate in the first year of a cohort substantially reduces the total amount of jobs and sales that cohort will add to the economy in the long run. Relative to foreign-owned firms, the survival rate among domestic firms has always been and continues to be lower, and this gap is particularly large in the first years of any cohort. This is one area where detailed investigations into the nature of this process would be important. It may be that a significant number of the firms being started are not economically viable, in which case the survival rate is to be expected. On the other hand, there may be particular barriers to new enterprises whose removal can assist new firms or an inexperience among entrepreneurs about how to manage a new business that is reducing the survival rate. If the latter explanation is true, it would suggest more training and education in entrepreneurial activities and management are appropriate policy initiatives.

A serious concern identified in our analysis is the increase in the real wages being paid in the state-controlled sector, which are not being matched by the total output per worker, as measured by our real sales data. Figure 3.9 and the statistical results in Tables 3A.8–10 indicate quite steady yearly increases in wages in the state-managed sector that exceeded those among domestic firms, independent of productivity. Furthermore, these increases in state firms are more weakly related to productivity levels than in private firms. The latter relationship reinforces the observation that annual wage increases in this sector are decided primarily on the basis of a proportional increase in previous wages rather than productivity differences.

The lack of market discipline among state-managed firms could be a problem in the long run for the Polish economy. If continued, this behavior means the very scarce resources in the economy are being allocated to less productive enterprises with poorer histories of providing growth in either sales or jobs. Our results consistently indicate that the faster that resources can be shifted to the process of improving the birth, survival, and growth rate of new firms, the faster the whole economy will grow and the faster the transition will be to a full market economy.

Appendix 3A: Models for Birth, Survival, and Growth Rates and Wage Rates

This appendix, comprising Tables 3A.1–10, presents the statistical estimations of the models for the entry, survival, and growth of de novo firms described in Equations 3.6 to 3.8 and for wage changes as shown in Equation 3.9.

Table 3A.1. *Domestic-Firm Birthrates*

Variables	Manufacturing		Trade & Services		Other	
	Coeff.	Std. Error	Coeff.	Std. Error	Coeff.	Std. Error
Log(farm)	−0.135	0.059	−0.073	0.060	−0.452	0.082
Log(density)	0.042	0.115	0.091	0.125	−0.414	0.170
Log(SOE emp/work force)$_{90}$	−0.050	0.080	−0.134	0.071	−0.234	0.105
West	−0.168	0.058	−0.017	0.057	−0.140	0.101
Warsaw	−0.201	0.084	−0.277	0.103	−0.023	0.128
Log(dev. agencies)	0.136	0.068	0.135	0.066	0.122	0.067
Log(bank offices)	0.077	0.057	0.140	0.055	0.306	0.072
Log(bank coops)	−0.157	0.052	−0.155	0.052	−0.234	0.062
Log(roads/km^2)	−0.148	0.187	−0.107	0.156	−0.115	0.218
Log(telephone/cap)	0.216	0.088	0.175	0.107	0.059	0.147
Log(education)	0.381	0.513	2.258	0.444	2.207	0.686
Year 91	1.067	0.245	0.465	0.252	0.708	0.240
Year 92	0.565	0.172	0.188	0.176	0.670	0.185
Year 93	0.274	0.122	−0.252	0.112	0.625	0.146
Year 94	−0.223	0.083	−0.656	0.078	0.133	0.147
Year 95	0.390	0.077	0.266	0.066	0.550	0.124
Year 96	0.843	0.071	0.683	0.059	0.838	0.087
Log(domestic firms/work force)	0.590	0.147	0.414	0.091	0.290	0.094
Log(foreign firms/work force)	0.046	0.027	0.051	0.018	0.064	0.024
Log($B_{t−1}$/work force)	0.151	0.112	−0.112	0.069	0.102	0.080
Log(work force)	−0.485	0.165	0.217	0.132	0.064	0.184
Constant	1.996	1.656	−0.474	1.472	−1.387	1.860
Log(α)	−2.630	0.110	−2.733	0.098	−2.352	0.143

Table 3A.2. *Foreign-Firm Birthrates*

Variables	Manufacturing		Trade & Services		Other	
	Coeff.	Std. Error	Coeff.	Std. Error	Coeff.	Std. Error
Log(farm)	−0.225	0.144	0.014	0.168	−0.241	0.209
Log(density)	−0.321	0.212	−0.161	0.279	−0.840	0.393
Log(SOE emp/work force)$_{90}$	0.410	0.206	0.459	0.252	−0.350	0.312
West	0.211	0.106	0.111	0.149	0.704	0.224
Warsaw	0.154	0.215	0.362	0.253	1.050	0.304
Log(dev. agencies)	0.077	0.105	−0.193	0.168	−0.013	0.180
Log(bank offices)	−0.088	0.177	0.021	0.207	−0.852	0.360
Log(bank coops)	−0.188	0.093	−0.460	0.135	−0.664	0.238
Log(roads/km^2)	0.108	0.225	0.008	0.270	0.200	0.421
Log(telephone/cap)	0.053	0.184	0.418	0.241	0.684	0.548
Log(education)	1.389	1.151	2.435	1.943	2.974	3.332
Year 91	−0.030	0.395	−0.580	0.800	−2.641	0.661
Year 92	0.918	0.276	1.542	0.521	−0.396	0.528
Year 93	0.336	0.230	0.327	0.449	−0.436	0.431
Year 94	0.427	0.206	−0.007	0.343	−0.187	0.466
Year 95	1.332	0.167	1.442	0.247	0.925	0.299
Year 96	0.795	0.149	0.721	0.214	0.397	0.257
Log(domestic firms/work force)	0.509	0.207	0.723	0.208	0.336	0.273
Log(foreign firms/work force)	0.404	0.107	0.423	0.101	0.399	0.134
Log(B_{t-1}/work force)	0.027	0.071	−0.042	0.080	−0.178	0.104
Log(work force)	−0.253	0.228	0.318	0.327	0.825	0.672
Constant	−7.971	2.744	−10.033	4.409	0.2794	7.950
Log(α)	−2.438	0.256	−1.976	0.369	−2.343	0.645

Table 3A.3. *Models for Number of Firms in 1990*

	Manufacturing		Trade & Service		Other	
	Domestic	Foreign	Domestic	Foreign	Domestic	Foreign
Log(farm)	0.111	−0.186	−0.062	−0.412	−0.131	−0.591
	(0.183)	(0.394)	(0.172)	(0.697)	(0.201)	(0.772)
Log(density)	0.461	0.562	0.207	0.389	−0.421	−0.627
	(0.334)	(0.699)	(0.322)	(1.098)	(0.364)	(1.363)
West	0.516	0.709	0.184	0.723	0.548	1.129
	(0.176)	(0.366)	(0.172)	(0.618)	(0.189)	(0.688)
Warsaw	0.161	1.190	0.163	1.509	0.174	0.417
	(0.380)	(0.723)	(0.357)	(0.915)	(0.393)	(1.278)
Log(SOE emp)$_{90}$	−0.233	−0.741	0.303	−0.768	0.275	−0.086
	(0.225)	(0.512)	(0.239)	(1.098)	(0.279)	(1.432)
Log(roads/km^2)	−0.472	−0.411	−0.365	−0.268	0.624	0.063
	(0.445)	(0.949)	(0.450)	(1.610)	(0.485)	(2.027)
Log(telephone/ cap)	−0.358	0.479	0.414	1.294	−0.209	0.413
	(0.247)	(0.529)	(0.254)	(1.0552	(0.273)	(1.199)
Log(education)	4.093	0.194	1.850	2.353	4.958	5.830
	(1.303)	(2.743)	(1.414)	(6.500)	(1.567)	(7.588)
Log(work force)	−0.208	0.787	0.486	1.652	−0.200	1.122
	(0.305)	(0.660)	(0.308)	(1.468)	(0.349)	(1.651)
Constant	−0.161	8.576	0.965	1.014	−12.398	−11.463
	(3.343)	(7.017)	(3.712)	(15.390)	(4.065)	(19.185)
Log(α)	−2.328	−1.123	−2.576	−1.698	−2.455	−1.140
	(0.214)	0.310	0.320	1.813	(0.314)	(1.243)

Note: Coefficient standard errors in parentheses under coefficients.

Table 3A.4. *Domestic-Firm Survival Rates: (Firms$_t$/Firms$_{t-1}$)*

Variables	Manufacturing		Trade & Service		Other	
	Coeff.	Std. Error	Coeff.	Std. Error	Coeff.	Std. Error
Log(farm)	0.062	0.070	0.127	0.085	0.060	0.089
Log(density)	0.086	0.117	0.169	0.108	0.369	0.143
Log(SOE emp/work force)$_{90}$	−0.125	0.077	−0.049	0.104	−0.213	0.166
West	−0.019	0.058	−0.005	0.075	−0.065	0.086
Warsaw	0.207	0.093	0.160	0.105	0.356	0.152
Log(bank offices)	−0.026	0.064	0.057	0.086	0.080	0.084
Log(bank coops)	−0.048	0.051	−0.016	0.077	−0.055	0.090
Log(roads/km^2)	−0.029	0.167	−0.179	0.178	−0.647	0.255
Log(telephone/cap)	0.104	0.078	0.157	0.127	−0.378	0.200
Log(education)	0.173	0.513	0.746	0.497	0.951	0.903
Log(dev. agencies)	0.068	0.066	0.010	0.076	−0.160	0.093
Log(cohort)	0.274	0.062	0.318	0.102	0.623	0.105
Cohort 1	0.146	0.059	0.200	0.085	0.450	0.146
Year 91	−0.249	0.206	0.173	0.249	−0.332	0.381
Year 92	0.059	0.158	0.541	0.204	−0.147	0.297
Year 93	0.453	0.131	0.573	0.168	0.447	0.232
Year 94	0.564	0.106	0.232	0.109	1.069	0.182
Year 95	0.731	0.087	0.451	0.091	1.144	0.129
Year 96	0.546	0.072	0.332	0.059	1.086	0.091
1/cohort age	−1.086	0.076	−1.206	0.130	−1.268	0.170
Log(emp/firm)$_{t-1}$	0.309	0.054	0.244	0.071	0.517	0.069
Log(sales/emp)$_{t-1}$	0.139	0.052	0.092	0.061	0.213	0.060
Log(firms in cohort)$_0$	0.026	0.043	−0.052	0.044	0.026	0.087
Log(domestic firms/work force)	−0.052	0.108	−0.212	0.088	−0.003	0.094
Log(foreign firms/work force)	−0.016	0.030	0.011	0.020	0.004	0.031
Log(work force)	0.043	0.100	0.350	0.143	0.118	0.118
Constant	0.539	1.672	−0.789	2.056	3.775	3.603
N	1,372		1,372		1,290	

Table 3A.5. *Foreign-Firm Survival Rates: (Firms$_t$/Firms$_{t-1}$)*

Variables	Manufacturing		Trade & Service		Other	
	Coeff.	Std. Error	Coeff.	Std. Error	Coeff.	Std. Error
Log(farm)	−0.341	0.174	0.617	0.219	−0.440	0.675
Log(density)	−0.420	0.226	0.777	0.244	0.951	0.591
Log(SOE emp/ work force)$_{90}$	−0.327	0.256	0.413	0.387	−0.956	1.146
West	−0.121	0.110	0.050	0.155	0.147	0.531
Warsaw	0.077	0.188	−0.518	0.311	−0.377	0.936
Log(bank offices)	0.228	0.137	0.667	0.275	−0.275	0.498
Log(bank coops)	−0.356	0.150	−0.225	0.414	−0.181	0.523
Log(roads/km^2)	0.482	0.319	−0.280	0.288	−0.364	0.603
Log(telephone/cap)	0.764	0.327	−0.089	0.545	0.483	0.866
Log(education)	0.672	1.734	−0.727	3.176	−0.820	5.869
Log(dev. agencies)	0.186	0.098	0.174	0.120	0.320	0.457
Log(cohort)	−0.432	0.196	0.563	0.288	0.211	0.718
Cohort 1	−0.676	0.230	1.199	0.347	−0.005	0.668
Year 91	−0.347	0.554	1.585	1.038	0.003	2.056
Year 92	−0.179	0.376	0.655	0.894	−0.037	1.552
Year 93	0.299	0.338	1.592	0.594	0.912	1.266
Year 94	0.446	0.245	0.785	0.457	0.633	0.905
Year 95	0.509	0.187	1.059	0.385	1.893	0.533
Year 96	0.482	0.159	0.536	0.260	0.946	0.373
1/cohort age	0.092	0.279	−1.235	0.225	−0.927	0.657
Log(emp/firm)$_{t-1}$	0.431	0.088	0.437	0.096	0.497	0.196
Log(sales/emp)$_{t-1}$	0.117	0.073	0.238	0.064	0.335	0.137
Log(firms in cohort)$_0$	0.065	0.084	0.261	0.079	0.146	0.279
Log(domestic firms/work force)	−0.062	0.188	0.039	0.304	0.526	0.410
Log(foreign firms/work force)	−0.244	0.110	−0.241	0.120	−0.453	0.236
Log(work force)	0.143	0.256	−0.268	0.422	−1.273	1.026
Constant	−7.410	4.179	2.673	6.515	14.648	16.021
N	1,062		565		373	

Table 3A.6. *Domestic-Firm Growth Rates: [(Employees/Firm)$_t$/*
(Employees/Firm)$_{t-1}$]

Variables	Manufacturing		Trade & Service		Other	
	Coeff.	Std. Error	Coeff.	Std. Error	Coeff.	Std. Error
Log(farm)	−0.007	0.008	0.015	0.020	0.008	0.023
Log(density)	−0.034	0.012	−0.026	0.029	0.046	0.041
Log(SOE emp/ work force)$_{90}$	−0.009	0.014	0.058	0.027	0.011	0.039
West	−0.009	0.008	−0.056	0.016	0.053	0.019
Warsaw	−0.025	0.015	0.007	0.023	0.085	0.031
Log(bank offices)	−0.002	0.014	−0.043	0.019	0.006	0.026
Log(bank coops)	−0.003	0.008	0.013	0.027	−0.006	0.021
Log(roads/km^2)	0.026	0.020	−0.008	0.044	−0.030	0.064
Log(telephone/cap)	−0.030	0.016	0.006	0.051	−0.014	0.048
Log(education)	0.246	0.114	−0.140	0.189	0.020	0.218
Log(dev. agencies)	0.006	0.010	0.017	0.013	−0.010	0.022
Log(cohort)	−0.003	0.019	−0.044	0.037	0.187	0.075
Year 91	−0.145	0.049	−0.071	0.110	0.238	0.205
Year 92	−0.107	0.039	−0.216	0.085	0.195	0.191
Year 93	−0.100	0.031	−0.177	0.055	0.149	0.132
Year 94	−0.101	0.024	−0.121	0.047	0.115	0.093
Year 95	−0.079	0.017	−0.086	0.034	0.053	0.067
Year 96	−0.059	0.011	−0.046	0.018	0.014	0.033
Cohort age/10	−0.374	0.093	−0.507	0.200	0.430	0.299
(Cohort age/10)^2	0.412	0.121	0.393	0.205	0.491	0.294
Cohort age = 1	0.183	0.014	0.078	0.021	0.247	0.029
Log(emp/firm)$_{t-1}$	−0.069	0.012	−0.148	0.098	−0.045	0.017
Log(sales/emp)$_{t-1}$	0.052	0.013	0.042	0.030	0.047	0.022
Log(firms in cohort)$_{t-1}$	−0.036	0.009	−0.018	0.011	0.030	0.032
Log(domestic firms/work force)	−0.008	0.016	0.003	0.024	−0.020	0.026
Log(foreign firms/work force)	−0.009	0.006	0.005	0.006	−0.008	0.007
Log(work force)	0.040	0.015	0.021	0.035	0.017	0.024
Constant	−0.472	0.283	0.560	0.615	−0.339	0.811
N	1,372		1,372		1,265	

Table 3A.7. *Foreign-Firm Growth Rates: [(Employees/Firm)$_t$/ (Employees/Firm)$_{t-1}$]*

Variables	Manufacturing		Trade & Service		Other	
	Coeff.	Std. Error	Coeff.	Std. Error	Coeff.	Std. Error
Log(farm)	−0.031	0.038	−0.177	0.058	−0.067	0.099
Log(density)	−0.017	0.041	−0.244	0.054	−0.100	0.126
Log(SOE emp/ work force)$_{90}$	0.037	0.053	−0.222	0.106	−0.018	0.138
West	−0.036	0.025	−0.089	0.044	−0.135	0.076
Warsaw	−0.039	0.050	0.045	0.073	−0.016	0.120
Log(bank offices)	0.001	0.040	0.046	0.070	0.085	0.104
Log(bank coops)	0.009	0.030	−0.004	0.095	−0.190	0.089
Log(roads/km^2)	−0.065	0.047	0.268	0.050	0.074	0.123
Log(telephone/cap)	−0.046	0.054	−0.066	0.134	0.084	0.189
Log(education)	0.275	0.260	1.267	0.730	−0.016	1.514
Log(dev. agencies)	−0.036	0.028	0.078	0.038	0.015	0.076
Log(cohort)	0.147	0.069	0.092	0.108	0.155	0.122
Year 91	−0.136	0.179	0.620	0.397	0.161	0.439
Year 92	0.073	0.132	0.341	0.363	0.224	0.318
Year 93	−0.014	0.092	0.048	0.231	0.305	0.267
Year 94	0.032	0.069	0.104	0.177	0.189	0.185
Year 95	0.046	0.048	0.081	0.122	0.118	0.104
Year 96	−0.030	0.032	−0.004	0.070	−0.053	0.059
Cohort age/10	−0.335	0.319	−0.025	0.422	−1.201	0.674
(Cohort age/10)^2	0.669	0.337	−0.105	0.469	2.246	0.788
Cohort age = 1	0.215	0.043	0.136	0.040	0.102	0.058
Log(emp/firm)$_{t-1}$	−0.019	0.016	−0.002	0.039	−0.125	0.035
Log(sales/emp)$_{t-1}$	0.034	0.010	0.080	0.024	0.085	0.026
Log(firms in cohort)$_{t-1}$	0.013	0.017	0.004	0.032	0.014	0.045
Log(domestic firms/work force)	−0.006	0.038	0.111	0.061	0.013	0.057
Log(foreign firms/work force)	0.002	0.025	0.001	0.049	−0.016	0.031
Log(work force)	−0.046	0.048	−0.140	0.098	−0.029	0.132
Constant	−0.081	0.780	−4.479	1.666	−0.639	3.302
N	1,034		536		357	

Table 3A.8. *Changes in Manufacturing Sector Wages*

Variable	Domestic		Foreign		State	
	Coeff.	Std. Error	Coeff.	Std. Error	Coeff.	Std. Error
Log(farm)	0.006	0.008	−0.034	0.017	0.010	0.006
Log(SOE emp/ work force)$_{90}$	0.031	0.010	−0.069	0.030	0.007	0.011
West	−0.012	0.007	−0.021	0.011	0.000	0.005
Warsaw	0.018	0.009	0.057	0.022	−0.002	0.011
% Unemployment	0.006	0.047	0.018	0.137	0.009	0.053
% De novo jobs	0.051	0.077	0.235	0.109	−0.006	0.055
Cohort 1	−0.009	0.008	−0.025	0.027	−0.006	0.010
Cohort age = 1	0.028	0.006	0.013	0.013	−0.013	0.009
Age	0.006	0.001	0.007	0.006	0.008	0.004
Log(work force)	−0.018	0.008	−0.015	0.019	0.004	0.007
Log(emp/firm)$_{t-1}$	0.014	0.012	0.006	0.011	0.001	0.006
Log(sales/emp)$_{t-1}$	0.060	0.010	0.060	0.012	0.031	0.005
Log[Δ(sales/firm)]	0.083	0.016	0.083	0.016	0.064	0.011
Log(wage$_{t-1}$/av. wage)	−0.214	0.066	−0.311	0.052	−0.179	0.035
Year 91	0.136	0.030	0.109	0.062	0.020	0.020
Year 92	0.126	0.012	0.183	0.043	0.135	0.013
Year 93	−0.059	0.008	0.022	0.031	0.033	0.012
Year 94	−0.039	0.007	0.037	0.026	0.066	0.009
Year 95	0.015	0.008	0.074	0.018	0.073	0.009
Year 96	0.032	0.009	0.076	0.017	0.090	0.006
Year 97	0.052	0.010	0.093	0.016	0.117	0.008
N	1,372		1,026		1,192	

Table 3A.9. *Changes in Trade and Service Sector Wages*

Variable	Domestic		Foreign		State	
	Coeff.	Std. Error	Coeff.	Std. Error	Coeff.	Std. Error
Log(farm)	0.024	0.011	−0.046	0.023	0.008	0.016
Log(SOE emp/ work force)$_{90}$	0.025	0.018	−0.089	0.057	−0.013	0.025
West	−0.042	0.019	−0.027	0.027	0.005	0.010
Warsaw	−0.048	0.019	0.116	0.041	−0.044	0.023
% Unemployment	−0.064	0.084	0.003	0.257	0.068	0.096
% De novo jobs	0.321	0.123	−0.264	0.218	0.286	0.150
Cohort 1	0.033	0.022	−0.099	0.033	−0.002	0.014
Cohort age = 1	0.049	0.008	0.127	0.040	0.025	0.013
Age	−0.001	0.005	0.034	0.009	−0.002	0.004
Log(work force)	−0.008	0.012	0.031	0.025	0.033	0.018
Log(emp/firm)$_{t-1}$	0.096	0.052	−0.010	0.014	−0.016	0.009
Log(sales/emp)$_{t-1}$	0.015	0.017	0.010	0.018	0.004	0.006
Log[Δ(sales/firm)]	0.057	0.026	0.042	0.024	0.036	0.014
Log(wage$_{t-1}$/av. wage)	−0.484	0.150	−0.264	0.046	−0.140	0.032
Year 91	0.129	0.056	0.178	0.062	0.045	0.032
Year 92	0.174	0.020	0.285	0.054	0.170	0.036
Year 93	0.003	0.027	0.098	0.048	0.046	0.032
Year 94	0.013	0.012	0.097	0.041	0.093	0.018
Year 95	0.047	0.010	0.106	0.032	0.065	0.023
Year 96	0.055	0.008	0.168	0.036	0.070	0.014
Year 97	0.090	0.012	0.164	0.044	0.117	0.022
N	1,372		527		963	

Table 3A.10. *Changes in Other Sector Wages*

Variable	Domestic		Foreign		State	
	Coeff.	Std. Error	Coeff.	Std. Error	Coeff.	Std. Error
Log(farm)	0.041	0.014	−0.002	0.040	0.019	0.009
Log(SOE emp/ work force)$_{90}$	0.008	0.025	−0.056	0.095	0.023	0.018
West	0.009	0.011	0.057	0.038	−0.016	0.012
Warsaw	0.051	0.020	0.082	0.077	−0.086	0.022
% Unemployment	−0.178	0.111	−0.636	0.304	0.074	0.107
% De novo jobs	0.462	0.160	0.742	0.245	0.501	0.160
Cohort 1	−0.007	0.013	−0.080	0.060	0.036	0.017
Cohort age = 1	0.032	0.016	0.082	0.022	−0.043	0.015
Age	−0.007	0.004	0.005	0.010	−0.012	0.005
Log(work force)	−0.017	0.018	−0.048	0.049	−0.012	0.017
Log(emp/firm)$_{t-1}$	0.025	0.011	0.017	0.017	0.007	0.006
Log(sales/emp)$_{t-1}$	0.032	0.010	0.029	0.013	−0.004	0.009
Log[Δ(sales/firm)]	0.067	0.014	0.059	0.022	0.043	0.013
Log(wage$_{t-1}$/av. wage)	−0.168	0.020	−0.200	0.047	−0.169	0.038
Year 91	0.137	0.038	0.067	0.134	−0.021	0.044
Year 92	0.111	0.029	0.201	0.122	0.158	0.031
Year 93	−0.042	0.015	−0.036	0.042	0.041	0.024
Year 94	−0.029	0.014	0.064	0.063	0.067	0.021
Year 95	0.015	0.010	0.039	0.041	0.035	0.014
Year 96	0.001	0.013	−0.010	0.035	0.052	0.015
Year 97	0.015	0.014	−0.034	0.048	0.073	0.013
N	1,255		353		1,079	

4

The Social and Distributional Costs of Transition

The Polish transition, though successful in the aggregate, did not happen without considerable pain, and the success was not uniformly distributed throughout the country and among all segments of society. Table 2.2 shows that the unemployment rate escalated dramatically during the early reform years, reaching 17 percent in 1993, and even by 1997 was still close to double digits. Real wages, though they increased after 1993, did not return to prereform levels. These data indicate that, even though GDP exceeded prereform levels and grew at impressive rates, there were still reasons to be concerned about the quality of economic life, even several years after the reforms began. These aggregate conditions led some to question the pace, direction, and even the philosophy behind the reforms.

The previous chapter made it clear that some regions adapted more quickly and successfully to the transition. People in these areas were better equipped to start and grow new enterprises. Regions that entered the transition with good communications infrastructure, with higher levels of education, with a larger number of small private firms, and that created and expanded local development agencies and banks fared much better than other areas. The impact of the transition was also very unevenly distributed among individual Poles. One's age, work history, attitudes, and education were highly correlated with the ease or difficulty of the transition. Experiencing these benefits and costs naturally affected how one evaluated the reforms and how one began to affiliate politically.

These costs and benefits and their distribution need to be considered in any assessment of the reform process, in particular how they affected the political economy of transition. This discussion has three main topics: aggregate and regional unemployment and income levels, in a society that had not experienced measurable unemployment in more than forty years; the agricultural sector, which was poorly prepared to function in an environment of lowered tariffs and reduced subsidies; and some measures of public health, related to increases in unhealthy behaviors and decreased life expectancy, which occurred during some transitions to a market economy.

EMPLOYMENT SECURITY AND INCOME

During the transition, there was considerable variation in rates of unemployment and levels of income. Because the data in Table 2.6 show increasing correlations between new-firm creation and unemployment and wages, we sought systematic evidence that regions that were more successful at stimulating the entry and survival of new firms had more successful transitions, as measured by lower unemployment and higher incomes. We use individual data collected in the Polish General Social Survey (PGSS; Cichomski and Morawski, 1999) to develop and estimate multivariate statistical models to explore both measures.

Unemployment

The unemployment rate in 1993 of 17 percent was unprecedented in Poland and caused considerable distress even beyond those unemployed or those who feared they were next. There was a marked regional variation, ranging from the lowest rate of 7.6 percent in Warsaw to more than 30 percent in Olsztyn and Suwalkie. Table 4.1 shows the national rate and variations in the regional rates in unemployment for the period 1991 to 1997. After peaking in 1993, the national rate fell to about 10 percent in 1997, although it was still more than 20 percent in the hardest hit areas.[1]

The high aggregate levels resulted jointly from the difficulty in the transition from state-owned to free-market enterprises, the introduction of strict budget constraints to drive the transition, and the austere macroeconomic measures adopted in the early 1990s to stabilize and liberalize the economy. The high variations are the result of regional differences in adapting to the new economic rules and structure. To illustrate this point we developed a probit model for the probability of an individual being unemployed, using data from the Polish General Social Survey (people

---

1 We note that the unemployment level began rising dramatically after 1997, returning to the 16 and 17 percent level by 2001. Our discussion here focuses on the 1990–97 period. We discuss the conditions after 1997 in Chapter 8.

Table 4.1. *Regional Variations in Percent Unemployed*

	1991	1992	1993	1994	1995	1996	1997
Highest	18.6	24.1	30.3	29.8	28.4	25.7	21.2
National mean	11.4	13.6	16.4	16.0	14.9	13.2	10.3
Lowest	4.2	5.9	7.6	6.5	5.4	4.1	2.7
Lowest excluding Warsaw	5.6	7.9	7.7	8.4	7.7	6.7	3.4

who are retired or not looking for work are omitted).[2] The equation includes individual characteristics, such as age, education, gender, living in Warsaw, and being a private farmer, as well as two characteristics of the economic structure in the respondents' voivodship, the number of new firms relative to the size of the work force divided by 1,000 and the proportion of state-owned firms in 1990. All continuous variables are expressed as deviations from their annual means so the constant term represents the value of the probit function for the probability of being unemployed in 1997 for a nonfarming male with the average education and age, and who lives in a region with the average rate of new-firm creation and SOEs at the start of the transition. The results are shown in Table 4.2. The right-hand column shows the expected difference in the probability of being unemployed for a one standard deviation increase in the variable in 1997, if all the continuous variables are at their means. For the dichotomous variables, such as being female, and the year dummies the change is based on the dichotomy.

For our purposes the important relationships are between unemployment and the structure of the local economy. The new-firms variable measures the amount of new economic activity in the region without measuring job creation per se, which obviously reduces unemployment. The coefficient implies that relative to an average region, people living in an area with a standard deviation difference in more new firms have a 0.015 lower probability of being unemployed than an otherwise identical person. At an aggregate level, this is equivalent to a 1.5 percent lower unemployment rate. The relationship with the concentration of state-owned enterprises is quite small and not statistically significant. The coefficient indicates that an increase of one standard deviation in the proportion of

2 We want to stress that this is not a theoretically derived model of unemployment but simply a descriptive way of showing the characteristics associated with being unemployed. The estimation procedure uses a probit model with clustering by voivodship and robust standard errors.

Table 4.2. *Probability of Unemployment*

Variable	Coefficient	Standard Error	Probability
Constant	−1.312	0.085	
Year 93	0.104	0.059	0.019
Year 94	0.200	0.087	0.038
Year 95	0.134	0.085	0.025
Year 97	0.085	0.076	0.015
Warsaw	−0.179	0.079	−0.027
Schooling	−0.142	0.011	−0.050
$(\text{Age} - \overline{\text{age}})/100$	−1.755	0.306	−0.028
Age < 25	0.480	0.099	0.108
Age < 25, year 97	−0.328	0.145	0.009
Private farmer	−1.764	0.198	−0.094
Female	0.149	0.061	0.028
$\text{Log}[(\#\text{new firms}_t - \#\text{new firms}_t)/\text{work force}]$	−0.232	0.086	−0.015
$\text{Log}[(\#\text{SOE firms}_{90} - \#\text{SOE firms}_{90})/\text{total firms}_{90}]$	0.105	0.201	0.003
N	5,099		

state-owned firms in a region relative to the average increased the likelihood of being unemployed by less than 0.5 percent.[3]

The variations in being unemployed varied with the individual variables in the expected manner. More schooling was strongly associated with lower unemployment. A standard deviation difference in the years of schooling (2.7 years) decreased the probability of being unemployed by 0.05. The relationship between age and the probability of unemployment is a complex function but not a totally unexpected one. This probability decreased with age at a fairly steep rate, being about 0.03 for a ten-year difference in the middle age range. For people younger than twenty-five during 1992 to 1995, however, the unemployment rate for those looking for work is significantly higher, by about 11 percent. This difference dissipated in 1997. In 1997 the expected unemployment rate for those younger than twenty-five is higher than other ages, but only by an amount that is consistent with all age differences. (Several other piecewise versions of the equation were tried for all age ranges, and all gave the same results and a comparable fit to the model in Table 4.2.) Women were much

3 Variations were tested to see if either the coefficients on the new-firm and the individual and regional state-firm variables varied by year. No measurable variation was observed.

Table 4.3. *Regional Variations in Average Monthly Gross Salary*

	1991	1992	1993	1994	1995	1996	1997
Highest	127.3	145.2	146.7	152.4	157.5	169.4	187.6
Highest excluding Warsaw	127.3	145.0	142.9	152.4	154.4	158.9	164.8
National mean	103.1	119.0	118.5	120.5	124.1	131.0	139.0
Lowest	90.1	99.8	96.6	97.6	99.3	104.8	110.3

Note: In real 1990 new Polish złotys.

more likely to be unemployed as otherwise similar men. Private farmers were less likely to be unemployed. (We discuss the situation for farmers in more detail in the next section.) And Warsawians were less likely to be unemployed than residents in the rest of the country.

The yearly differences in the probability of being unemployed show that the likelihood of being unemployed was higher in 1994 and even in 1995 than in 1992 and 1997. Given that the PGSS surveys were conducted early, in the years 1992 to 1995, these coefficients correspond to the national unemployment pattern, with the highest unemployment being observed in late 1993. It is important to keep in mind that we control for the yearly differences in the average number of new firms in each voivodship each year, which was increasing (see Table 2.5).

Family Income

A second way to assess the distress associated with the economic transition and the shock therapy policies is by examining income levels. Table 4.3 shows average monthly wages and salaries in real new Polish złotys for the nation and for the poorest and the richest voivodships (including and excluding Warsaw). (These data are presented in a different manner in Table 2.6.) Even without data from Warsaw, average wages and salaries in real terms rose consistently beginning in 1994 and in the poorest regions by 1996 and 1997. The ratio between the worst- and best-paid regions, excluding Warsaw, and between the best-paid and the average regions increased through 1994 and then decreased after that. The ratio of the poorest-paid to the average regions fell during the early 1990s and remained fairly constant after 1994.

We can use the PGSS data to examine how individuals' incomes are affected by the transition by comparing incomes across regions for similar individuals. The PGSS survey asks respondents for their monthly income from their main job if they are working and their total family income from all sources regardless of whether they are working. We use these data for two different analyses, one of monthly incomes for workers and the other for the total family incomes of households where the respondent and/or a spouse is retired. These analyses provide two different views of how economic situations are affected by the transition. The obvious interest is in the income of those who find jobs and how that income is related to where they work and the local economic characteristics. Retired individuals' income has been a major concern during the transition as they have fewer protections against some of the transition's effects, such as the early inflation, the decline of many large enterprises where they once worked, and the restrictions on the state budget. Retired individuals are often dependent on other family members for support, so the growth of the local economy should benefit retired workers as well as current workers.

The models relate individual and family incomes to the individual variables used to model unemployment plus variables to indicate the ownership of the enterprise where the person works, or did work if retired, and the amount of hours worked or the number and composition of the workers in the household for retired respondents. We also include three measures of local economic conditions: the number of de novo firms relative to the size of the work force each year, the proportion of state-owned firms in 1990, and the annual unemployment rate. We include the local unemployment rate as a further test of the proposition put forth in Chapter 3 that local wages will vary inversely with the unemployment rate. We did not find evidence of this in Chapter 3 when looking at aggregate wages, but we examine this again, along with the proposition that higher rates of new-firm creation will stimulate demand for workers and thus raise wage rates. We include the proportion of state firms in the model as their presence may exert an upward pressure on wages, given their high wage levels. The results are shown in Table 4.4.

The evidence is stronger with the individual data showing that local labor-market conditions are related to incomes. New-firm creation and unemployment are positively and negatively associated with both worker and family incomes respectively. In each case the magnitudes of the elasticities are about 0.1 for new firms and about −0.07 for unemployment. A 1 percent change in new-firm creation is associated with about 0.1 percent change in income, and a 1 percent change in unemployment (as distinct from a change in the unemployment rate of 1 percent) is associated with a 0.7 percent change in incomes. The density of state-owned firms at the

Table 4.4. *Real Monthly Income*

Variable	Employed[a]		Retired[b]	
	Coeff.	Std. Error	Coeff.	Std. Error
Constant	1.872	0.226	3.575	0.207
Year 93	−0.022	0.038	0.013	0.024
Year 94	−0.106	0.043	−0.057	0.017
Year 95	−0.172	0.050	0.038	0.021
Year 97	0.010	0.057	0.082	0.037
Warsaw	0.070	0.027	−0.078	0.054
Schooling/10	0.747	0.033	0.357	0.030
Age/100	4.482	0.718	1.425	0.389
(Age/100)^2	−4.622	0.895	−0.547	0.317
Female	−0.282	0.028	−0.041	0.015
Log(number of hours worked)	0.127	0.032		
Log(number of incomes in household)			0.808	0.024
Private farmer	−0.536	0.067	−0.109	0.026
Pvt farmer * (farmsize − $\overline{\text{farmsize}}$)/10	0.465	0.091	0.021	0.007
State farmer	−0.151	0.071	0.000	0.026
Work in industrial SOE	0.200	0.035	0.061	0.022
Work in industrial SOE * (92 & 93)	−0.092	0.039		
Work in nonindustrial SOE	0.030	0.035	0.034	0.017
Work in foreign-owned private firm	0.444	0.067	0.293	0.057
Work in domestic private firm	0.208	0.041	0.085	0.036
Self-employed	0.290	0.041	0.014	0.028
Don't know ownership type	0.225	0.052	0.029	0.042
Work full time	0.429	0.031		
Respondent or spouse never worked			−0.080	0.033
Spouse works			0.104	0.033
Respondent retired, spouse not retired			−0.179	0.029
Both retired			−0.004	0.031
Log(new firms/work force)	0.120	0.034	0.100	0.024
Log(SOE 1990/total firms 1990)	0.127	0.061	0.122	0.068
Log(% unemployed)	−0.066	0.028	−0.078	0.048
R^2	0.36		0.57	
N	4,193		3,351	

[a] Log of monthly income from main job, if employed, in real PLN (1990 = 1).
[b] Log total family income, including any transfers, pensions, etc., in real PLN (1990 = 1).

beginning of the transition is positively related to income levels, although there is more uncertainty about this relationship.

Where individuals work makes an important difference in their incomes, both when they are working and when they retire. Current and former employees of foreign-owned firms have the highest incomes, as we observed with the firm data in the previous chapter. Among the employed, the self-employed have the next highest incomes, but the lowest retirement incomes, other than private farmers. The self-employed category includes the owners of private enterprises (who are really proprietors or owners), some of whom are successful entrepreneurs, which raises the average income for this group considerably. (Jackson and Mach, 2002, show that the incomes of the so-called self-employed who employed more than three workers are considerably higher than the incomes of the self-employed with fewer workers.) Those employed by private firms have about the same income as workers in state industrial enterprises, both when they are working and when they retire. An exception is workers in state-owned industrial firms in 1992 and 1993, when the popiwek was in effect. The base group are workers in cooperatives, and they and workers in nonindustrial state enterprises are the lowest-paid groups, other than farmers.

The relationships with the individual characteristic variables are what one would expect and are statistically significant. Working full-time and the number of hours worked are positively related to incomes for the working group. Similarly, among the retired respondents incomes are higher where there are more wage earners in the family and when the spouse works, and lower if either the respondent or spouse never worked and if the respondent is the retired member of the family. Women have lower incomes than men, particularly among those currently employed, because a woman's income is expected to be 75 percent of a similar man's income. Among the retired this expected difference is only about 0.95, though the difference is statistically significant. Among the retired respondents, what appears to be a quadratic relationship between income and age is effectively a monotonically increasing function with diminishing marginal changes, indicating that incomes among the retired individuals steadily increase with age.[4] Lastly, the better-educated retired have higher incomes than the less-well-educated.

The relationships between income and age and education among the employed merit special attention, as they reveal an interesting implication of the transition. The results shown in Table 4.4 indicate a strong positive relationship between incomes and education, as one would expect, and a quadratic relationship with age, such that incomes peak among

---

4 The peak value for the quadratic relationship is 130 years of age, well outside the sample values. A variable that is the log of age matches the fit of this quadratic form, suggesting the likely relationship between income and age for retired individuals.

forty-five-year olds. Neither of these results is surprising, particularly that involving education, where one expects positive returns to investments in human capital. This is only the beginning of the story, however. Diewald and Mach (1999) found higher returns to education in the market economy than in the planned economy, because it is a more valued attribute in the former. Jackson and Mach (2002) find further corroborating evidence in an analysis of a longitudinal panel of Polish workers between 1988 and 1998.[5] Diewald and Mach also expected lower returns to work experience after the transition, suggesting a decreased relationship between age and income, but did not find evidence for this proposition; however, Jackson and Mach did. We examined these propositions with the PGSS data by including interaction terms between the education, age, and age-squared variables and the year of the survey and whether the person worked in the private sector. (Being self-employed and working for a foreign or a domestic firm are combined to create a single variable measuring if the respondent worked in the private sector.) If the Diewald and Mach propositions are correct, the coefficient on education will increase between 1992 and 1997 and the relationship between income and age will flatten. If the changes occur only for those working in private firms, then the interaction coefficients for type of employer should be significant and those for the year should be close to zero. We have also included an interaction term between year and a private-sector job and the female and number of de novo firms variables. These terms test whether other important relationships in the study also changed during the transition. If these coefficients change over time or with the type of employer, it also has substantive importance.

The results reveal very interesting patterns consistent with this set of predictions for age and education. Table 4.5 shows the estimated coefficients for the age, education, female, and new-firm variables and for the interaction terms. (The coefficients on all the other variables are virtually identical to those shown in Table 4.4, so we choose not to reproduce them.) The quadratic relationship between income and age is greatly reduced, and there is no interaction between age and type of employer. The implication is that by 1997 there is a monotonic relationship between

5 The Jackson and Mach data partially overlap the Diewald and Mach data as both use the 1988 to 1993 wave of the Polish Social Structure and Social Mobility Panel. Jackson and Mach also use the 1993 to 1998 wave of the same study and a different statistical model. Diewald and Mach also use longitudinal data from the former GDR.

Table 4.5. *Age, Education, Gender, and New-Firm Coefficients, with Interactions*

Variable	Main Effect[a]		(Year − 1992)		Private[b]	
	Coeff.	Std. Error	Coeff.	Std. Error	Coeff.	Std. Error
Age	6.731	1.322	−0.867	0.466	0.538	1.425
Age^2	−7.319	1.650	1.082	0.606	−1.020	1.802
Years of schooling/10	0.559	0.067	0.044	0.022	0.265	0.059
Female	−0.288	0.043	0.000	0.012	0.008	0.043
Log(new firms/ work force)	0.117	0.048	0.005	0.017	−0.028	0.037

[a] Coefficient shows the relationship between the log of income and the variable for 1992 for someone not self-employed nor employed in a domestic or foreign private firm.
[b] Combines the self-employed and foreign-owned and domestically owned variables to create a single private-sector variable.

income and age where there are some but much smaller income differences between a twenty-year-old and a fifty-year-old in 1997 than in 1992.[6] The income difference associated with more years of schooling increases substantially each year, by a factor of about 40 percent between 1992 and 1997. Furthermore, the returns to education are significantly higher in the private sector. The private sector values education more than the other sectors do, and this appears to have pushed up returns to education throughout the labor market. There were no interaction effects between incomes and the female and new-firm creation variables, suggesting these relationships were similar over time and across type of employer. Women continued to face income discrimination, even accounting for hours worked, and the increased entry of new firms continued to be associated with higher incomes. The transition appears to be increasingly rewarding education and devaluing work experience, at least during this period when most work experience is likely to be in the former state enterprises.

The overall picture is one where residents in regions making a successful transition, as indicated by the rate of de novo firm creation, are economically better off. They are less likely to be unemployed and can expect higher incomes when working. Retirees in these successful regions

6 The model with the best statistical fit includes a log(age) term for 1997 with a relatively flat slope, suggesting incomes increase with age but relatively slowly and at a decreasing rate. The sharp quadratic form still fits the 1992 to 1995 period.

can also expect to be better off, at least compared with retirees in regions without new firms. There are also very clear differences related to education, age, and gender. Early in the transition, younger respondents, at least those under twenty-five, were more likely to be unemployed. But as the transition proceeded this gap diminished and once they got a job there was a smaller wage premium given to age. There is also an increasing gain for education, and particularly for those entering the private sector. These relationships will work to the advantage of younger Poles, who are becoming better educated and more likely to work in the private sector. These variations among individuals and among regions will become important as we begin to examine attitudes toward the reforms and support for the different political parties.

AGRICULTURE

Polish agriculture during the transition warrants special discussion because of both its economic and enduring political significance. One important aspect of Polish farming before 1989 was its mix of private and collective farms. At the end of World War II, in many areas land was given to individuals who previously had worked the land as paid employees on larger farms. The parcels given were usually quite small and created a large number of small private farms, averaging about four to five hectares per farm. This policy exacerbated an existing problem of farms that were too small in eastern and southern Poland because of the historical pattern of dividing farms equally among the children as land was passed to subsequent generations. These private farmers resisted efforts by Communist governments to force them into cooperatives or into state-owned farms. The situation in the area acquired by Poland from Germany at the end of World War II and resettled with farmers from Ukraine is quite different. Communist governments had a much easier time in those areas creating state-owned and cooperative farms, and consolidating these into a smaller number of larger farms. Between 1965 and 1980, the number of state agricultural enterprises dropped from 6,500 to 2,100 even though the acreage increased by 700,000 hectares. The average state farm exceeded 1,500 hectares and employed more than 200 farmers, quite a contrast to the private farms with fewer than 10 hectares and operated by a single person or family.

The social structure of these two types of farms was radically different. The state farm, was much more similar to a factory than to a farm, and the farmers were more similar to workers in state industrial enterprises than they were to the private-sector farmers. The state farm provided its "workers" with living quarters, basic social services, and recreational and cultural centers, as did the state-owned industrial firms. Even the length of the workday for state farmers was closer to that of the industrial workers than that of the private farmers. The joining of the hammer and the sickle clearly applied to these two sets of employees in state-owned units.

The economic situations were both similar and different. The private farms were not fully private in that they sold their output at prices fixed by the government, as did the state farms. The private farms were also obligated to fill quotas that went directly to the government, in effect a tax. The agricultural prices bore no resemblance to "real" prices, as they were routinely manipulated by the government to placate whichever constituencies it felt it had to satisfy. Private farms also suffered on the input side, as they could not buy necessary factors, such as machinery or fertilizer, on an open market or apply directly for credit. In the economy of shortage created by central planning, farms had to get governmental approval, or coupons, in order to be eligible to obtain goods. Under the rationing systems, the state-owned farms generally received more favorable treatment than the private farmers.

The economic transition began with two distinctly different agricultural sectors, neither very well equipped for what was to come. The private sector was populated by farms that were far too small to be efficient, with little capital equipment, and with no experience buying and selling goods on open markets. The state sector, though better capitalized with larger farms, was actually less efficient than the private farmers in terms of output per hectare. Both sets of farmers were used to fixed prices, no competition, and extensive subsidies in both buying and selling goods. All this changed dramatically after 1989. Subsidies were withdrawn, markets were opened to foreign competition, inputs were sold at real prices, and capital was suddenly and abruptly loaned at real interest rates. The change in credit policies was particularly hard on the state-owned farms because interest rates were allowed to increase on outstanding loans, leaving farmers with dramatically increased payments. This change affected state farms more severely because the private farms were generally self-financed.

Beginning in 1991, there was a serious depression in the agricultural sector. The output of state farms fell 9.8 percent in 1991 and 12.7 percent in 1992. The combination of foreign competition, liberalized prices and floating interest rates, the withdrawal of subsidies, and declining output led to extensive bankruptcies and unemployment on the state farms. By 1994 more than 4,000 farms had been taken over by the state treasury, yet there was no formal policy for restructuring these farms and moving them into the fully private sector. These properties were eventually returned to agricultural use, largely through leasing arrangements.[7] Employment on these farms dropped by over 250,000 between 1990 and 1992. The consequence has been very high levels of unemployment in these rural areas, as the former state farm workers generally had low education levels and were located in areas with little industrial infrastructure. As we saw in Chapter 3, these were also the areas experiencing the greatest difficulty generating new firms and jobs. These circumstances explain the result in Table 4.4 showing that workers on state farms had lower monthly incomes compared with workers in state jobs and with private farmers with an average-sized farm.

Private agricultural output and income did not suffer as badly as that of the state farms. Output was essentially flat in 1991, declined by 8.2 percent in 1992, and did not fully recover until 1995, with recovery most evident on the larger farms. Incomes of private farmers, though low, have been better than among the workers on state-owned farms. There is one group of private farmers who suffered considerably. Many of the farmers on the smallest farms also had industrial jobs in nearby towns to supplement their farm income. This holding of two jobs was particularly encouraged during periods of intense industrialization, as in the 1970s. The census even created a separate classification for the "employee-farmers." When the state-owned industrial firms faced tightening budgets and liquidity problems, these employee-farmers were some of the first individuals terminated under the assumption that they retained a source of income that nonfarmers, would not have. If their farm income proved insufficient, though, the poor conditions for these employee-farmers was exacerbated because most of these layoffs occurred in poorly developed regions where job creation was low. Even by 1996 this group had one of the lowest family incomes, comparable with retirees and those on social welfare.

Farming remains a difficult sector with low output per farmer, small farm size, and a low capital-labor ratio. The farmers' response has been what one sees in most countries – politically directed pleas for greater subsidies, more protection, and a resistance to become more efficient or to leave farming. These demands and political actions are a significant

---

7 The process here, though different from the restructuring and privatizing of state-owned industrial firms, had some similarities in that the entities became wards of the government, which then tried to find private leasers or buyers while the workers were left to their own devices to find alternative employment.

part of the politics of the Polish transition. These issues and associated political demands remain a concern, as was evidenced in the debate and vote about joining the European Union.

PUBLIC HEALTH

One of the significant corollaries of the transition to market economies among the East-Central European countries and the former Soviet republics has been changes in public health, which can be evaluated through measures such as life expectancy, the incidence of alcoholism and other socially destructive behaviors, and the number of suicides. Any assessment of the Polish transition and of its distributional consequences must examine these same statistics in comparison with some of the other transitional countries and over time and cross-sectionally within Poland. The health statistics evident in some of the transitional countries, particularly the states of the former Soviet republic, are particularly alarming (see Brainerd, 2001).

National Comparisons

The data from the economically more successful transitional countries are relatively encouraging. Figure 1.2 graphs comparative data on the life expectancy of forty-five-year-old males and females in Poland and other transition countries. This age is selected because it is the prime working age; males in particular constitute the cohort most expected to be suffering from the loss of jobs and increased uncertainty associated with the economic reforms. Both the Czech Republic and Poland show significant increases in life expectancy for both males and females, with the patterns being relatively monotonic, at least after 1991. (The 1990 data for the Czech Republic likely understate the actual life expectancy and thus overstate the increase between 1990 and 1997 because the data for that year but not subsequent years include the Slovak Republic.)

Several important comparisons are evident in these plots. First, life expectancies increased most in the Czech Republic, the country that suffered the least from the transition, at least until 1997 and 1998. Significantly less unemployment and a lower decline in income were recorded there in comparison with rates in the other countries. The opposite was true for Hungary, which experienced some of the same distress as Poland but not the early success (see Figure 1.1). Hungary's increasing growth after 1995 and 1996, however, is reflected in markedly increasing life expectancy after those years. Poland, which had the sharpest declines in the initial years and then the fastest growth, shows a significant increase from 1991 onward. Russia, on the other hand, experienced serious declines in life expectancy during the early transition period, with the life expectancy of males falling by almost five years during the period 1990 to 1994. A second important comparison is that in Poland, the Czech Republic, and Hungary life expectancy for males increased more than for females. This is significant in that it is expected that working-age males experienced the most acute distress and were the ones most likely to engage in self-destructive behaviors, such as excessive alcohol consumption. These results contrast sharply with those from Russia, which show decreasing life expectancy, particularly among working-age males.

These broad comparisons suggests that a failing or static economic transition contributes to distress, whereas a successful transition improves the chances for a healthy life. The declines in Polish life expectancy between 1980 and 1990 evident in Figure 1.2 further suggest that economic health, rather than job security or the type of economic system, is the likely contributor to life expectancy.

Individual Differences

If the initial observations from examining variations in life expectancy over time among the transitional countries are valid, there should be similar associations at the individual and regional level, with people and regions succeeding in the transition faring better. We begin these comparisons with individual responses to a question in the PGSS data asking people, "Would you say your own health, in general, is excellent, good, fair, or poor?" This question was asked each year, permitting individual and temporal comparisons. Our expectation is that the responses to this question should become more favorable over time, as implied by the national statistics, and among the individuals and regions we have identified as becoming better off during the transition. In purely aggregate percentages, 65 percent said they had excellent or good health in 1992 and this rose to 71.5 percent in 1997, while those saying they had poor health dropped from 8 to 6 percent.

The statistical analysis includes some of the variables used in the discussions of unemployment and income plus a variable measuring frequency of church attendance. Studies of social correlates with health all indicate that people with strong social connections are healthier. (See House, Umberson, and Landis, 1988, and Stansfeld, 1999.) One of the strongest organizations to which most Poles are connected is the Catholic Church. Initial results indicated that retired and nonretired individuals constitute very different statistical populations; hence, the analysis is done and reported separately for each group. Interestingly, except for the relationship with age, there is no statistical difference between the respondents who are in the work force, even if unemployed, and those not in the work force but not retired. (The predominant members of this group are students and housewives who are not working outside the home. We refer to this entire group as the eligible work force, as distinct from those who are retired.) With two exceptions discussed later, the difference between men and women is well represented by the female dummy variable. The three different SOE employer (industrial, farm, and other) and the three private-sector ownership variables (foreign, domestic, and self-employment) are each combined to create single SOE and private-sector variables. State-sector employment is used as the base category so that all coefficients compare the self-assessment of health for specific employment groups relative to those working or who had worked in the state sector. The results are shown in Table 4.6.[8]

Several results are relevant for our discussions, though most of these are the absence of large differences. The unemployed and the nonworking in most age ranges have the same assessments of their health as those working full-time. Only those working part-time report having worse health than full-time workers. There are no differences among the eligible work force related to the employer type, other than private farmers and cooperative workers, who both report their health is worse than other employed individuals. Among the retired respondents, those who worked in the private sector report having better health than state workers, but otherwise there are no differences. There are no regional differences, including living in Warsaw, with the exception of the relationship with de novo firm creation among women. Thus individuals living in distressed regions and those experiencing personal economic distress, other than private farmers and cooperative workers and the small proportion of part-time workers, do not report having any worse health than those living in less-distressed regions or working people.

---

8 Estimation was done with an ordered probit model where the thresholds estimate the cutting points dividing the respondents' assessments into the ordinal groupings, for example, the first threshold divides those who said their health was poor from those who said it was fair, and so on. The results have been rescaled so that the threshold separating fair from good is fixed at zero. This rescaling makes the constant terms comparable for each group.

Table 4.6. Health Self-Assessments

	Not Retired		Retired	
	Coeff.	Std. Error	Coeff.	Std. Error
Constant	2.482	0.263	−0.156	0.760
Year 93	−0.020	0.046	0.049	0.086
Year 94	0.046	0.039	0.070	0.080
Year 95	0.078	0.061	0.023	0.077
Year 97	0.020	0.067	0.122	0.115
Warsaw	−0.020	0.035	−0.029	0.115
Schooling/10	0.271	0.071	0.554	0.077
Log(income)	0.108	0.027	0.209	0.035
Age/100: work force/female	−6.309	0.835	6.918	1.649
$(Age/100)^2$: work force/female	4.207	1.004	−5.320	1.317
Age/100: non–work force/male	−4.549	1.114	−1.859	2.208
$(Age/100)^2$: non–work force/male	0.772	1.221	1.933	1.890
Female	−0.499	0.057	−2.885	0.788
Church attendance	0.132	0.046	0.340	0.051
Unemployed	−0.016	0.058		
Work part-time	−0.229	0.047		
Not in work force	−0.207	0.297		
Private farm	−0.172	0.057	0.129	0.069
Private employer	−0.039	0.035	0.246	0.108
Cooperative	−0.111	0.056	0.043	0.060
Never worked	−0.098	0.084	0.022	0.098
Don't know ownership type	0.053	0.103	0.289	0.198
Log(de novo jobs/work force)	−0.048	0.056	−0.008	0.091
Female*log(de novo jobs/work force)	0.189	0.052	0.104	0.073
Log(SOE firms)$_{1990}$	−0.099	0.074	0.110	0.149
Log(% unemployment)	0.059	0.037	0.042	0.104
Poor/fair threshold	−1.206	0.266	−1.244	0.760
Fair/good threshold	0		0	
Good/excellent threshold	2.073	0.260	1.611	0.743
N	6,012		2,898	

Individual differences are broadly what are expected, though there are some interesting variations in the relationship between well-being and age. Among both the retired and those in the eligible work force there are large positive associations between reported health and education and income. There is also a strong positive association between frequency of church attendance and reported health, as predicted. The relationships with age vary considerably among the different subgroups. Among the working members of the eligible work force well-being declines monotonically with age, though at a decreasing rate. (The quadratic form implies that well-being increases after age seventy-five, which is well beyond the retirement age for most Poles. Only 6 of 4,000 full-time workers are older than seventy-five, but they report they are very healthy.) Among those who are not retired or working or looking for work, health declines linearly with age. Among the retired there is virtually no relationship between age and health for males. Female's health assessments are lower than males and follow a sharp quadratic pattern, with the best health being reported by women who are sixty-five, which is just past the legal retirement age for women in Poland. Lastly, there is no systematic variation with the year of the transition, despite the data on life expectancy and the aggregate distributions among the PGSS respondents. This suggests that the observed changes in the aggregate measures are likely coming from changes in individual characteristics, such as improving education or a changing age distribution.

Women's assessments of their health are lower than men's for all ages and situations. The one interesting pattern is that women living in regions with a higher rate of new-firm creation report better health. This pattern does not hold for men. The relationship is not statistically significant among retired women, but the pattern is the same for both groups. It may be that women are more sensitive than men to the conditions in their local environment.

Overall, then, we see results suggesting that health assessments are strongly related to individual factors such as age, education, and income but are not strongly related to measures that might indicate economic distress, such as unemployment, type of workplace, or local unemployment. The possible exceptions to these broad statements are private farmers, part-time workers, and women living in areas with different rates of new-firm creation.

Regional Health Measures

Our last comparisons deal with changes in life expectancy at the regional level. The motivating question is whether areas having a difficult transition to a market economy are likely to have decreases in life expectancy, particularly among males. Poland collectively had increasing life expectancy beginning in 1991, so the question is whether there is any decrease in life expectancy, or at least smaller improvements in regions experiencing economic hardship. The available data severely constrain this discussion, unfortunately. Life expectancy data for age-specific groups are not

Table 4.7. *Variations in Life Expectancy from Birth among Voivodships*

Group/Period	1976–80	1981–85	1986–90	1991–95	1997
Women					
Highest	76.1	76.9	77.1	77.6	78.3
National mean	74.6	75.1	75.3	75.8	77.0
Lowest	73.7	73.9	73.9	74.3	75.7
Highest – lowest	2.4	3.0	3.2	3.3	2.6
Men					
Highest	68.7	69.1	68.5	69.1	71.1
National mean	66.5	66.9	66.8	66.9	68.5
Lowest	65.1	65.4	65.3	64.9	66.3
Highest – lowest	3.6	3.7	3.2	4.2	4.8

available on a regional basis, so the only data we can compare is the life expectancy for all age groups for men and for women. Table 4.7 shows the mean life expectancy for men and for women at birth in the periods 1976–80, 1981–85, 1986–90, 1991–95, and 1997 and the lowest and highest levels among the voivodships.

These data on the variations in male and female life expectancy reveal some significant patterns. Female life expectancy improved throughout the twenty-year period, on average and among regions with the lowest and highest rates. The rate of improvement slowed noticeably in the 1986–90 period, however. The national average for male life expectancy improved slightly from the late 1970s to the early 1980s and then was essentially flat between 1981–85 and 1991–95. Life expectancy in the lowest and highest regions declined in the 1986–90 period, and for the lowest region this decline continued into the 1991–95 period. Life expectancy among both men and women had increased markedly by 1997. The gains for men in these years were greater than those among women both nationally and in the healthier regions. In the regions with the lowest life expectancy in the late 1980s, the gains for women exceeded the gains for men between 1986–90 and 1991–95 and for the entire period.

Table 4.7 also shows the changes in the regional variation over time, defined as the gap between the regions with the highest and the lowest life expectancy. The voivodship gaps are smaller for women than for men. These differences increased in every time period, except for a short aberation among men between 1986 and 1990 when there was a decline in the highest region and for women between 1991–95 and 1997. These numbers indicate a widening gap in regional life expectancy that goes back to the 1980s, particularly for males. This widening gap, particularly after 1991 when life expectancy among males was increasing, indicates that the regions where males already had a longer life expectancy increased those values faster than regions with lower levels. These initial comparisons suggest that local factors are very likely contributing to changes in life expectancy, particularly for men. The question is whether these factors are related to the economic transition, and if they are, can we corroborate that with available data.

We estimate a statistical model relating the proportional gains in male and female life expectancy by voivodship to a series of variables, including wages and salaries, unemployment, and new-firm creation to try to get a picture of how these aspects of the economic transition may have affected life expectancy. (The left-hand side variable is the ratio of life expectancy in 1997 to that for the 1986 to 1990 period.) The unemployment variable included is the 1993 unemployment in the voivodship, which marks the period of greatest stress. Variables for the education level, age of the population, and average frequency of church attendance plus proxies for the quality of health care are also included in the model. These proxies are the change in the number of physicians per 100 people between 1991 and 1997 and the change in infant mortality between 1988 and 1997. The first variable should assess the improvement in the quantity of health care in the region and the second should proxy improvements in the broader health standards in the locality, allowing us to focus on the relationships with the economic variables. The results are shown in Table 4.8. (Variables are expressed as deviations about their means so the constant term is the expected improvement in life expectancy in an average voivodship.)

The results for changes in life expectancy are particularly revealing. Unemployment and salary changes were unrelated to changes in life expectancy. The unemployment variables in the men's equation and the change in salary in the women's equation had the unexpected sign and were not statistically significant. The coefficient on unemployment in the equation for women's life expectancy had the expected sign but was not statistically significant. Particularly given the proposition that the distress associated with the transition should affect men more strongly than women, the general conclusion could be that changes in Polish life expectancy during the 1990s for both men and women are unrelated to the distress associated with the economic transition. For unemployment, these results mirror the patterns observed in individual health assessments.

In substantive and statistical terms, the relationships between changes in life expectancy and the amount of job creation in new firms are

Table 4.8. *Changes in Life Expectancy*

Variable	Male		Female	
	Coeff.	Std. Error	Coeff.	Std. Error
Constant	1.022	0.001	1.020	0.001
% Unemployment$_{93}$	0.040	0.034	−0.022	0.022
Salary$_{97}$/salary$_{91}$	0.010	0.020	−0.015	0.014
New firms$_{97}$/work force$_{97}$	0.178	0.085	0.134	0.056
Years schooling/10	0.073	0.027	0.000	0.018
Mean age/100	−0.448	0.148	−0.277	0.098
(Doctors/pop)$_{97}$/(doctors/pop)$_{91}$	0.042	0.023	0.034	0.015
ΔInfant mortality (1988–97)	0.013	0.006	0.007	0.004
Church attendance	0.031	0.014	−0.000	0.009
R^2	0.69		0.47	
N	49		49	

Note: Changes in life expectancy measured as the ratio of life expectancy at birth in 1997 divided by life expectancy at birth between 1986 and 1990.

substantial and statistically significant for both men and women. A higher level of job creation that corresponds to a standard deviation in the observed proportion among the voivodships is associated with a 0.4 and 0.3 percent increase in life expectancy for men and for women, respectively. Given the average 1988 life expectancy, these translate into about a quarter of a year longer life.

The variables included to measure the other factors that contribute to changes in life expectancy had the expected coefficients except for years of schooling and church attendance in the equation for women's longevity. Improvements in infant mortality, as reflected in a decreased rate per 1,000 births, were strongly associated with increases in life expectancy, capturing, we hope, many of the other broad factors that might be contributing to better personal and public health.[9] The change in the number of physicians per 100 people was positively related to changes in life expectancy and was statistically significant. Mean age in the voivodship was negatively related to increases in life expectancy, indicating that regions with an older population saw smaller proportional increases in life expectancy. Church attendance and years of schooling were positively

9 The improvement in infant mortality was not related to economic conditions, so the significance of this variable in the life expectancy equations is not masking the relationship between life expectancy and the economic variables.

related to increases in men's life expectancy but were unrelated to changes among women.[10]

Overall, the aggregate data do not support the proposition that regional distress in making the economic transition is related to decreases in life expectancy. The most substantial result was that areas making a faster and better adjustment, as represented by the proportion of de novo firms, had larger increases in life expectancy than areas with smaller rates of new-firm creation. From these results, we do not want to diminish the important concerns expressed about the health costs of the transitions in Central and Eastern Europe. We do suggest caution in what lessons are drawn from the data and that one examine carefully the transition's path.

Several factors may make the Polish case an important exception to the broader pattern. First, as noted in Chapter 1, life expectancy for Poles, and particularly Polish men, had decreased during the 1980s during the hardships that followed the martial law period. Thus, some of the improvements we noted reflect a recovery from that difficult period. The regional data, however, suggest that the recovery was larger and faster in areas that were making a faster transition to the new economic system. A second factor that may be important in Poland's experiences is the combination of a highly centralized political system and aggregate economic success. A centralized government means that health and social services can be widely and fairly evenly distributed, in contrast to a more federal system. This was particularly true of the health care system, at least until the reforms that were initiated in 1995 but not fully implemented. A growing aggregate economy means the government has resources, though quite limited, and a provisioning system that permits it to raise the national health level and to protect areas less well off. The distinctions then are not between the areas lagging in the transition and the rest of the nation but between the nation as a whole and the areas making the fastest transition, where life expectancy was improving the fastest. Overall, given the aggregate data from Poland, the Czech Republic, and Hungary and the regional data from Poland, we want to suggest that the connections between the transition to a market economy and public health are more

---

10 The models were also estimated including a Warsaw variable. The coefficients on this variable were not statistically significant. The standard errors on other variables, such as the proportion of new firms, increased but the magnitudes of their coefficients did not change appreciably. We then decided to omit the Warsaw variable as we think the equations in Table 4.8 give better estimates of the relationships with life expectancy, given the included variables.

complicated than often recognized and possibly relate to the level and pace of the creation of the de novo economy.

CONCLUSION

The aggregate data for Poland, both economic and social, give a picture of a country that is making a successful economic transition and in a relatively short time. The progress, at least in the early and mid-1990s, was based almost exclusively on the creation of new enterprises and their survival and growth. The market economy was built largely by creating a new economy and only in a small way by transforming the old one. This process of destruction and creation carries with it considerable social and distributional costs. The individuals, enterprises, and regions that were well established in the state-dominated economy found it very hard to function in a capitalistic economy where the ability to develop and market products that consumers wanted to buy is a far larger determinant of economic success than physical labor and bureaucratic and political position. In addition to the general proposition about creative destruction rewarding some and punishing others, the particular macroeconomic policies adopted by the early reform governments contributed their own costs and hardships.

We have summarized some of the groups and areas most affected, positively and negatively, by the transition. Agriculture in general and the former state-owned farms in particular were unprepared for the level of competition created by the open markets, by the removal of various subsidies, and by the significantly higher costs of credit and input factors. Younger Poles were more likely to be unemployed early in the transition. But once employed, they experienced increasing returns to education and a decreasing age premium as the transition proceeded.

There were considerable regional disparities in the responses to the transition. Obviously, nonfarming areas with a concentration of more highly educated individuals were more likely to prosper, given the individual differences just noted. The regional differences extend beyond these individual-level differences, however. We noted in Chapter 3 the considerable agglomeration effects, whereby areas that already had established small private enterprises had much higher birthrates for new firms than areas that started the transition without such a base. Even though after 1993 unemployment decreased and incomes increased throughout Poland, the differences among voivodships increased as the successful areas built on that success and the lagging areas fell further behind.

These individual and regional differences are important for their own sake and particularly in a country that values equality of well-being and opportunity. Beyond their descriptive value, these individual and regional differences are politically important as they help structure the political cleavages that are important in helping to understand Polish politics during the transition. The distribution of the costs and benefits of the transition, along with the high social costs nationally, sets the stage for a protracted and at times unpredictable political debate and electoral outcomes. The remainder of the book examines how different constituencies evolved from these distributional consequences of the transition and the importance of these constituencies in the series of elections beginning in 1991.

5

Individual Attitudes and Voting

The evolution of attitudes about the economy and about who should govern is an integral part of the transitional dynamic in Poland. To integrate the development of Polish attitudes toward various economic and social institutions with our model of the economic evolution, we first consider economic institutions because they affect a wide range of attitudes and perceptions and place substantial constraints on the actions of different political parties. Thus, the Polish transition was based on developing not only a new economic order but also a new set of political institutions and procedures. These political and economic changes are deeply interrelated, and their development and ultimate properties are pieces of a single process. To illustrate this process, we begin with an analysis of two individual attitudes that are central to the Polish political transformation.

Chapter 2 gave a brief description of the political events, and particularly the elections, in Poland since the transition began. Central to these events are the individual's attitudes toward private enterprise and its role in the new Polish economy and about Communism and former Communist officials. This attitude is particularly important as the main opposition to the economic reforms came from parties composed of former Communist officials. This meant that voters who might be opposed to the economic reforms had to vote for a former Communist to express that opposition. Opinions about communism were also likely influenced, in part, by the assessment of the reforms.

We also include attitudes toward the Catholic Church in the electoral model but do not examine the structure of these attitudes. Although the church was not a significant fixture in the economic debates, it became a critical aspect of Polish elections. Various priests and church officials were important contributors to Solidarity and expected to play a major role in any post-Communist government. This, however, became a political issue in itself, with parties divided over how much influence the church would, and should, wield in policy making. Understanding Polish elections requires that we consider opinions about the political role of the church.

CONFIDENCE IN PRIVATE ENTERPRISE

The success of the economic transition, as we have seen, depends on the ability to build a capitalist economy where private ownership is the central feature. Confidence in the ability of this private economy to provide jobs and income for owners and workers is vital for its success, both econom- ically and politically. The greater the confidence, the more willing people are to start firms and to work for new firms and the more willing they will be to vote for political parties that adopt policies that stimulate and encourage private business. A lack of confidence leads in just the opposite direction – namely, support for efforts to maintain subsidies for the state- owned enterprises, both industrial and agricultural, and votes for parties that will maintain these subsidies.

The evolution of people's confidence in private versus state enterprises is a central part of our proposition that the development of new enter- prises will foster its own pro-reform constituency. The faster and more widespread this development, the larger and better distributed this con- stituency. Three critical elements in this evolution are the performance of the aggregate economy during the transition, the movement of people into the new private sector, and the ability of individuals to benefit from the opportunities provided by a market economy, as reflected by respon- dents' education, income level and age, and residence in an area that is making the transition. The Polish populace's support suffered on the first two grounds because of the poor aggregate economic situation during the early 1990s and by the pace at which new firms were created to replace the jobs in the state sector.

Data from the Polish General Social Survey can be used to monitor this confidence over time and to correlate different levels of confidence with individual and regional characteristics. The PGSS survey asked a two-part question that forms the basis for our analysis: "I am going to name some institutions in this country. Would you say you have a great deal of confidence, only some confidence, or hardly any confidence at all in them, or you don't know?" Institutions included state firms and private firms. Appendix 5A shows the details of how the responses to these two questions were recoded to provide a measure of confidence in private

Table 5.1. *Confidence in Private versus State Enterprises and Size of Private Sector*

Measure	1992	1993	1994	1995	1997	1999
Mean	0.419	0.384	0.366	0.359	0.368	0.376
(% Neg – % pos)[a]	25.7	35.0	42.0	43.8	41.2	38.1
% Private[b]	23.8	23.5	31.6	34.6	42.9	43.4
% Unemployed[c]	13.1	16.7	17.2	15.7	13.5	18.3
% De novo jobs/work force	3.7	4.7	5.6	7.4	11.7	
National unemployment rate	13.6	16.4	16.0	14.9	10.3	

[a] Percentage expressing more confidence in state enterprises minus percentage with more confidence in private firms.
[b] Percentage of PGSS sample employed by foreign or domestic private firm plus self-employed relative to those working or looking for work.
[c] Percentage of PGSS sample unemployed relative to those working or looking for work.

relative to state enterprises. The variable ranges from zero, indicating hardly any confidence in private firms and a great deal of confidence in state firms, to one indicating the reverse. Two important hypotheses are represented in these data: first, that at the aggregate level this confidence should increase as the new private sector becomes more successful; and, second, that at the individual level, people employed in new private firms should express more confidence in private firms than people employed in enterprises remaining in the state sector, and this category should be expanding over time. Unfortunately this question does not distinguish between people's confidence in new private firms and in the privatized state firms, whose evaluations could be different.

Table 5.1 shows the mean of the confidence variable and the difference in the proportions of the respondents having more confidence in state enterprises than in private firms. The table also shows the proportion of the PGSS sample in the work force (either working or not working but looking for work, which excludes students, retirees, and others not looking for work) in private nonfarm firms and the proportion unemployed. The last two rows show the proportion of the work force employed in de novo firms, based on the data in Chapter 3, and the national unemployment rate. Unfortunately, there was no survey conducted in 1996; hence data for that year are missing. We include data from the 1999 PGSS survey to indicate that the trends observed between 1995 and 1997 continued, at least until 1999. Confidence in private firms eroded substantially following the hardships of the early 1990s at the beginning of the transition. By 1997 and 1999, when the aggregate economy was improving, a significant

Table 5.2. *Confidence in Private versus State Firms*

Explanatory Variable	Coefficient	Standard Error
Constant	0.387	0.009
1993	−0.032	0.010
1994	−0.056	0.008
1995	−0.066	0.009
1997	−0.052	0.009
Private farmer	0.091	0.010
SOE farmer	0.014	0.018
Domestic private company	0.032	0.008
Foreign private company	0.067	0.022
Self-employed	0.102	0.009
Cooperative	0.013	0.009
Never worked	0.067	0.011
Don't know employer type	0.074	0.021
Retired	0.010	0.008
Years of schooling/10	0.090	0.010
Log(income)	0.011	0.004
Age/100	−0.700	0.081
$(Age/100)^2$	0.689	0.075
Village	−0.011	0.005
Unemployed	−0.018	0.011
Female	−0.010	0.004
Church attendance	0.008	0.005
German partition	−0.007	0.008
Russian partition	−0.018	0.008
% Unemployed in voivodship	−0.105	0.056
% De novo jobs in voivodship	0.050	0.071
% State firms$_{90}$	0.046	0.050
N	8,910	
R^2	0.067	

proportion of the work force was in the private sector, evidence of new-firm creation was substantial, and confidence in private firms increased.

The analysis of the individual responses reveals the emergence of a group with increasing confidence in private firms, a significant part of which is working in private firms. Table 5.2 shows the results of a statistical analysis relating this confidence variable to a range of individual and regional variables. The continuous variables, such as age, education, and income, and the regional variables are included as deviations from their yearly means so that the constant term and year dummies indicate the expected confidence for a male respondent with average age, education, income, and church attendance who works in a state enterprise and lives in a region with average unemployment, proportion of state firms, and de novo jobs for that year.

Not surprisingly, but importantly, respondents employed in the private sector express more confidence in the private sector than do workers in the state-owned sector. The gap is particularly large for the self-employed, those in foreign-owned firms, and private farmers. On the 0 to 1 confidence scale, the self-employed and private farmers have an expected confidence that is 0.10 higher than respondents in the state sector, whereas for those in foreign and domestic firms the differences are 0.07 and 0.03, respectively. Those who have never worked express more confidence in private firms than state-enterprise workers, with an expected difference of 0.06. The magnitude of these relationships contrasts with other relationships, which are on the order of 0.01 for females and those living in villages and less than 0.02 for the unemployed.

The other variables related to economic interests had the expected coefficients, though not all are statistically significant. Unemployed individuals and respondents living in areas with high unemployment expressed less confidence in private firms. These relationships were fairly small, however. An unemployed person was expected to have less than a .02 lower level of confidence than an employed state-sector worker, and respondents in areas whose unemployment level differed by 10 percent only differed in their confidence by about 0.01. Areas that differed in their rate of de novo job creation and in their concentration of state-owned firms in 1990 did not have any significant differences in their residents' confidence in private firms.

Confidence, or lack thereof, in private firms was not simply a matter of economic conditions or circumstances. Levels of education and income are strongly related to the level of confidence, with the better-educated and the better-off being more confident in private firms. The relationship with education may reflect individuals' expectation that a market economy will value human capital more highly than the command economy, or it may be reflecting a belief by the better-educated that a private economy will perform better for everyone than the previous economy. People living in villages and women had less confidence in private firms, while confidence increased among the more frequent church attendees. Two variables not included in the analysis in Chapter 4 have been added. These indicate whether the respondent resided in the sections of Poland occupied by the Russians, Germans, or Austrians (the omitted category) during the nineteenth century. Many studies of Polish social and political culture comment on the enduring effects these occupations had on various attitudes and institutions (see Tworzecki, 1996). In this case there is no difference in the confidence level of residents in the former German and Austrian partitions, but residents in the former Russian sector have less confidence in private firms.

The relationship between confidence and age is particularly revealing. The results showed a very definite quadratic pattern, with confidence reaching its lowest point about age fifty, an age at which one has the most difficulty dealing with an abrupt economic transition. At this age, retirement is still a number of years away, seeking new employment can be difficult, and family responsibilities may still be significant. A second explanation derives from the socialization into the political and economic system that respondents received. Fifty-year-olds in the early 1990s would have been born in the early 1940s so that virtually all their socialization would have taken place during the Communist years. Older respondents would have had some exposure to the pre-Communist period, although that was not a particularly optimistic period for Poles. At the other end of the age scale, the later one was born, the larger a proportion of one's life was spent during the period of resistance during the 1980s, which would likely have undermined the attachment to the socialist system.

One possible way to discriminate between these two propositions is to examine whether, and how, the age at which confidence reaches its lowest point changes over the period of the surveys. If the socialization hypothesis is the most likely explanation, then this age should increase between the early and the late surveys, as the population most socialized into the old system is aging. A different pattern for the quadratic form would suggest that other forces, in addition to or besides socialization, were contributing to the different confidence levels. To examine this question, we included interaction terms between the year of the survey and the age and age-squared variables.[1] These interactions allow the coefficients on the two age variables to shift systematically each year. Table 5.3 shows the estimated coefficients, the implied yearly coefficients for the age and

1 Formally, the year of the survey is normalized so that the 1992 survey is coded as zero, the 1993 survey as one, and so forth until the 1997 survey, which is coded as five. If we denote this time variable as year, age, and age-squared as the respective age of respondent and its square variables, and X as the other variables, then the model is: $Pvt.\ Conf = XB + (A_{11} + A_{21}*Year)*(Age/100) + (A_{12} + A_{22}*Year)*(Age/100)^2$. The age where confidence reaches its lowest level is $(A_{22} + A_{21}*Year)/[2*(A_{12} + A_{22}*Year)]$.

Table 5.3. *Confidence and Age, by Survey Year*

	Age[a]	Year*Age	Age^2	Year*Age^2	
Coefficient	−0.961	0.100	0.902	−0.082	
Standard error	0.104	0.033	0.101	0.033	
	1992	1993	1994	1995	1997
Age	−0.961	−0.861	−0.760	−0.660	−0.459
Age^2	0.902	0.821	0.739	0.657	0.493
Age*[b]	53.2	52.4	51.5	50.2	46.5
Confidence at age*[c]	0.376	0.347	0.326	0.320	0.339

[a] All age variables are age in years divided by 100.
[b] Age* indicates age at which confidence is at its minimum.
[c] For a male respondent working in a state-owned factory with average income, education, and church attendance living in an average region.

age-squared terms, and the associated age for the lowest confidence level.[2] (We only show the relationships with age, as the other coefficients are virtually identical.)

The age at which confidence reaches its lowest level decreases from 1992 to 1997, contrary to what is expected by the socialization hypothesis. The results seem more consistent with an explanation that experiences, likely painful ones, are the cause of the lack of confidence. This minimum confidence in private firms, or the most confidence in state firms, occurs at younger and younger ages, which are likely including the workers increasingly threatened by the transformation and the uncertainty it creates. One might also speculate that the attraction of the free market in terms of the quantity and range of goods it was providing was decreasing, both because the novelty was wearing off and because the prices of goods were beyond the incomes of many Polish workers. The second aspect of the model that we show in the last row in Table 5.3 is the overall decline in confidence between 1992 and 1995 and the subsequent increase in 1997. We observed this in Table 5.1, and it is implicit in the constant terms and age coefficients. So even for the average respondent at the age where confidence reached its minimum, that person's level of confidence decreased the most between 1992 and 1993 and then increased between

[2] The estimation was also done with separate coefficients for the *Age* and *Age^2* for each year. There was no statistical difference between this model and the one shown in Table 5.2, and the ages for the minimum confidence were nearly identical. We have kept the version in Table 5.2 for parsimony.

Table 5.4. *Opinions of Communism as a Form of Government (%)*

Attitude	1992	1993	1994	1995	1997
Worst form[a]	34.8	28.5	22.5	31.6	34.1
Good, good for some[a]	17.5	23.9	26.4	21.9	23.2
Don't know	14.4	13.0	13.7	11.7	14.1

[a] Percentage among those who have an opinion.

1995 and 1997. These changes coincide with changes in the aggregate economy.

ATTITUDES TOWARD COMMUNISM

The second attitude strongly related to the consequences of the economic reforms and to people's basic ideology is their assessment of communism as a form of government. This evaluation would encompass one's opinion of a centrally planned economy, as well as other related dimensions, such as one's attitude toward democratic reforms and one's opinions of the Communist leaders. The prospect of electing former Communist officials was a significant issue during Polish elections in the 1990s, raised in particular by President Wałęsa and the more right-wing nationalist parties.

The PGSS survey asked people the following question: "Thinking about all different kinds of governments in the world today, which of these statements comes closest to how you feel about Communism as a form of government? worst form; bad, but no worse than some; good for some countries; good form; don't know."[3] Table 5.4 shows the distribution of responses.

Among the respondents expressing an opinion, favorable and unfavorable evaluations mirrored the changes in economic conditions. Communism was increasingly looked upon favorably during the hardest times in 1993 and 1994 and then with less favor in 1995 and 1997. The proportion saying that communism was a good form of government or a good form for some countries actually exceeded the proportion calling it the worst form in 1994. There are relatively small changes in the proportion

3 Half the 1997 sample was asked a slightly different version than was used previously. In this case, respondents were given a more explicit Don't know or Don't have an opinion option. Statistical tests indicated that responses to this new format differ from the earlier format so that for the rest of this section we only use responses to the original form. The differences are discussed in Appendix 5A.

with no opinion over this time period. This is somewhat surprising given the efforts by the SLD to position itself as a center-left party in the tradition of the German Social Democrats and the British Labour Party. One might think these efforts would leave respondents increasingly indifferent to this question, although Wałęsa in 1995 and the right in 1997 campaigned partly on the issue of removing former Communists from the government.

The statistical analysis of attitudes toward communism as a form of government uses the same variables as were used to describe confidence in private firms. The constant term and the coefficients on the yearly dummy variables indicate the evaluations of an average respondent living in an average voivodship. We also examine how the relationships between these opinions may have changed between 1995 and 1997. The results are shown in Table 5.5

Among the occupational variables, with the exception of being employed in a foreign-owned firm, respondents in the private sector including private farmers before 1997 have less favorable opinions of commumism than workers in state enterprises. The self-employed are particularly less sympathetic to the old regime. Private farmers were less favorable through 1995 but were more likely to see it as a good system in 1997.[4] Two of the regional economic variables are related to opinions about communism. Respondents in areas with a large number of de novo jobs were less favorable, whereas those in regions with high unemployment were more favorable toward communism, as one might expect.

Most of the individual characteristics associated with evaluations of communism are in the expected direction. Support for communism decreased with income and sharply with education. Frequent church attendees also thought it to be a poor form of government and that sentiment became even more pronounced between 1995 and 1997, possibly a consequence of the campaigns waged by Wałęsa in 1995 and the AWS in 1997. Women, villagers, and residents in the former Russian and German partitions were more likely to think favorably of communism than men, more urban dwellers and residents in the former Austrian region.

Lastly, associations between age and evaluations of communism followed the quadratic pattern found in the associations between age and confidence in private firms. The most favorable opinion of communism occurred about age forty-six, which is about four years younger than the

---

4 Other statistical analyses indicated that the breakpoint came between the 1995 and 1997 surveys, not before 1995.

Table 5.5. *Model of Opinions of Communism a Good Form of Government*

Variable	Coefficient	Standard Error
1993	0.138	0.041
1994	0.249	0.038
1995	0.083	0.041
1997	−0.065	0.067
Private farmer	−0.099	0.047
Private farmer, 1997	0.293	0.127
SOE farmer	0.058	0.090
Domestic private company	−0.119	0.037
Foreign private company	0.016	0.116
Self-employed	−0.169	0.050
Cooperative	0.011	0.044
Never worked	−0.047	0.044
Don't know employer type	−0.073	0.074
Retired	−0.045	0.038
Years of schooling/10	−0.681	0.044
Log(income)	−0.076	0.024
Age/100	1.701	0.515
$(Age/100)^2$	−1.849	0.523
Village	0.109	0.046
Unemployed	−0.023	0.048
Female	0.107	0.025
Church attendance	−0.145	0.029
Church attendance, 1997	−0.176	0.087
German partition	0.005	0.058
German partition, 1997	0.243	0.083
Russian partition	0.119	0.057
Unemployed in region/work force	0.514	0.264
De novo jobs in region/work force	−1.731	0.451
% SOE firms$_{90}$	−0.015	0.258
Threshold 1	−0.521	0.062
Threshold 2	0.600	0.056
Threshold 3	1.056	0.055
Threshold 4	1.739	0.058
N	7,719	

age for the minimum confidence in private firms. The test for whether this age for the high point in favoring Communism changed over time produced an interesting and unexpected result. The age where support for communism peaked declined slightly over time, from about forty-eight years to forty-five and a half years of age, which is less of a shift than for confidence in private firms. But the differences among different age groups sharpened considerably, which was not particularly true for the confidence variable, which if anything flattened over time. In 1992 the expected difference between a twenty-year-old and a fifty-year-old in their views on communism is 0.06, whereas in 1997 it expanded to 0.21. There is a similar increase in the gap in the evaluations of a fifty- and an eighty-year-old. The results suggest that middle-aged respondents, who are likely having the most difficulty with the transition are maintaining, or developing, stronger attractions to the old system than older or younger individuals, who for different reasons may be having an easier time adjusting.

Many of the same factors that are related to attitudes toward private firms are associated with opinions about communism. Although there are differences between the two, as seen in the changing relationship with age and the different associations with the type of ownership variables, both tap similar assessments of the reform process. The correlation between the predicted outcomes for both variables from the statistical analysis was about −0.6 from 1992 to 1995 and −0.55 in 1997. Individuals who themselves were suffering from the effects of the transition or who were doing better at making the transition and people residing in regions doing poorly or well had similar views about private versus state firms and about communism as a form of government. The interesting speculation is how, on balance, these two factors weigh in the elections because a majority did not have confidence in private firms, as seen in Table 5.1, while a majority did not evaluate communism favorably. A post-Communist party opposing the economic reforms and an economically liberal but clearly anti-Communist party both present the electorate with conflicting choices. How these conflicts played out in the elections during the 1990s is the theme for the next section.

INDIVIDUAL VOTE CHOICE IN POLISH ELECTIONS, 1991–1997

The remainder of the chapter examines the Polish elections from 1991 to 1997 to test the proposition that the attitudes favoring private firms and opposing communism are related to how people voted in the successive Polish elections. If these attitudes are consistently related to how people vote, then the voters holding these attitudes form a constituency favoring liberal economic policies and vote for parties that will pursue those policies, or at least be sufficiently visible to constrain the actions of parties that are less sympathetic to liberal policies. To anticipate our findings in this section, at the level of individual voters making choices among the competing parties and candidates, these new economic interests play a consistent role in Polish elections. There is a high degree of stability in voters' positions on key issues and on how these issues relate to voting patterns, suggesting an important continuing role for this constituency.

Poland conducted three parliamentary elections, in 1991, 1993, and 1997 and one presidential election, in 1995, during the period 1991 to 1997.[5] Chapter 2 gives a chronology of the elections and the contending parties. We present only a brief summary of that discussion here. The political issues during this period reveal a considerable degree of continuity. In 1991, the major issues were the role of the Catholic Church in Polish civil and political life and the role for former Communist leaders. Some parties, most notably the post-Communist SLD, were also campaigning against the effects of the stringent macroeconomic policies adopted by the incumbent reform coalition led by the UD. By 1993 the liberal reform economic policies and their consequences had become a major issue. These three issues – the role for the church and church teachings in the government, the political access for former Communists, and the pace and direction of economic reforms – would be the major political fault lines, though with different degrees of emphasis, through all four elections. (For an extended discussion of the 1993 election, see Chan, 1995, and Powers and Cox, 1997. Slay, 1994, and Tworzecki, 1996, have good discussions of the 1991, 1993, and 1995 elections.)

The configuration of contending parties and candidates was much less stable through these elections. Table 2.7 shows the major parties and candidates and their shares of the votes in each election, grouped roughly by their political orientations and backgrounds. The economic liberals associated with the radical reforms were led by the UD and were joined in the government by the smaller KLD party. These two merged in May 1994 to form the UW after the KLD did not win any seats in the 1993 election. Jacek Kuroń was the UW's candidate for president in 1995.

In the 1991 and 1993 elections the votes for the UD and KLD are combined to form, in effect, a single party supporting liberal economic policies. This treatment makes the vote choices in these two elections

---

5 There was a presidential election held in 1990 that is not part of our analysis. In that election, Lech Wałęsa defeated the UD leader and Prime Minister Tadeusz Mazowiecki in the first round and the political unknown Stanisław Tymiński in the second round.

comparable with choices in 1995 and 1997, which occurred after these two parties formally joined. A vote for either party in 1991 is also effectively a vote for the coalition partners as these two parties formed part of the governing coalition during much of the 1991 to 1993 period.

The SLD and the PSL are two so-called post-Communist parties because their leaders had been party officials in the Communist Party before 1989. In 1991 the SLD campaigned strongly against the economic reforms and in favor of state intervention to protect Poland's heavy industry (see Tworzecki, 1996, p. 59). Its economic platform became less opposed to the promarket economic reforms with each election, although it was continually seen as opposing the liberal policies and even now its economic leaders disparage the economic policies pursued by the liberal governments between 1989 and 1993, often referred to as the Balcerowicz Plan (see Kołodko, 2000). The SLD leader in 1993, Aleksander Kwaśniewski, successfully ran for the presidency in 1995, defeating the Solidarność icon Lech Wałęsa in a very close second round. The PSL is an agriculturally and rurally based post-Communist party. It strongly opposed the economic reforms and campaigned strongly for continued subsidies for farmers and state-owned firms. The PSL leader, Waldemar Pawlak, was the first prime minister in the SLD-PSL coalition government and was a minor candidate for president in 1995.

The right-wing parties were an amalgam of organizations remaining from Solidarność that, with the exception of 1997, could not unite into a single coalition. One group of parties was church-related, and the other was associated with the trade-union movement. Prior to the 1997 elections the trade-union leader Marian Krzaklewski organized the AWS coalition that united the two factions. The AWS also built its support on Wałęsa's presidential campaign that made a strong appeal to these two factions. Independent organizations loosely associated with Wałęsa contested the 1991 and 1993 elections, first the Center Alliance (PC) and then the BBWR.

The UP is an interesting party, taking positions on economic reform and the role of the church that matched those of the SLD, yet it was anti-Communist, reflecting the roots of some of its leaders in the Solidarność movement. The UP hoped to attract voters who opposed the economic reforms but would not vote for the SLD because of its Communist background. As evidenced in Table 2.7, this strategy did not prove viable. Lastly, there is a series of strongly nationalistic parties, the KPN and the ROP most notably, that before 2001 managed to win only a small portion of the vote and a few seats in parliament. In addition to their nationalism, these parties advocated very populist economic programs in opposition to the liberal reforms, were strongly anti-Communist, and generally were sympathetic to the church leaders. There were attempts in 1997 to get the ROP to join the AWS coalition, but its leader, Jan Olszewski, chose to run separately.

The description of the major issues and contending parties and candidates in Chapter 2 and summarized in Table 2.7 should help predict the likely vote choices of individuals supporting the economic reforms and with strong confidence in private firms. These people are most likely to support the UD/UW Party and Kuroń's presidential candidacy. We can expect them to be unlikely to support the SLD, the PSL, and the UP among the left parties and the Solidarity trade union on the right. In the choice between Wałęsa and Kwaśniewski in the presidential election, they are most likely to support Wałęsa rather than the SLD leader. The pro-reformers may be somewhat ambivalent about the Catholic parties, which did not support the liberal reforms but were part of the early pro-reform government and which did not take highly visible positions on the economy.

We analyze individual vote choices for the various elections using data collected as part of the Polish General Social Survey (Cichomski and Morawski, 1999). The individual data allow us to relate vote choices to specific attitudes that cannot be observed at the aggregate level. With the survey data, the dependent variable is the log-odds the person said he or she voted for one of the competing parties relative to the UD or the UW in the 1991, 1993, and 1997 parliamentary elections and for one of the presidential candidates relative to Jacek Kuroń in the 1995 election. The shortcoming of the survey data is that these assessments of how people voted are based on their recall, in two instances with a definite time lag between the election and the survey.[6]

The central variable in our analysis of individual vote choices is the one measuring respondents' confidence in private relative to state firms. We would expect variations in this attitude to be strongly related to individual vote choices, particularly as the transition proceeds and as economic issues begin to be an important part of the political debate. This issue should differentiate between the strongly pro-reform parties and candidates (i.e., the UD and KLD, Jacek Kuroń, and the UW) and parties opposed to the

---

6 Comparisons of the marginal distributions in the survey responses with the actual vote distributions suggest that most differences are likely just sampling error, with the exception of a larger reported nonvoting (or Don't recall) group than the actual proportion of registered voters not voting.

reforms (i.e., the SLD and PSL, the UP, and the Solidarity trade union). Attitudes toward private firms should offer less discrimination between the pro-reform parties and the Catholic parties, between Kuroń and Wałęsa, and between the UD and the parties aligned with Wałęsa. The full statistical results are shown in Appendix 5B. The important substantive results are discussed here.

The private confidence variable is included with separate relationships for private farmers and for all other respondents. Table 5.2 shows that private farmers expressed considerably more confidence in private relative to state firms than did other workers, except those in private foreign firms and the self-employed. Yet, given the impact of the economic reforms on agriculture, it is hard to expect farmers to vote for the UD or UW, despite their attitudes toward private firms. The expectation is that for private farmers these attitudes either will not be related to how they vote or will be related to voting for different parties than for nonfarmers.

The voting models include a second aspect of economic voting. The logic behind most of the arguments that simultaneous economic and political reforms would be difficult if not impossible is the concept of retrospective voting. (See Fiorina, 1981, and Lewis-Beck, 1988. Stokes, 2001, has an excellent summary of this literature and propositions about why it has limited applicability in the transitional countries.) In its simplest form this proposition argues that voters hold the incumbent administration accountable for economic performance. If conditions have worsened, they vote for the opposition party, and if things are improving, they vote for the incumbent. There are important debates about whether voters are more attentive to changes in their personal situations or to changes in the national economy, but the main argument is that the election is a referendum on the incumbent administration's handling of the economy. The connection to propositions about economic voting in the transitional countries is quite direct. The hard measures required to reform the economy lead to hardship, at least in the short run, with increased unemployment, higher prices, and lowered output and incomes. Following the retrospective voting arguments, observers predicted this would lead the people to vote against the incumbent reform governments and to install an antireform party, most likely some version of the former Communist parties.

Stokes (2001) argues that the conventional retrospective model requires strong assumptions about how voters use recent economic performance to project the likely consequences of voting for the incumbent government or its challengers. These assumptions, however, are more problematic in transitional countries than in Western democracies. In the transitional countries much of the debate is about whether short-run costs are necessary and will lead to stronger future economic growth and whether the incumbent government should be held responsible for the problems inherited from previous regimes. Voters will attempt to evaluate the government's policies and performance based on their assessment of these circumstances and vote accordingly and not simply on the basis of whether conditions have gotten better or worse over some recent interval.

Consistent with Stokes's critique, empirical studies of elections in various transitional countries have not found as strong support for the retrospective voting arguments as have studies in the U.S. and Western Europe. In their study of the 1993 Polish election, Powers and Cox (1997) conclude there is an association between people's assessments of their economic situation and their votes in that election but that these relationships are small relative to other considerations, such as religious and regional factors. Harper (2000), in a study of elections in Hungary, Bulgaria, and Lithuania, similarly finds a weak association between personal and aggregate retrospective evaluations. Furthermore, he finds stronger associations between respondents' vote choices and their ideological evaluations of the democratic and market reforms than with their retrospective evaluations. Przeworski (2001) shows that in the early years of the Polish transition increasing unemployment seriously eroded support for Balcerowicz's economic plan and for the pro-reform government but that inflation had the opposite effect. His unemployment results are consistent with the retrospective voting propositions, but they are also consistent with a policy model of voting, as are the findings about inflation. All these results suggest that voting in the transitional countries may be more strongly rooted in people's assessments of the reforms as policy than in their retrospective assessments. Mach and Jackson (2003) analyze a panel study of Polish voters in the 1991, 1993, and 1997 elections and conclude that policy is more significant than retrospective voting.

We incorporate the retrospective propositions in our voting models to provide a further comparison of these different views of economic voting. The models for all three parliamentary elections and the 1995 presidential election include a variable based on people's responses to the question, "During the last few years, has your financial situation been getting better, getting worse, or has it stayed the same?" Responses are coded as 1 if they had gotten worse, 0 if better, and 0.5 if they had stayed the same or if the person volunteered an "I don't know." In 1997 the PGSS included a comparable question about the Polish economy, "In your opinion, compared with the period before three years ago, is the present state of the Polish economy definitely better, somewhat better, more or less the same, to some extent worse, or definitely worse than three years ago?" The responses to this question are coded from 0 to 1 with those who responded "I don't know" coded as 0.5 along with those who said "more or less the same."[7] The associations between individual vote choices and these retrospective variables, when compared with the association with the confidence and communism variables, should give a good picture of the amount of retrospective voting versus ideological, prospective voting in these Polish elections.

The variable measuring respondents' assessment of communism as a form of government is included in all the models because the role to be accorded the former Communists was a significant political issue in all these elections. It was a major theme in Wałęsa's 1995 campaign and in the AWS campaign in 1997. These assessments should distinguish between voting for the two post-Communist parties, the SLD and the PSL, and other parties, but not among the latter group of parties, most of which had roots in the Solidarność opposition and campaigned, in varying degrees, against the former Communists.

As we have indicated, considerations related to the economic and political reforms were not the only cleavage in the Polish electorate. People were divided over the role to be played by the Catholic Church. To incorporate this issue, the analysis includes responses to a question asking, "Do you think that churches and religious organizations in this country have far too much power, too much power, about the right amount of power, too little power, or far too little power, or don't you know?" The values of the variable ranges from 0 for those saying the church had far too little power to 1 for those who said the church had far too much power with a mean of 0.678. People who thought the church had too much power would be most likely to vote for the SLD or the UP, both of whom had taken positions opposite to those of church leaders, particularly on the abortion issue. Those who disagreed that the church had too much power would be most likely to vote for the Catholic party or its coalition. UD and UW leaders and parliament members divided on the church issues, occupying a middle ground, allowing for a limited church influence.

In addition to the three attitude variables, we include several variables to capture specific aspects of each campaign and party strategy. Three variables indicate whether respondents are private farmers, farmers on

---

7 There was no statistical difference between this coding and an alternative estimation with the Don't know as a separate variable.

state farms, and/or live in a rural village. We expect the private farm and village variables to be strongly related to votes for the PSL. We separate the state farmers from the private farmers, because we saw in Chapter 4 their economic situation was more similar to that of workers in state-owned industries.

We also include variables to indicate if respondents live in the home district of one of the parties' leaders or candidates to capture any localized campaign effects. A variable is included in the 1997 analysis to indicate if the respondent resided in one of the nine voivodships where Wałęsa received more than 40 percent of the vote in the first round of the 1995 presidential election. The proposition is that the Wałęsa campaign formed an important element of the organizational base for the church and Solidarność trade-union coalition that formed the AWS. Voters in these districts are more likely to vote for the AWS than comparable voters in other regions. It is important to keep in mind that we are trying to capture the organizational influences that might exist in these regions, not simply to relate an individual's vote in the previous election to his or her 1997 vote.

STATISTICAL RESULTS

The full estimated models are shown in Appendix 5B. We discuss the economic voting models first, with the primary interest being the role of people's confidence in private versus state firms in their vote choices. These associations are then compared with those based on retrospective evaluations. The relationship between voting and the opinions of communism and of the Catholic Church follows the discussion of economic voting, with the understanding that opinions about communism are partially rooted in people's economic positions during the transition.

Economic Voting

Confidence in Private Firms. Our primary interest is in the association between people's confidence in private firms relative to state-owned firms and their vote choices. Table 5.6 shows the expected difference in vote proportions among a group of representative respondents who don't know how much confidence they have in both private and state firms (scored a .5) and a comparable group who have a great deal of confidence in private firms and hardly any confidence in state firms (scored a 1.0). The respondents in these groups are not farmers, do not live in a rural village,

Table 5.6. *Confidence in Private Firms and Differences in Vote Choices*

Party/Candidate	1991	1993	1995	1997
UD+KLD/Kuroń/UW	3.4	17.0	9.9	18.6
SLD/Kwaśniewski	−2.1	−9.1	−14.4	−6.6
PSL/Pawlak	−0.1	−4.3	0.1	−0.8
UP/Zieliński	1.1	−2.4	−0.9	−2.5
Catholic/Wałęsa	−0.8	1.2	6.3	
Solidarność/AWS	−1.0	−3.1		−9.7
Other[a]	0.4	0.7	−0.9	1.0

Note: Entries are the expected difference in percentage voting for each party or candidate for a 0.5 difference in level of confidence in private relative to state-owned firms.
[a] Other category includes BBWR in 1993 and ROP in 1997.

and have the average retrospective evaluations and attitudes toward communism and the Catholic Church among this set of respondents. (This set comprises between 65 and 75 percent of the voters in each of the surveys.)

There are important comparisons in Table 5.6. Considerations of confidence in the private sector played only a small role in the 1991 election, which was held after the start of the stringent reforms but before the full scope of their costs became apparent. Even in that election, those with more confidence in private firms were more likely to vote for the pro-reform coalition represented by the UD and KLD and less likely to vote for the SLD or the Solidarność trade union. In percentage terms among a group of typical voters, these magnitudes are a 3.4 percent gain for the UD+KLD, a loss of 2.1 percent for the SLD, and a 1.9 percent loss for Solidarność. The reverse differences would be true for respondents with more confidence in state firms. The relatively small differences in vote probabilities associated with differences in this attitude suggest this issue was not a particularly salient one in 1991. Increases in vote differences associated with differences in this attitude in subsequent elections suggest that the salience of this issue emerged during the course of the transition and are not spuriously reflecting some other difference among voters.

Beginning with the 1993 election the differences in expected vote choices associated with different levels of confidence in private firms are fairly substantial and consistent. Respondents with more confidence in private firms were more likely to vote for the UD+KLD/UW and less likely to vote for the SLD, the PSL, or the Solidarność trade union and to a lesser extent the UP. They were also more likely to vote for Kuroń or Wałęsa and less likely to vote for Kwaśniewski in the first round of the presidential election. Again, if we think in terms of homogeneous groups of average voters who differ only in their confidence in private firms, the UD/UW share would have been 17 and 18.5 percent higher in the more-confident group in 1993 and 1997, respectively. The SLD share would have been 9 and 7 percent lower in the two elections, and the AWS share almost 10 percent lower in 1997. It is significant to note here that increasing confidence in private firms reduced the vote of the AWS more than it did the SLD in 1997, suggesting that the AWS may have been seen as even less supportive of the new private sector than the SLD among the nonfarmer and nonrural respondents. In the first round of the 1995 presidential election, Kuroń's and Wałęsa's shares would have been 10 and 6 percent higher, and Kwaśniewski's share 14 percent lower in the more-confident group.

A modest trend in increasing support for the UD/UW as confidence increases is accompanied by deceasing support for the Solidarity/AWS over time. The 1995 presidential election is a bit anomalous, as the contest in the first round quickly became a contest between Kwaśniewski and Wałęsa for entry into the runoff. Many pro-reform voters were not confident about Wałęsa's policies but saw him as preferable to Kwaśniewski, the post-Communist leader. (Some portrayed this election as a choice between yesterday and the day before yesterday, referring to both candidates as being tied more to Poland's past than to its present or future.) This led to a certain amount of strategic voting with people voting for their second or third preference rather than their first preference, based on candidate viability. Our interpretation of these results is that from 1993 onward, people's confidence in private relative to state-owned enterprises played an important, though not determinative, role in vote decisions and that this role was relatively stable over these three elections.

Private farmers' votes are not related to their level of confidence in private firms. Statistical tests never rejected the null hypothesis that these relationships are zero. This was true for individual party choices as well as for the pattern among all parties. The only statistically significant relationship in all four elections was a small positive association between the confidence variable and votes for the Other party category in 1993. On the basis of these results across all elections, we feel confident concluding that these attitudes are not related to how private farmers voted, that this variable could be omitted from the analysis for farmers, and that the dummy variable indicating whether the respondent was a private farmer was the best way to compare his vote choice with the choices of other

Table 5.7. *Voting and Retrospective Evaluations That Economy Is Worse*

Party/Candidate	Personal				Aggregate	
	1991	1993	1995	1997	1995	1997
UD+KLD/Kuroń/UW	−7.2	−2.9	−0.8	−5.4	−3.2	−7.3
SLD/Kwaśniewski	2.4	0.0	−0.8	3.5	−7.4	−7.4
PSL/Pawlak	0.4	2.3	−0.0	−0.1	0.1	0.8
UP/Zieliński	0.5	−0.2	−0.3	−0.0	−1.9	2.2
Catholic/Wałęsa	−0.9	−0.1	3.3		11.4	
Solidarność/AWS	0.4	1.5		0.3		9.3
Other[a]	4.4	−0.5	−1.4	1.8	1.1	2.3

Note: Entries are the expected difference in percentage voting for each party for a 0.5 difference in assessment of the changes in economic conditions.
[a] Other category includes BBWR in 1993 and ROP in 1997.

respondents. Omission of the confidence variable for farmers did not alter the coefficients on the other variables, including the confidence variable for nonfarmers.

Retrospective Voting. The second dimension of economic voting is the role played by evaluations of the changes in personal and aggregate economic conditions. Table 5.7 shows the expected differences in the vote proportions for our representative citizen groups in each of the elections based on differences in their retrospective evaluations. (Now they have the average amount of confidence in private firms.) The differences are 0.5 in magnitude, which corresponds to the differences used in Table 5.6. For the assessment of personal and aggregate conditions, this difference is equivalent to comparing those who say conditions have stayed the same with those who say conditions are worse.

Several results are noticeable in this table. Variations in people's assessments of how their personal situations have changed are only weakly associated with vote choices. The largest association is a lower probability of voting for the UD in 1991, at the beginning of the reforms, and again in 1993, though the magnitude is substantially smaller in 1993. There is a higher probability of voting for the SLD in 1991 and the PSL in 1993 among those who say their financial situation has worsened. These associations, however, are consistently negative for the UD and the UW, even when they are not part of the government (e.g., 1997) and are positive for the SLD in 1997, when they are the dominant party in the government. In several other cases, the associations are contrary to the one predicted by retrospective voting models. In the first round of the 1995 presidential election, those who said their situation had worsened were more likely to report voting for Wałęsa, the incumbent president. In 1993 the Solidarność trade union was part of the governing coalition, yet people who assess their conditions as worsening are somewhat more likely to vote for them. In 1993 the trade-union members made it clear they opposed the economic reforms and were partially responsible for the fall of the reform government. A vote for them in the 1993 election is at least as much an assessment of prospective policy choices as a retrospective evaluation. Taken together, these relationships are more suggestive of prospective policy voting, with people whose financial situations have worsened deciding not to vote for the economic liberals and to vote for the post-Communists or the trade union regardless of which parties are in office.

The relationships between assessments of the changes in the national economy and voting are larger than those for personal assessments, but they are no more consistent with the retrospective voting proposition. Only in the 1997 parliamentary election, where those who say the economy has gotten worse are more likely to have voted for the challenging AWS party and less likely to vote for the incumbent SLD, do we see the classic retrospective voting result. These disaffected individuals are less likely to vote for the UW, which was a challenging party and had been the formal parliamentary opposition to the SLD+PSL coalition. This, again, seems more indicative of policy-directed than retrospective voting.

Opinions about Communism

In comparing the relationship between attitudes about communism and votes, we compare the differences in the proportions voting for each party or candidate between representative groups of members who say they don't know whether communism is a good or bad form of government (coded as 0.5) and those who think that communism is a good form (coded as 1). Table 5.8 reports the differences in vote proportions for these two groups.

There are several contrasts here among the patterns observed between votes and confidence in private firms. First and as expected, this issue is strongly associated with voting differences in all the elections. The probability of voting for the SLD is consistently higher among those with a more positive evaluation of communism as a form of government. The party with the most support among respondents with negative views of communism varied from election to election. In 1991 the pro-reform UD+KLD

Table 5.8. *Communism as a Good Form of Government and Vote Choices*

Party/Candidate	1991	1993	1995	1997
UD+KLD/Kuroń/UW	−11.9	−10.4	−3.0	−10.4
SLD/Kwaśniewski	19.5	19.1	26.4	34.7
PSL/Pawlak	1.1	2.2	−0.1	−0.4
UP/Zieliński	0.8	−1.6	−1.1	−2.2
Catholic/Wałęsa	−1.1	−1.1	−18.5	
Solidarność/AWS	−2.5	−0.4		−19.8
Other[a]	−5.8	−7.7	−3.8	−1.9

Note: Entries are the expected difference in percentage voting for each party for a 0.5 difference in beliefs about communism as a form of government.
[a] Other category includes BBWR in 1993 and ROP in 1997.

protoparty gained the most votes among those with negative evaluations. In 1993 the UD and the group of other parties had more support among those with more unfavorable attitudes toward communism. The Other category in that election included both the BBWR, the Wałęsa-backed group of nonparty candidates, and the KPN, a far-right nationalistic party. In 1995 and 1997 it was Wałęsa and then AWS, the Catholic–Solidarność trade-union coalition, that gained the most votes among the more anti-Communist voters. The increased differences and shifts in 1995 and 1997 correspond to the efforts by Wałęsa and then the AWS leaders to campaign explicitly against former Communist officials.

Other Variables

The coefficients on the other variables matched expectations or were not important. Assessments of the influence of church organizations played a large and consistent role in people's vote decisions. (For more on the church role in 1993, see Powers and Cox, 1997.) Those who thought the church had too much power were much more likely to vote for the SLD, which most strongly opposed the positions advocated by church leaders. Conversely, those who thought the church had too little influence were much more likely to vote for the Catholic party in 1991, the Catholic coalition party or Solidarność trade union in 1993, Wałęsa in 1995, and the AWS in 1997. Private farmers and villagers were more likely than other respondents to vote for the PSL in all the parliamentary elections and for Pawlak in 1995 and, to a lesser extent, for the AWS in 1997. Farmers on state-owned farms were more likely to vote for Kwaśniewski in the second round of the 1995 presidential election; however, other than that vote, their vote choices were not significantly different from nonfarm workers. (Recall that the attitudes of state farmers on private firms and communism closely matched those of workers in state enterprises.)

THE EVOLUTION OF A LIBERAL ECONOMIC CONSTITUENCY

Voters expressing confidence in private firms consistently supported parties and candidates advocating liberal economic policies, and this group was increasing by 1997. This constituency was fueled by the growth of the new private sector, which was contributing to the improving economy by 1997. Even though the UD and the KLD in 1993, Jacek Kuroń in 1995, and the UW in 1997 did not receive a plurality of the votes, and in fact consistently placed third, this emerging constituency was positioned to exert influence on the political process and the actions of the governing parties. (We talk more about this phenomenon in the next chapter when we discuss voting returns and the allocation of seats.) The second round of the 1995 presidential election in which Mr. Kwaśniewski defeated President Wałęsa by 51.7 to 48.3 percent offers an opportunity to illustrate this point. In this close election, relatively small shifts in vote choices could have tipped the election to Wałęsa.

The statistical result showing that self-employed individuals and those working in private firms had more confidence in private firms and a lower opinion of communism than workers in state firms and farms suggests that this group should be an important part of Wałęsa's constituency. The analysis of individual vote choices indicates that the size of this group and the salience of the economic issues in its voting decision was an important factor in the election. Our contention is that this constituency is important in two ways. The obvious way is that by voting for liberal parties and candidates it increases the number of seats held by these parties. But at least as important, the growth of a liberal constituency constrains the actions other parties may take when in office, even if the liberals do not control a majority of the seats.

We examine how critical the pro-reform constituency might have been in this election by asking how important would this issue have to have been to switch the average voter to being a Wałęsa supporter, given that those with more confidence in the private sector were more likely to vote for Wałęsa? Appendix 5C shows that in a model of sincere individual voting where voters choose the candidate whose platform is closest to their preferred policies and whose dislike for a candidate increases with the square of the deviance of that candidate's policies from their preferred position, movements of a candidate's platform on an issue change the relative importance of that issue in people's voting decision.[8] Such a change then alters the relative weight of that issue in affecting the election outcome. The implication here is that if the SLD's and Kwaśniewski's policies after winning the 1993 election had been less supportive of economic reform, the issue of private confidence might have had a larger association with how people voted in 1995.

To estimate how large the coefficient on the private confidence variable would have needed to be to swing the expected vote of the average voter to Wałęsa, we assume that with Wałęsa getting 48.3 percent of the votes the value of the logit for the average voter is −0.068.[9] The mean of the private confidence variable among voters in the second round is 0.37, implying that the coefficient on this variable needed to be larger by 0.184 to make the expected logit positive. The second column under the Wałęsa heading in Table 5B.1 shows that the estimated coefficient on the private confidence variable in the voting model for the second round of the presidential election, which only included Kwaśniewski and Wałęsa, is 1.40 with a standard error of 0.34. The value of 0.184 then is a relatively small increase in the magnitude of this coefficient, on the order of 13 percent, or about three-fifths the coefficient's standard error.

Our inference here would be that if the model in Appendix 5B is applicable, a relatively small change in Kwaśniewski's, or the SLD's, positions might have had a significant impact on the election by raising the relative weight voters gave to economic policies in the 1995 election.[10] Again,

---

8 It is entirely appropriate to consider voters as sincere in this case as there are only two candidates, reducing any gains for strategic voting.

9 We are assuming a symmetrical distribution of preferences so that the mean and median voters' preferences are identical.

10 The model in Appendix 5B suggests that a change in Kwaśniewski's or the SLD's positions of less than this magnitude might have had the same effect. This discussion ignored the change in the constant term that would result from a change in a candidate's positions, which would also have raised the average logit, meaning a smaller shift than needed to raise the coefficient on private confidence to 1.50 might have altered the election. Also, if individual utilities were not separable, it is likely that the joint effect of attitudes about private firms and communism interacted positively, meaning that utility increased further for candidates who favored private firms and opposed Communists, or vice-versa. If this is the case, a shift by Kwaśniewski or the SLD opposing the development of private firms would also have raised the coefficient on the communism variable in the vote equation, further increasing the average logit.

we do not want to try to use these results to predict an outcome for this election under an assumption that the SLD might have followed different economic policies between the 1993 and 1995 elections. We do think this exercise is useful to illustrate how the growth of the pro-reform constituency builds incentives for parties and candidates who hope to win successive elections to constrain their positions and ultimately even to recognize this constituency.

CONCLUSION

This chapter examines whether the growth of a group of voters with a strong stake in the emerging private sector evolves into a constituency that supports parties advocating and pursuing liberal economic policies. This emerging constituency, the size of which depends on the growth rate of the de novo firms sector, helps to offset the constituency that becomes frustrated and impatient with the reforms as their cost becomes evident. Many writers assumed this latter constituency, particularly given its organizational advantage derived from its roots in the older state enterprises and unions, would dominate the political process and lead to the election of parties that would severely slow or halt the reforms. There is certainly evidence of that process in some of the transitional countries. We contend, however, that such situations result because the de novo firm creation was not rapid enough to generate a significant liberal constituency. One of the keys to the Polish success during the 1990s is its de novo firm creation and its developing constituency supporting market reforms. This constituency is evident in the individual survey data, both in the attitudes expressing confidence in private firms and in the vote choices of respondents with more confident attitudes. The next step is to examine the actual vote returns and parliamentary seat allocations to judge the role of this constituency.

Appendix 5A: Coding of Private Confidence and Communism Measures

The scientists conducting the PGSS conducted several experiments with the question format in the 1997 study. They asked each version, labeled X for the traditional question and Y for the new version, in half the sample. Our concern is if, and possibly how, these changes alter our results

Table 5A.1. *Coding for Confidence Measure*

Response: Form X	Code[a]	Response: Form Y	Code[a]
A great deal of confidence	2	Definitely a great deal of confidence	2
Only some confidence	1	Only some confidence	1
		Neither confidence nor lack thereof	0
Don't know	0	Don't know	0
Hardly any confidence at all	−1	Not much confidence	−1
		Definitely no confidence	−2

[a] Coding for confidence in private enterprises. Coding for confidence in state enterprises is −1 times coding for confidence in private enterprises.

as the questions about confidence in private and state enterprises and the question about Communism as a form of government are part of this experiment. This appendix analyzes how the two forms might affect our model of attitudes and the estimates of the voting models. The summary result is that the changes in the confidence questions do not change either the attitude or the voting equations. The changes in the communism question alter the attitude but not the voting equation.

The measure of confidence in private relative to state enterprises is constructed from the two-part question, "Would you say you have a great deal of confidence, only some confidence, or hardly any confidence at all in them, or don't you know?" Institutions included state firms and private firms. The coding becomes slightly complicated because for half the respondents in the 1997 survey the PGSS used an experimental form for the question. Table 5A.1 shows the response categories used in the 1992, 1993, 1994, 1995, and one-half of the 1997 survey, form X, and those used in the second half of the 1997 study, form Y.

Rather than delete the cases where form Y was used, which would severely reduce the information on which to base the statistical analysis and results, we tried to match the coding to the two different response categories as closely as possible. There are two problems created by the use of the two forms. The easier, relatively, to handle is the alteration of the wording in categories that might otherwise be the same. We ignored this problem and decided that choosing "A great deal of confidence" would be equivalent to choosing "Definitely a great deal of confidence." Similarly we combined "Hardly any confidence at all" and "Not much confidence." (We subject all these decisions to a statistical test shortly.)

The more serious problem is created by the addition of the "neither confidence nor lack thereof" and "Definitely no confidence" categories to create a five-point scale where only a three-point scale was used previously. We treat the Don't know responses in both forms as equivalent to the explicit "Neither confidence nor lack thereof" option in form Y. More respondents opted for the "neither" option than responded Don't know – about 30 percent for the private firms and 17.5 percent for SOE's compared with between 6.5 and 7.5 percent for the various Don't know's on form X and on form Y in 1997. This distribution means that a higher proportion of the respondents are located in the middle of the scale using the Y form, but that does not imply a bias in assessing people's confidence in private firms. Lastly, we decided that the addition of the category "Definitely no confidence" in form Y separated respondents already at the bottom of the confidence scale into two groups rather than combining them into a single category. Without any way to distinguish among these two sets of people in the early surveys and with form X in 1997, we code them identically. In 1997 with form Y, where we can distinguish those with definitely no confidence from those with not much confidence, we do so.

The changes in the format of the communism question appear to be more benign, on the surface. Form Y included an explicit, "I don't have an opinion." Form X did not explicitly offer a "Don't know" or "No opinion" option, though if respondents volunteered that response it was coded as such. Table 5.4 shows that about 12 to 14 percent of respondents volunteered this response. This proportion increased to more than 30 percent with the Y form, with the largest drops being among those saying that communism is the worst form or is bad but no worse than some other forms of government. With both forms we treated the Don't knows as a middle category, placed between those who say communism is bad but no worse than some other forms and those who say it is good for some countries. Again the question is whether respondents answering form Y can be pooled with those answering form X when estimating both our model of attitudes and the voting models for 1997.

We conducted three tests to examine if any statistical differences are associated with the two forms. The first two tests related the coded responses for each form to a set of exogenous variables to see if the relationships differed between the two codings. If these associations are the same, it suggests that the findings and discussion about how confidence varies among individuals and has evolved over time are not affected by use of the two questionnaires. The exogenous variables are the ones included in Tables 5.2 and 5.5. The first analysis used the confidence measure and compared the fit of an OLS regression on the pooled 1997 sample with the

Table 5A.2. *Estimations with Form Y of Confidence and Communism Measures*

	Prob: H_0[a] Coefficient	Form Y Dummy[b]	Standard Error
OLS estimation of confidence	0.86	0.0006	0.0089
Ordered probit estimation of confidence	0.86	0.0276	0.0430
Ordered probit estimation of communism	0.004	0.1549	0.0438
Ordered probit of communism excluding no opinion	0.017	0.0605	0.0518
Vote			
1995, round 1	0.79		
1995, round 2	0.71		
1997	0.87		

[a] Probability of results if null hypothesis of no difference is correct.
[b] Model with only the form Y variable included.

fit when the model was estimated separately for respondents asked each question type. A model was also estimated with the pooled sample with an intercept dummy variable for form Y. The second analysis estimated an ordered probit model for both the confidence and communism measures using the same explanatory variables. The first estimation constrained all the coefficients to be the same, the second included the dummy intercept variable for form Y, and the third estimated separate coefficients for all variables for each form. The last analysis reestimated the vote choice models for 1995 and 1997 with a slope dummy variable on the confidence and communism variables for respondents answering form Y. If the co-efficients on these two variables are different from zero it indicates that our inferences about the relationship between these attitudes and how people voted are affected by the question form. The statistical test is the null hypothesis that the coefficients on the form Y variables are zero. The results of these tests are shown in Table 5A.2.

The first column in Table 5A.2 indicates the probability of getting a worse fit by chance when separate models are estimated relative to the null hypothesis that there is no difference between the relationships with form X and form Y codings. With the confidence variable there is a substantial probability that the differences in the statistical relationships modeling individual attitudes could have happened by chance. The estimation of a dummy intercept variable for form Y in these two estimations also produced the equivalent of a null result. The estimated coefficients estimating whether there was any bias in the expected mean response, conditioned on the values of the explanatory variables, were virtually zero in magnitude and far smaller than their estimated standard errors. From these results we are comfortable pooling the respondents asked the different forms. With the communism measure, however, the relationships with the explanatory variables are likely different for the two forms, even when respondents with no opinion on each form are excluded. Furthermore, the differences are not just in the intercept, which could be accommodated by the form Y dummy variable. Based on these results we decided to estimate the attitude model only using respondents asked the form X version so that comparisons would be comparable for the 1992 to 1997 period.

The results of the tests with the voting equation indicate that the relationships between respondents' votes and the two attitude variables are not affected by the question form. The statistical differences could easily have occurred by chance. We ran separate tests for the confidence and communism questions and got the same results. From these statistical results we conclude that it is very unlikely that our voting results are affected by the change in question format.

Appendix 5B: Statistical Model of Individual Vote Choices

The probability of voting for one of the contending parties or candidates is modeled as a multinomial logit equation depicting the log odds of voting for party or candidate j rather than for the liberal party, the UW, or candidate, Kurón. The parties denoted by j in the analysis are the SLD, PSL, UP, Catholic coalition, and the Solidarność trade union. In 1997 these latter two parties formed a coalition that ran as the AWS. Votes for all other parties are combined into a single Other category so that all vote probabilities sum to one. The dependent variable in the analysis is the log of the probability of person i choosing party j relative to the probability of choosing the UW, $\log(P_{i,sld}/P_{i,uw})$, $\log(P_{i,psl}/P_{i,uw})$, $\log(P_{i,up}/P_{i,uw})$, $\log(P_{i,cath}/P_{i,uw})$, $\log(P_{i,solid}/P_{i,uw})$, or $\log(P_{i,aws}/P_{i,uw})$, and $\log(P_{i,other}/P_{i,uw})$. Each of these log odds ratios is then related to a set of explanatory variables, denoted as X_i, which includes the attitude variables, so for 1993 we have;

$$\log(P_{i,sld}/P_{i,uw}) = X_i B_{sld} + U_{i,sld} \qquad (B2.1)$$

$$\log(P_{i,psl}/P_{i,uw}) = X_i B_{psl} + U_{i,psl} \qquad (B2.2)$$

$$\log(P_{i,up}/P_{i,uw}) = X_i B_{up} + U_{i,up} \qquad (B2.3)$$

$$\log(P_{i,cath}/P_{i,uw}) = X_i B_{cath} + U_{i,cath} \tag{B2.4}$$

$$\log(P_{i,solid}/P_{i,uw}) = X_i B_{solid} + U_{i,solid} \tag{B2.5}$$

$$\log(P_{i,other}/P_{i,uw}) = X_i B_{other} + U_{i,other}. \tag{B2.6}$$

A nonstandard feature is that the variable indicating the respondent resides in the UW leader's home district appears in the other parties' equation with the same negative coefficient. Formally, $\text{Prob}(V_j = 1) = P_j = e^{XB_j}/D$ and $\text{Prob}(V_{uw} = 1) = P_{uw} = e^{XB_{uw}}/D$, where D is the denominator that scales the log-odds equations so that all probabilities sum to one. This gives, $\log(P_j/P_{uw}) = (XB_j - XB_{uw}) = X(B_j - B_{uw})$. Thus, a variable that is related only to votes for the UW appears in the log-odds equations for all parties, but with the same coefficient. The estimated equations are shown in Table 5B.1.

Table 5B.1. *Individual Vote Choice Equations*

	SLD/Kwaśniewski				PSL/Pawlak			
	1991	1993	1995	1997	1991	1993	1995	1997
Confidence in private firms	−1.03 (0.53)	−2.34 (0.61)	−2.38 (0.56)	−1.98 (0.52)	−0.28 (0.84)	−2.92 (0.70)	−0.76 (0.84)	−1.80 (0.66)
Retro personal	1.06 (0.28)	0.25 (0.27)	0.14 (0.28)	0.88 (0.34)	0.88 (0.38)	0.76 (0.37)	−0.18 (0.57)	0.47 (0.31)
Retro collective			0.58 (0.73)	−0.14 (0.45)			1.75 (1.14)	1.33 (0.66)
Communism	2.76 (0.38)	2.56 (0.49)	1.76 (0.55)	2.98 (0.37)	1.59 (0.71)	1.88 (0.66)	0.31 (0.66)	1.22 (0.47)
Church power	4.27 (0.76)	2.72 (0.54)	2.33 (0.62)	4.06 (0.43)	0.82 (0.68)	0.44 (0.77)	0.18 (1.26)	1.08 (0.71)
Private farmer	0.29 (0.72)	1.02 (1.26)	0.09 (0.77)	−0.90 (0.56)	1.72 (0.52)	2.18 (1.17)	1.41 (0.84)	0.92 (0.66)
SOE farmer	0.59 (0.64)	0.37 (0.71)	0.65 (0.98)	0.73 (0.72)	−0.32 (0.85)	−0.28 (0.55)	−0.32 (1.51)	0.32 (1.08)
Village	−0.87 (0.49)	0.09 (0.36)	1.05 (0.36)	0.63 (0.26)	2.04 (0.40)	1.86 (0.37)	4.11 (0.81)	2.29 (0.33)
Wałęsa voiv.				−0.56 (0.18)				
UD candidate	−0.58 (0.08)	−1.01 (0.11)		−0.44 (0.11)	−0.58 (0.08)	−1.01 (0.11)		−0.44 (0.11)
Party candidate		0.78 (0.13)	−0.21 (0.11)	0.95 (0.15)	2.02 (0.27)	2.10 (0.22)		0.21 (0.22)

	Catholic Parties		BBWR	Wałęsa		Solidarity		AWS
	1991	1993	1993	1995 (1)	1995 (2)	1991	1993	1997
Confidence in private firms	−0.45 (0.58)	−0.16 (0.92)	−0.60 (0.97)	−1.04 (0.59)	1.40 (0.34)	−0.44 (0.52)	−2.59 (0.61)	−1.72 (0.37)
Retro personal	−0.00 (0.28)	0.14 (0.65)	−0.45 (0.36)	0.35 (0.24)	−0.07 (0.15)	0.39 (0.26)	0.69 (0.40)	0.58 (0.25)
Retro collective				1.51 (0.76)	1.06 (0.34)			1.28 (0.49)
Communism	0.27 (0.47)	−1.61 (1.07)	−1.28 (1.00)	−1.04 (0.47)	−2.88 (0.26)	0.30 (0.32)	1.35 (0.87)	−0.99 (0.40)
Church power	−4.88 (0.72)	−6.48 (1.11)	−3.37 (1.19)	−1.86 (0.63)	−4.50 (0.30)	−1.23 (0.49)	−3.45 (1.12)	−2.53 (0.47)
Private farmer	0.72 (0.59)	2.47 (1.26)	−20[a]	0.66 (0.68)	0.45 (0.26)	0.31 (0.43)	−0.49 (1.47)	0.03 (0.44)
SOE farmer	−20[a]	−20[a]	−0.07 (1.03)	−0.50 (0.97)	−0.82 (0.30)	0.40 (0.36)	−0.30 (0.94)	−0.61 (0.85)
Village	0.20 (0.37)	−0.48 (0.62)	−0.34 (0.73)	0.92 (0.39)	−0.14 (0.16)	0.41 (0.25)	0.71 (0.43)	0.70 (0.24)
Wałęsa voiv.								0.44 (0.17)
UD candidate	−0.58 (0.08)	−1.01 (0.11)	−1.01 (0.11)			−0.58 (0.08)	−1.01 (0.11)	−0.44 (0.11)
Party candidate				0.05 (0.06)	0.74 (0.10)			−0.11 (0.11)
Kwaśniewski					−0.17[b] (0.10)			

(continued)

Table 5B.1 *(continued)*

	UP/Zieliński				Olszewski/ROP	
	1991	1993	1995	1997	1995	1997
Confidence in private firms	0.50	−1.48	−1.94	−2.00	−2.38	−0.83
	(0.94)	(0.90)	(0.51)	(0.47)	(0.65)	(0.93)
Retro personal	0.68	0.21	0.03	0.56	0.05	0.27
	(0.50)	(0.29)	(0.51)	(0.35)	(0.43)	(0.62)
Retro collective			−0.65	1.37	1.68	1.78
			(1.04)	(0.75)	(0.75)	(0.81)
Communism	1.12	1.14	0.15	0.85	−1.93	−0.96
	(0.77)	(0.77)	(0.62)	(0.56)	(0.71)	(0.77)
Church power	−1.10	1.15	0.85	1.55	−1.53	−1.37
	(1.00)	(0.89)	(0.82)	(0.66)	(0.93)	(0.89)
Private farmer	−20[a]	0.14	−0.97	−0.21	0.22	0.42
		(1.54)	(1.41)	(0.74)	(0.87)	(0.68)
SOE farmer	0.91	−0.22	0.52	1.08	0.24	−20[a]
	(0.84)	(0.92)	(1.48)	(0.80)	(1.44)	
Village	−0.23	0.27	0.51	0.41	0.39	1.30
	(0.58)	(0.34)	(0.56)	(0.33)	(0.46)	(0.48)
UD candidate	−0.58	−1.01		−0.44		−0.44
	(0.08)	(0.11)		(0.11)		(0.11)
Party candidate		1.16				
		(0.18)				

	Other			
	1991	1993	1995	1997
Confidence in private firms	−0.11	−0.95	−1.16	−0.95
	(0.39)	(0.62)	(0.68)	(0.86)
Retro personal	0.68	0.32	−0.27	1.12
	(0.19)	(0.26)	(0.40)	(0.41)
Retro collective			0.82	1.06
			(0.98)	(0.80)
Communism	0.12	0.89	0.11	1.37
	(0.31)	(0.47)	(0.61)	(0.56)
Church power	−0.21	−0.56	−0.60	0.46
	(0.42)	(0.71)	(0.69)	(0.80)
Private farmer	0.94	1.27	0.82	0.94
	(0.41)	(1.20)	(0.88)	(0.63)
SOE farmer	0.16	−1.86	2.04	−0.00
	(0.36)	(1.20)	(1.17)	(1.35)
Village	0.48	0.62	0.05	0.31
	(0.27)	(0.27)	(0.65)	(0.43)
UD candidate	−0.58	−1.01		−0.44
	(0.08)	(0.11)		(0.11)

[a] Coefficient set to −20 because no respondents in that group voted for that party.
[b] Coefficient refers to respondents in Kwaśniewski's voividship.

Appendix 5C: Candidate Policies and Individual Voting

It is a fairly easy task to show that individual voting decisions, if based on a metric relating how far candidates are from voters' preferred policies, in effect weights these issues proportionally to how distant the candidates' platforms are from the voter's preference. If we use the conventional quadratic loss function, then we can estimate the voting decision of the mean voter and also show that the weight given by this central voter is proportional to the distance the candidates' policies are from the average preference. Together, these points suggest that the further a candidate gets from the mean preference, the greater the weight that issue gets in affecting the election's outcome.

Begin with the stipulation that voters have a utility loss for candidate X, U_i^x, based on the distance from that candidate's platform, denoted by P_x, to the voter's preferred policy, denoted by P_i, where $U_i^x = -\alpha(P_x - P_i)^2$. There is a similar utility loss, U_i^y, associated with the platform of candidate Y, denoted by P_y. Ignoring any stochastic elements for the sake of this demonstration, person i votes for the candidate associated with the higher utility. The margin by which candidate X is preferred to (or dominated by) Y is given by,

$$U_i^x - U_i^y = -\alpha(P_x - P_i)^2 + \alpha(P_Y - P_i)^2 = 2\alpha(P_X - P_Y)P_i - \alpha(P_x^2 - P_y^2).$$
$$(5C.1)$$

If the probability of person i voting for candidate X, V_i^x, is proportional to this utility difference, say $V_i^x = f(U_i^x - U_i^y)$, we might write this relationship in logistic form as

$$\log[V_i^x/(1 - V_i^x)] = L_i^x = 2\alpha(P_x - P_Y)P_i - \alpha(P_x^2 - P_y^2). \qquad (5C.2)$$

If we think of this as a logit equation for the individual voting decision, such as we have been estimating, then across individuals we have an equation with an effective constant term, $\alpha(P_x^2 - P_y^2)$, and a coefficient on the individual preferences given as $2\alpha(P_x - P_Y)$. Both these terms are constant across individuals. One can think of the coefficients we estimated on the variables measuring people's confidence in private firms, their assessment of communism as a form of government, and their opinion of the church's power as reflecting the relative weight of the issue in their utility function, the 2α term times the distance between the two candidates' positions and the constant term is proportional to the distance between the two parties' platforms.

Equations 5C.1 and 5C.2 are linear in terms of individual positions so the logit for the average voter is simply Equation 5C.1 with the mean preference, $\overline{P}$, substituted for P_i,

$$\overline{L}^x = 2\alpha(P_x - P_y)\overline{P} - \alpha(P_x^2 - P_y^2). \qquad (5C.3)$$

Any change in candidate X's position that increases the distance between the two candidates increases the magnitude of the effective coefficient on the mean preference, implicitly giving that issue more weight in affecting the election outcome. It also decreases the constant term, further reducing the likelihood the average voter votes for party X.

This development has used only a single issue, but the point generalizes to multiple dimensions with only two candidates. If the individual utility functions are separable, then we have the same results as noted previously. With nonseparable utility functions, the value of the logit is still linear in the preferred positions of the voter, and the mean logit is linear in the mean of the preference distributions. The implicit coefficient on each preference, however, becomes a function of the distances between the candidates on all the issues. This effectively means that changes in a candidate's position on one issue may alter the weights on all issues in the aggregate outcome equation, the equivalent for Equation 5C.3.

6

De Novo Job Creation and Election Returns

Individual attitudes and votes are only the beginning of the electoral process. How individual choices translate into votes for the different parties in their respective districts, and then how the district vote distributions determine the parties' shares of the seats in the parliament are critical issues. This chapter examines the district voting returns in Poland's 1993, 1995, and 1997 elections and the allocation of seats that followed from these votes. This analysis is the acid test for our proposition about the development of a constituency supporting the continuation of the market reforms. If this constituency cannot affect election outcomes and the parties' strength in parliament, then evidence about individual attitudes and behavior is interesting but insignificant.

The theme in this chapter is the continuing examination of the connection between new economic activity and support for economically liberal parties and whether this support will offset some of the opposition to the reforms generated by the economic hardships. We want to know both the magnitude of this association so that we can estimate how many votes more de novo jobs might have stimulated and the stability of the association. If the liberal constituency is to be influential, its presence must be evident over time and not just in one election. Evidence of a consistent relationship between measures of the de novo economy and votes for the reform party or parties would lend greater credence to our basic argument.

A MODEL OF AGGREGATE ELECTION RETURNS

The Polish elections in 1993, 1995, and 1997 provide a good test of our basic propositions about the relationship between the de novo economy and elections. The Polish electorate in 1993 and 1997 was divided into fifty-two electoral districts of vastly different population sizes and economic conditions.[1] As we noted in Chapter 4, there is considerable variation in how well each of these regions adapted to the transition and to developing new enterprises. These variations in unemployment, state-sector employment, and de novo job creation provide an excellent base for examining how the parties' votes varied with these measures of the transition. We use the statistical relationships between de novo job creation and votes for the economic liberals to explore how higher levels of job creation might have changed the voting results and ultimately altered seat allocations in the Sejm after each election.

Voting returns varied considerably among the forty-nine districts. For example, in 1993 the shares going to the UD and KLD combined range from 5 to 27 percent, the SLD share from 9 to 33 percent, and the PSL proportion from 5 to 44 percent. The central explanatory variable in the model of election returns is the amount of new-job creation in each voivodship. This is the critical variable in our model of the political economy of transitions. This variable is obtained from the GUS data used in Chapter 3 and used in the analyses in Chapters 4 and 5.

The statistical model estimated with the aggregate data is very similar to the individual logit model used in Chapter 5. The difference is that the left-hand-side variables are the log of the proportion of the votes in a voivodship received by a party, divided by the proportion of the votes received by the UD+KLD, by Jacek Kuroń, and by the UW in each of the sequential elections.[2] If we let V_{ji} denote the proportion of the votes received by party i in voivodship j, the equations estimated are:[3]

$$\log(V_{j,sld}/V_{j,ud}) = X_j B_{sld} + U_{j,sld} \tag{6.1}$$

$$\log(V_{j,psl}/V_{j,ud}) = X_j B_{psl} + U_{j,psl} \tag{6.2}$$

---

1 Forty-seven voting districts match the voivodships that form the basis for our measures of de novo firm creation and that match other data collected by the Polish Census Bureau. Two of the voivodships, Warsaw and Katowice, were divided into smaller electoral districts, two in Warsaw and three in Katowice. We aggregate the electoral data from these districts so there are forty-nine electoral districts that are co-terminous with voivodships, which matches the vote data to the measures of economic and social characteristics for each district.

2 Again, for the purposes of this analysis we have combined the votes for the UD and the KLD in the 1993 election. This makes the votes comparable with those received by the UW in 1997. When we analyze the seat distributions later in this chapter, we disaggregate these two parties' votes.

3 For a full development of this statistical model, see Jackson (2002).

$$\log(V_{j,up}/V_{j,ud}) = X_j B_{up} + U_{j,up} \qquad (6.3)$$

$$\vdots \qquad \vdots \qquad \vdots$$

$$\log(V_{j,othr}/V_{j,ud}) = X_j B_{othr} + U_{j,othr}. \qquad (6.4)$$

This specification incorporates the constraint that the proportion of all votes in a voivodship sums to 1, $V_{ud} + V_{sld} + V_{psl} + \cdots + V_{other} = 1$. The coefficients denoted by B indicate how the votes for each party or for all other parties relative to the votes for the UD vary with X.[4]

The specifications of the right-hand-side variables in Equations 6.1 to 6.4 parallel the results of the individual level analyses reported in Chapter 5. Among individuals, vote choices are related to the confidence in private relative to state enterprises, to attitudes about communism as a form of government, and to assessments of the political influence of the Catholic Church. These attitudes, in turn, vary with individual characteristics, such as working in the private sector, age, education, income, and church attendance. Beside the attitude variables, vote choices are also related to being employed as a private farmer and to residence in a village, in the home district of one of the party's leaders, and (for the 1997 election) in a voivodship that had been a stronghold for Wałęsa in 1995 and thus part of the AWS organizational base.

The economic measures used in the analyses of the election returns are the proportion of the total work force employed in de novo firms, the proportion of the nonagricultural work force employed in state-owned firms (which includes those that have been restructured but are still in government control) and the unemployment rate. The unemployment rate is included because it is a standard measure of the distress experienced by a region as a result of the economic policies associated with the transition. Both the variables measuring whether an individual was unemployed and the regional unemployment rate are only weakly related to attitudes about private enterprises and communism in the individual analyses reported in Chapter 5. These results suggest there may be only a weak relation between unemployment levels and vote shares at the aggregate level.

Two variables are used to represent the cleavages surrounding the role of the Catholic Church in Polish politics. The first, a measure of average frequency of church attendance in each voivodship, was constructed from data collected by the Polish General Social Survey because there are no

---

4 In precise terms, for a difference in X_k of $\Delta X_k = (X_k^* - X_k)$ the expected difference in the vote share for party x relative to the share for the UD is given by, $\log(V_x^*/V_{ud}^*) - \log(V_x/V_{ud}) = b_k \Delta X_k$, or $V_x^*/V_{ud}^* = (e^{b_k \Delta X_k})V_x/V_{ud}$.

published data on church attendance by voivodship. The five different surveys are pooled to give a sample size of 8,910 respondents. These are then grouped by voivodship, and the mean of the church attendance variable used in the individual analyses is computed for each voivodship. This is then used as the measure for regional church attendance. The second variable, the number of priests per 1,000 population, is included separately as it represents the church's local organizational strength. This variable is expected to be important in the early elections because church leaders, on the Sunday prior to the 1991 elections, openly urged people not to vote for the SLD. This pattern was not repeated as explicitly in 1993, although in some areas local church leaders made their preferences clear. The church as an organization largely withdrew from openly supporting or opposing candidates at this point, though the candidates and parties regularly made clear their positions on the proper relationship between the church and government policies. It is likely that any relationship between the organizational strength of the church, as distinct from individuals' attendance, and votes against the SLD will decline in elections after 1993.

Confidence in private firms and attitudes toward Communism are strongly related to age and education and moderately related to income in the individual analysis (see Tables 5.2 and 5.5), with the relationship with age being quadratic in form. Measures of the average years of schooling among the population older than seventeen, the proportion of this population in the thirty-five- to fifty-nine-year age range, and the mean wage and salary income in each voivodship are included in the vote model. A measure of the mean years of schooling is not reported in any of the statistical yearbooks published by the central statistical office. Consequently, we estimated the mean years of schooling from the Polish General Social Survey using the same method used to estimate mean church attendance. The proportion of the population older than seventeen between the ages of thirty-five and fifty-nine is used to reflect the quadratic relationship between age and attitudes at the individual level.[5] The relationship peaked in approximately the forty-five- to fifty-year age range for both attitudes. The variable based on the proportion of the population between thirty-five and fifty-nine will reflect the proportion of the population with the least confidence in private firms and the most favorable attitudes toward Communism.

---

5 Multinomial logit analysis of individual vote choices showed the same quadratic pattern as was observed in the analysis of attitudes toward private firms and about communism.

The last sets of variables relate to specific aspects of the campaigns. The proportion of the population employed as private farmers and the percentage living in villages are included in the equation for PSL support in all elections, reflecting the party's rural base. In addition, the percentage living in villages is included in the equation for Kwaśniewski in the first round in 1995 and in the equations for the AWS and the ROP in 1997. A variable measuring the proportion of the agricultural land owned by the state times the proportion of the labor force employed in agriculture is included in the model for Wałęsa's support in the second round of the 1995 presidential election. In all these cases, the results of the individual analysis in Chapter 5 show a significant relationship between these variables and the vote choices for the respective parties or candidates. The dummy variable indicating a voivodship where Wałęsa received more than 40 percent of the first round vote in 1995 is included in the equations for the SLD and the AWS in 1997. This variable indicates where the AWS had organizational strength gained from the Wałęsa campaign, as we observed in the individual-level analysis. Finally, a variable indicating the home voivodship of a party's leading candidate is also included when the individual analyses indicated such a relationship. The results of the statistical analysis are shown in Table 6A.1.[6] Table 6A.2 shows the estimated relationships for the 1993 election when the UD+KLD vote is separated, with the UD running alone and the KLD vote added to that for the Other parties.

STATISTICAL RESULTS

In our investigation of the relationships between vote shares and the economic variables measuring the transition, a key result is that the variable measuring the amount of de novo job creation is strongly related to the

6 These specifications differ from those in a previous article that analyzed just the 1993 election (Jackson et al., 2003a). The model in that paper did not include the church attendance variable and included variables for whether the voivodship was in the partition controlled by Austria, Germany, or Russia during the nineteenth centrury; a variable for the proportion female in only the Other party equation; a variable estimating membership in Solidarność in the SLD and PSL equations; and a variable estimating membership in the OPZZ in the Other party equation. The latter is the former Communist union and part of the SLD coalition. The partition variables were conceptually unnecessary with the addition of the church attendance variable as they were only included to represent unmeasured cultural variations. The female and union variables were of questionable significance in the 1993 analysis and unimportant in the analysis of the 1995 and 1997 elections. They were then omitted for the sake of parsimony, without altering the substantive results.

Table 6.1. *Additional Job Creation and Mean Changes in Vote Shares*

Parties/Candidates	1993		1995 (1)	1995 (2)	1997
	UD	UD+KLD			
UD/Kuroń/UW	1.66	2.98	0.51		3.10
	(0.64)	(0.84)	(0.57)		(0.99)
SLD/Kwaśniewski/SLD	−1.72	−1.71	−3.14	−4.14	−0.14
	(0.99)	(1.00)	(1.77)	(2.53)	(1.29)
PSL/Pawlak/PSL	−0.39	−0.49	−1.09		0.05
	(0.92)	(0.91)	(0.44)		(0.90)
UP/Zieliński/UP	0.08	0.08	−0.13		−0.08
	(0.46)	(0.46)	(0.16)		(0.39)
Catholic[a]/Wałęsa	0.78	0.78	3.82	4.14	
	(0.61)	(0.61)	(1.90)	(2.53)	
Solidarność[a]/AWS	−0.45	−0.45			−1.67
	(0.37)	(0.37)			(1.42)
BBWR	0.42	0.42			
	(0.44)	(0.44)			
KPN/Olszewski/ROP	−1.04	−1.04	−0.68		−0.42
	(0.46)	(0.46)	(0.55)		(0.52)
Other	0.66	−0.57	0.71		−0.84
	(1.25)	(1.12)	(0.52)		(0.66)

Note: Standard deviations in predicted vote shares for 10,000 simulations given in parentheses under coefficients.
[a] The coalition of Catholic parties combined with Solidarność in 1997 to form the AWS.

votes for the different parties. The coefficients assessing these relations are statistically significant and have the expected sign and magnitude. The relationships are strongest for the two post-Communist parties, particularly in 1993, the Solidarity trade union in both 1993 and 1997, and the far-right party in all elections. The regional unemployment variable is not statistically significantly related to parties' vote shares and most often has the wrong sign. Lastly, employment in state-managed firms is weakly related to vote returns but generally has the expected coefficient. The results suggest that de novo job creation is an important factor in building electoral support for liberal parties, as we saw with the individual data in Chapter 5.

De Novo Job Creation, Economic Conditions, and Votes

The important findings relating new-job creation to vote shares are summarized in Table 6.1, which shows the expected change in national vote proportions for each party or candidate if there had been a 50 percent increase in the number of new jobs as a proportion of the work force between 1990 and the year of the election.[7] (See note 4 for the precise expression used in making these calculations.) The method used to project the vote associated with increased job creation estimates both the expected changes in vote shares and the uncertainty associated with that estimate. The uncertainty arises because of the uncertainty associated with the coefficients on de novo job creation in the model for vote shares, as estimated by their standard errors. The methodology captures this uncertainty by drawing 10,000 values for each coefficient from a distribution whose variances and covariances match those of the estimated coefficients.[8] The expected shifts in vote shares are then calculated for each set of coefficients. The uncertainty of the predicted changes in vote shares is indicated by the standard deviation of the 10,000 predicted shares, shown parenthetically in the second row for each party or candidate in Table 6.1.[9]

The results indicate that increasing job creation in new firms would have increased the UD and the UD+KLD and the UW vote shares in 1993 and 1997, respectively, and Kuroń's and Wałęsa's shares in the first round of the 1995 presidential election and Wałęsa's share in the second round. These gains would have come primarily at the expense of the SLD and Kwaśniewski in 1993 and 1995 and the AWS in 1997 and the far right in all elections. The expected increased shares for the economic liberal parties in the parliamentary elections are on the order of 1.5 to 3 percent. These differences are two to three times the size of the standard deviation of the distribution of the predicted vote shares, indicating that it is unlikely that these levels of job creation would not have led to significantly increased vote shares for the liberal parties. These standard deviations indicate the

---

7 This is a substantial number of new jobs but is useful for illustrative purposes. When viewed in terms of the rates of birth, survival, and growth of new firms, such an increase requires relatively modest increases in these three rates over four to eight years. See Jackson et al., 1997.

8 There is also uncertainty in likely vote shares associated with the stochastic term in each equation. We omit this uncertainty from our simulations in order to concentrate on the relationship between additional de novo job creation and the expected shift in votes.

9 The uncertainty in the prediction of each party's vote share does not translate directly into our uncertainty about whether additional job creation would have changed the distribution among the shares of all the parties. A test of the null hypothesis that additional job creation is not associated with any changes in vote shares is a test of the null hypothesis that *all* the changes are zero. If this proposition is rejected, then the standard deviations simply provide guidance about the range of the expected shifts in vote shares.

range of the likely shifts in vote shares, with approximately two-thirds of the changes being within plus or minus one standard deviation of the expected change shown in Table 6.1.

If the UD and the KLD had merged prior to the 1993 election, they would have increased their share of the actual vote and benefited even more from any additional job creation. The additional job creation evaluated in Table 6.1 is associated with almost a 3 percentage point gain for the combined party, rather than the 1.7 percent gain for the UD running by itself. If the UD and the KLD had merged, the expected shares for the PSL would have declined slightly, and the expected shares for all the catchall Other parties, which now would not include the KLD, would have declined by about .5 percent.

The expected losses for the SLD in 1993 and the AWS in 1997 are about 1.7 percent. These differences are important in magnitude, as we will see when we talk about how changes in vote shares are associated with changes in seat shares. The standard deviation in the simulated vote shares indicates that we could expect two-thirds of the possible changes in vote shares to be within a range of .7 to 2.7 percent for the SLD in 1993 and .25 to 3.0 percent for the AWS in 1997.

The relationships between job creation and voting in the two rounds of the presidential election are more uncertain. The coefficients measuring these associations are statistically significant in several instances in the first round but not in the second. The standard deviations, relative to the expected vote changes, reflect this uncertainty. This uncertainty is particularly evident in the second round, where two-thirds of the expected vote changes for Wałęsa are between 1.6 and 6.7 percent. Remember that if 1.7 percent or more of the electorate had voted differently in the second round, Wałęsa would have won the election. In our simulations, about 70 percent of the trials produced shifts of that magnitude or more. From this we infer that additional job creation of the magnitude we have analyzed might have swung the election to Wałęsa.

The negative relationship between additional job creation and votes for the right-wing AWS is important on several grounds. The relationship with the AWS voting is consistent with the results observed with the individual data analyzed in Chapter 5, lending credibility to both results. Table 5.5 shows that expected vote losses associated with more confidence in private firms were larger for the AWS than for the SLD. The individual and aggregate results both suggest that the growing economically liberal constituency had greater reservations about the AWS than about the SLD. This result should not be surprising as new-business creation grew dramatically during the latter years of the SLD-led government (Table 3.1).

The observed association between greater de novo job creation and support for the ultraright parties and candidates (the KPN, Olszewski, and the ROP) is particularly suggestive. In all three elections, the shares for the far-right parties and candidates decreased under the scenario of more job creation. In 1993 and possibly in 1997 the shift might have reduced their national vote share below the 5 percent threshold required to obtain seats in the next parliament. At a minimum it would have substantially reduced their representation, as we shall see in the next section.

These results showing that more job creation is associated with less support for the right-leaning parties, when combined with the association between job creation and votes for the SLD and PSL in 1993, have a broad and important implication. Higher rates of de novo firm creation increase the votes for liberal economic parties, which are also the most centrist political parties. Furthermore, these increased vote shares come from both the left and the right parties, limiting the centripetal forces within the political structure and institutions. The possible exception to this pattern is the relatively small association between de novo job creation and votes for the SLD in 1997, which is after the SLD had moved toward the center and continued many of the economic reforms while it led the government. Grzymała-Busse (2002) in her book about the regeneration of post-Communist parties refers to the SLD's continual move to the economic center and says, "The party's 1997 program, developed over the course of 1996, marked an even bigger turn toward the free market" (pp. 166–67).

Swings of a few percentage points may not seem large, but in the context of Polish elections and the electoral laws in place, these differences are significant. We explore how vote shares translate into the distribution of seats in the Sejm shortly, but we simply suggest here that changes of this magnitude can shift an important number of seats. If the vote shifts resulted in any of the parties failing to pass the threshold for being represented in the Sejm, the consequences would have been quite profound. In the 1995 presidential election's second round, most of the predicted vote shifts would have more than offset Kwaśniewski's margin of victory and have given the election to Wałęsa. Although we may be discussing relatively small statistical differences, their consequences can be substantively large.

The second economic factor represented in the model is the proportion of the nonfarm work force remaining in state-owned or restructured firms.

Including this variable produces an interesting but entirely plausible result. The strongest associations between this variable and vote outcomes were higher support for the Solidarność trade-union party and the KPN in 1993 and for the AWS and the right-wing ROP in 1997. The trade unions and their workers in the large state-owned enterprises were a key element in the Solidarność movement that led to the removal of the Communist government. As a consequence they remained anti-Communist but were opposed to the liberal economic reforms. (Remember it was members of the Solidarność trade union that withheld their support of the Suchocka government, leading to the 1993 elections.) Thus it would be expected that workers in these large state enterprises would support the Solidarność party in 1993 and the AWS in 1997, as these parties were opposed to the liberal policies as applied to the state enterprises and were also anti-Communist. The Communist-backed union, the OPZZ, was part of the SLD coalition party, although, it had a smaller membership than did Solidarność.

The regional unemployment variable was either not related to vote returns or, in the analysis of the first round in 1995, had an unexpected sign and was statistically significant.[10] This lack of a relationship between unemployment and votes is evident in the individual analysis, where there were only small differences in attitudes between the unemployed and those who were working in state-owned enterprises. A broad explanation for the lack of results is a sociotropic one. The majority of Poles, not just those who were unemployed, were concerned about the impacts of the reforms and the hardships they created. These concerns then manifest themselves in support for the SLD or other opposition parties throughout the country, not just in the areas with high unemployment (Przeworski, 2001). The exceptions to this pattern are individuals in regions where the de novo firms were making a positive contribution to the economy. These are the individuals and regions exhibiting the greatest support for the parties and candidates promoting liberal economic programs.

The relations between individual votes and the responses to the question about retrospective evaluations of the Polish economy reported in Chapter 5 are partially consistent with this proposition. Unfortunately this question was asked only in 1997, but in that election respondents who

---

10 We conducted a number of diagnostic tests on the 1995 results, such as successively deleting each voivodship and examining residuals in the estimation with and without unemployment and the residuals in an equation for unemployment. The results were robust to all these alternatives.

thought the economy was getting worse are more likely to vote for the AWS and less likely to vote for either the UW or the SLD. We interpreted these results as a form of policy voting rather than purely retrospective voting, which is the proposition being offered here. A possible explanation for the 1995 results, where the coefficients are larger and statistically significant but show Jacek Kuroń, the UW candidate, doing better in areas with high unemployment, is that he represents the social democratic rather than the economically liberal wing of the Freedom Union and claimed he wanted to "put a human face on capitalism." That claim and his historic role as one of the leading figures in the Solidarność movement may have attracted votes in areas with higher than average unemployment. Or the results showing Kuroń doing better than other candidates in areas with high unemployment may be spurious.

The aggregate analyses support the conclusions reached with the individual data and provide estimates of how much vote shares might have changed if there had been a higher rate of de novo firm creation. Both analyses indicate that, from 1993 on, economic considerations related to the development of new enterprises are an important and consistent aspect of voters' evaluations of parties and candidates and of their voting decisions. As with the individual results, the pattern of support and opposition to parties supporting liberal economic policies is relatively stable. This analysis suggests that this economic success did not particularly benefit the incumbent parties, but as people gained confidence in the private sector and as more new jobs were created, they were more likely to support economically liberal parties, which were the primary opposition between 1993 and 1997. De novo firm growth was the key to job creation and economic expansion, which in turn strengthened the liberal economic and centrist political parties.

Vote Results in Their Broader Context

The Polish elections took place within a broader context of issues, candidates, parties, and ideologies than measured by the economic variables. These additional dimensions are discussed in our summary of the elections in Chapters 2 and 5 and are very evident in the analyses of individual votes in Chapter 5. The full specifications for Equations 6.1 to 6.4 and the statistical models presented in Appendix 6A contain measures for these aspects of the elections. The statistical results assessing these relationships conform to expectations and are consistent with the results of the individual analyses in Chapter 5. Church attendance is strongly and negatively related to votes for the SLD, the UP, and the PSL in both 1993 and 1997 and for Kwaśniewski and Pawlak in 1995 and strongly and positively related to votes for Wałęsa in both rounds in 1995. The votes for the SLD are also negatively related to the number of priests per 1,000 population in 1993 and weakened after that, as expected to the point that this variable is omitted from the second round in 1995 and the 1997 models.[11]

Education levels are negatively related to the votes for all major parties relative to the UD or the UW, although the coefficient for the Catholic coalition in 1993 is not statistically significant. These results indicate that increasing years of schooling are associated with increased vote shares for the Democratic Union/Freedom Union and that these increases are associated with decreases for all the other parties. The schooling variables' coefficients indicate that increased education is most strongly negatively related to voting for the PSL and Solidarity/AWS. There is very little consistent association between wages and salaries and vote distributions. The associations are negative with votes for the SLD in all elections but only statistically significant in 1997. These results suggest that income differences are not the basis for the political cleavages observed in the early stages of the transition. This may be a consequence of the fact that workers in state enterprises are consistently well paid, both before and after the transition, as noted in Chapter 3. The variable assessing the proportion of the population between the ages of thirty-five and fifty-nine is negatively associated with votes for the Catholic coalition in 1993, for Wałęsa in both rounds in 1995, and for the AWS and the ROP in 1997. These were the most strongly anti-Communist of the contending parties and candidates, so this result is expected. Age is positively associated only with voting for the PSL in 1993 and Kwaśniewski in 1995.

The campaign-related variables have the expected coefficients. The proportions of the population that farmed and/or that lived in a rural village are positively associated with voting for the PSL, the party that specifically campaigned for more and larger farm subsidies. The percentage living in a village is positively associated with votes for Kwaśniewski and negatively associated with votes for Wałęsa in the first round of presidential voting in 1995, as we observed with the individual data. The only instances where these results do not agree with the individual results are the negative associations between the proportion living in villages and the

---

11 If the priests per population variable is included in the two equations, its coefficients and standard errors are 0.06 and 0.32 for 1995 and 0.004 and 0.18 in 1997.

votes for the AWS and the ROP in 1997, although the latter coefficient is not statistically different from zero. These associations are positive in the individual model and negative here. The associations between votes for a party and the voivodship being the home for its leader are all in the direction observed with the individual data and are larger in 1993 than in subsequent years. Lastly, the voivodships that voted most strongly for Wałęsa in the first round in 1995 also voted heavily for the AWS in 1997, as we observed with the individual data.

The fact that these measures for the noneconomic factors related to voting in these elections have the expected coefficients and that the models estimated with the actual election data correspond very closely to the individual analyses provides greater confidence that the coefficients on the economic variables are also what one should expect. Lastly, with the exception of the votes for Zieliński, the UP presidential candidate in 1995, these equations explain a high proportion of the variance in the dependent variables. This suggests that the models include most of the important factors related to these votes, lending further credibility to the results. If the coefficients on the economic variables and particularly for the de novo firm job creation are correct, at least within sampling variations of the true values, we are then in a good position to use our results to explore counterfactual questions about how the electoral outcomes might have differed with different amounts of job creation.

JOB CREATION AND SEAT ALLOCATIONS

We now explore how the altered vote shares associated with more job creation might have altered the shares of seats in parliament. There is a twofold purpose to this discussion. One is to illustrate that the shifts in vote shares associated with additional job creation shown in Table 6.1 have important consequences for the representation of liberal and non-liberal interests in parliament. The second is to introduce a focus on the ultimate electoral objective, which is not vote shares per se but membership in parliament. We extend this discussion substantially in the next chapter.

Table 6.1 and the associated discussion argue that an increased rate of de novo job creation would have shifted vote shares toward the economically liberal parties and away from both the post-Communist and right-wing parties. Although the proportion of votes that would have shifted is not large, the important question is what would have been the distribution of seats if there had been these additional jobs in new enterprises?

The simulations of the expected seat allocations if there had been more de novo job creation follow the simulations done for Table 6.1. In 1993 we examine these changes for the set of parties that competed in the election and for a scenario where the UD and KLD combine to form a single economically liberal party. A distribution of expected vote shares is calculated for each voting district using the same distribution of coefficients that generated the distribution of national shares in Table 6.1 and with the assumption of a 50 percent greater number of de novo jobs in each district.[12] This scenario is consistent with the agglomeration effects shown in Chapter 3 because it produces, on the one hand, a very small increase in jobs, and thus a small change in vote shares, for regions with little job creation and, on the other, more job creation, and vote shifts, in regions that already had a large proportion of jobs in new firms.

Once the new vote shares for each district and for the country are calculated, the seat distributions for each district and for the national list are calculated using the same thresholds for getting seats in parliament and the d'Hondt rule for allocating seats among the eligible parties as were used in the 1993 and 1997 elections.[13] Using the thresholds for getting seats works against the KPN in 1993 as there are many simulations where it fell below the threshold for getting any seats. Conversely, there are simulations where the Catholic and Solidarity trade union parties in 1993 and the UP in 1997 surpassed the threshold and are given simulated seats. Table 6.2 shows the expected distribution of seats if job creation had been 50 percent higher in each district. The entries are the mean number of seats each party received in the 10,000 simulations, the standard deviation in the number of seats, and the difference from the actual number of seats. For the scenario with the merged UD and KLD, the "actual" number of seats is the seat allocation this coalition would have attained had the d'Hondt formula been applied with their combined actual vote shares in each district and to the national list.

The biggest expected change if there had been more new jobs is an increased seat share for the UD or UW. In 1993 these gains would have

---

12 The actual districts in Warsaw and Katowice are used in these simulations, rather than the aggregated districts used in the statistical analysis. The de novo job creation observed for the whole voivodship is assumed to describe each of the smaller districts.

13 Recall that in 1993 and 1997 parties had to receive more than 5 percent and coalitions had to get more than 8 percent of the national vote to get any seats in the next parliament and parties and coalitions that won seats had to get more than 7 percent of the national vote to be eligible for seats from the national list.

Table 6.2. *Seat Allocations with Greater Job Creation*

Party	Actual Seats	More Jobs		
		Seats	Standard Deviation	Difference
1993				
SLD	171	157.9	10.7	−13.1
PSL	132	133.8	8.1	+2
UD	74	91.9	6.1	+17.9
UP	41	41.6	7.1	+0.6
KPN	22	4.7	7.9	−17.3
BBWR	16	20.3	5.4	+4.3
Catholic	0	4.4	14.5	+4.4
Solidarity	0	1.3	4.5	+1.3
1993				
SLD	161	145.9	10.33	−15.1
PSL	128	121.2	7.9	−6.8
UD+KLD	97	128.5	8.9	+31.5
UP	37	34.6	6.4	−2.4
KPN	19	4.0	6.8	−15.0
BBWR	14	16.9	3.8	+2.9
Catholic	0	3.8	12.6	+3.8
Solidarity	0	1.0	3.6	+1.0
1997				
AWS	201	186.3	10.7	−14.7
SLD	164	161.8	8.4	−2.2
UW	60	82.2	6.6	+22.2
PSL	27	24.7	5.6	−2.3
ROP	6	2.2	2.4	−3.8
UP	0	0.7	1.5	+0.7

been at the expense of the SLD and the right-wing KPN. The KPN's large losses result because with more jobs its vote share falls dramatically; for 73 percent of the simulations it is below the threshold for being allocated seats. The UD running without the KLD on average gains eighteen seats while the SLD loses thirteen seats and the KPN loses seventeen seats. The other significant gainers are the BBWR and the Catholic party, which each gain an average of four seats. The shifts become more substantial if the UD had merged with the KLD, a possibility we discuss in more detail in the next chapter. If there had been the additional job creation, the merged UD+KLD would have picked up thirty-one and a half seats relative to what we predict this coalition would have had without the additional job creation. The SLD and the KPN would each have lost fifteen seats and the PSL seven seats, as in the previous simulation. In

1997, the UW would have gained twenty-two seats, with most of the losses accruing to the AWS. The ROP would have lost four seats and the SLD and PSL two each. The large standard deviations in the seat allocations arise because of the discontinuities in seat allocations for the minor parties created by the thresholds. Seat shifts of these magnitudes would not have threatened the ability of the SLD and the PSL to form a coalition government. They would, however, strengthen the position of the economically liberal parties.

CONCLUSION

We conclude that additional de novo job creation would have helped the liberal economic interests. It would have shifted votes and seats away from the less liberal post-Communist, trade-union, and right-wing parties. The evidence for this conclusion began with the analysis of individual attitudes where people employed in the de novo firms constituted a strong constituency favoring private firms and voting for economically liberal parties. This section has extended this proposition to show that new-job creation is linked to the actual election returns in all the elections between 1993 and 1997. Finally, we can trace higher rates of de novo job creation to shifts in representation in parliament that follow from the expected vote differences. These results form the core support for our argument that a constituency supporting liberal economic policies will evolve from the new-firm creation that is the key to successful economic reform.

Appendix 6A: Estimated Election and Vote Share Models

This appendix presents the statistical estimations of the models for the aggregate vote shares received by the parties competing in the 1993 and 1997 parliamentary elections and the candidates competing in both rounds of the 1995 presidential election. The equations being estimated are discussed in the text and shown as Equations 6.1 to 6.4, with the parties and candidates specific to each election.

Table 6A.1. *Estimated Election Models*

	SLD 1993	Kwaśniewski 1995	SLD 1997	PSL 1993	Pawlak 1995	PSL 1997
New jobs	−9.80	−3.44	−2.97	−7.84	−8.24	−2.89
	(3.02)	(1.48)	(1.24)	(2.83)	(3.51)	(1.89)
% Unemployed	−0.80	−1.46	−0.27	0.04	−5.23	−1.38
	(0.98)	(0.69)	(1.11)	(0.99)	(1.55)	(1.59)
% Jobs in SOEs	0.28	−0.12	0.54	0.77	0.86	−0.27
	(0.65)	(0.38)	(0.80)	(0.58)	(0.87)	(1.09)
% Farming				4.02	3.34	1.94
				(0.89)	(1.20)	(1.21)
% Village		0.99		1.70	2.00	3.53
		(0.29)		(0.54)	(0.90)	(0.79)
Schooling	−0.23	−0.20	−0.20	−0.37	−0.23	−0.27
	(0.11)	(0.07)	(0.09)	(0.10)	(0.15)	(0.13)
Wage and salary	−0.18	−0.07	−0.12	−0.29	−0.17	0.03
	(0.19)	(0.06)	(0.06)	(0.18)	(0.14)	(0.09)
% Age (35–59)	0.01	0.06	0.05	0.14	0.03	0.01
	(0.04)	(0.03)	(0.04)	(0.05)	(0.09)	(0.07)
Church attendance	−1.85	−1.45	−1.47	−1.20	−2.37	−2.22
	(0.53)	(0.34)	(0.48)	(0.47)	(0.75)	(0.62)
Priests/1,000	−0.48	−0.13				
	(0.24)	(0.15)				
Wałęsa, 1995			−0.15			
			(0.10)			
UD candidate	−0.66		0.09	−0.66		0.09
	(0.18)		(0.22)	(0.18)		(0.22)
Party candidate	0.66	0.31	0.09	0.98	0.96	
	(0.19)	(0.13)	(0.17)	(0.21)	(0.34)	
R^2	0.79	0.81	0.71	0.91	0.90	0.91

(continued)

Table 6A.1. *Estimated Election Models*

	Catholic 1993	BBWR 1993	Wałęsa 1995 (1)	Wałęsa 1995 (2)	Solidarity 1993	AWS 1997
New jobs	−2.63	−4.05	1.31	3.82	−10.16	−3.60
	(3.76)	(2.97)	(2.16)	(2.38)	(3.29)	(1.23)
% Unemployed	−0.40	−0.91	−0.67	0.84	−0.62	0.23
	(1.23)	(0.97)	(0.99)	(1.08)	(1.08)	(1.09)
% Jobs in SOEs	−0.04	064	0.48	0.52	1.54	1.08
	(0.82)	(0.75)	(0.55)	(0.60)	(0.72)	(0.79)
% Village			−0.82	−1.59		−1.49
			(0.33)	(0.58)		(0.39)
% State farms*%farm				−1.79		
				(1.45)		
Schooling	−0.12	−0.21	−0.12	0.14	−0.29	−0.31
	(0.13)	(0.10)	(0.09)	(0.11)	(0.12)	(0.09)
Wages and salary	0.22	0.04	0.12	0.15	0.03	−0.01
	(0.24)	(0.19)	(0.09)	(0.09)	(0.21)	(0.06)
% Age (35–59)	−0.20	−0.05	−0.20	−0.22	0.00	−0.16
	(0.05)	(0.04)	(0.04)	(0.05)	(0.04)	(0.04)
Church attendance	0.30	0.27	1.45	2.80	0.74	−0.11
	(0.58)	(0.46)	(0.41)	(0.47)	(0.51)	(0.47)
UD candidate, District	−0.66	−0.66			−0.66	0.09
	(0.18)	(0.18)			(0.18)	(0.22)
Party candidate, District			0.03	0.32		−0.18
			(0.15)	(0.28)		(0.12)
Kwaśniewski's District				−0.27		
				(0.26)		
Wałęsa, 1995						0.48
						(0.10)
R^2	0.75	0.65	0.79	0.82	0.71	0.84

Table 6A.1. *Estimated Election Models*

	UP 1993	Zieliński 1995	UP 1997	Other 1993	Other 1995	Other 1997
New jobs	−6.30	−2.11	−3.18	−7.72	0.75	−4.48
	(2.55)	(1.57)	(1.36)	(3.18)	(2.22)	(1.42)
% Unemployed	−0.10	−1.38	−0.02	−0.20	−1.22	−0.50
	(0.85)	(0.73)	(1.21)	(1.04)	(1.03)	(1.26)
% Jobs in SOEs	0.80	0.19	0.64	0.27	−0.14	0.30
	(0.57)	(0.41)	(0.86)	(0.69)	(0.58)	(0.90)
Schooling	−0.21	−0.08	−0.24	−0.25	−0.14	−0.12
	(0.09)	(0.07)	(0.10)	(0.11)	(0.10)	(0.10)
Wage and salary	−0.02	−0.02	−0.08	0.02	0.08	−0.04
	(0.16)	(0.06)	(0.07)	(0.20)	(0.09)	(0.07)
% Age (35–59)	0.03	0.03	0.00	−0.11	−0.08	−0.03
	(0.03)	(0.03)	(0.04)	(0.04)	(0.04)	(0.04)
Church attendance	−1.73	−0.16	−1.61	−1.88	−0.05	−0.37
	(0.39)	(0.30)	(0.44)	(0.49)	(0.42)	(0.46)
UD candidate	−0.66		0.09	−0.66		0.09
	(0.18)		(0.22)	(0.18)		(0.22)
Party candidate	0.89					
	(0.21)					
R^2	0.60	0.20	0.65	0.76	0.42	0.67

(continued)

Table 6A.1. *Estimated Election Models*

	KPN 1993	Olszewski 1995	ROP 1997
New jobs	−13.87	−3.74	−4.05
	(3.93)	(3.05)	(1.73)
% Unemployed	−1.22	−1.68	1.07
	(1.28)	(1.42)	(1.52)
% Jobs in SOEs	1.01	0.79	1.70
	(0.86)	(0.79)	(1.06)
Schooling	−0.06	−0.07	−0.16
	(0.14)	(0.13)	(0.13)
Wage and salary	0.07	0.29	0.03
	(0.25)	(0.13)	(0.09)
% Age (35–59)	−0.03	−0.32	−0.27
	(0.05)	(0.06)	(0.05)
Church attendance	0.36	−1.28	−2.01
	(0.61)	(0.58)	(0.57)
UD candidate	−0.66		0.09
	(0.18)		(0.22)
% Village			−0.41
			(0.66)
R^2	0.63	0.78	0.78

Table 6A.2. *Estimated Vote Share Model for UD Only in 1993*

	SLD	PSL	UP	KPN	BBWR	Catholic	Solidarity	Other
New jobs	−8.34	−6.14	−4.82	−12.40	−2.58	−1.16	−8.69	−4.22
	(2.94)	(2.69)	(2.66)	(3.99)	(3.26)	(3.67)	(3.54)	(3.13)
% Unemployed	−0.40	0.65	0.28	−0.84	−0.52	−0.01	−0.23	0.21
	(0.95)	(0.94)	(0.89)	(1.30)	(1.07)	(1.20)	(1.16)	(1.02)
% Jobs in SOEs	0.12	0.60	0.64	0.86	0.49	−0.20	1.39	−0.01
	(0.63)	(0.55)	(0.59)	(0.87)	(0.71)	(0.80)	(0.77)	(0.68)
% Farming		4.36						
		(0.86)						
% Village		1.55						
		(0.52)						
Schooling	−0.25	−0.38	−0.22	−0.08	−0.23	−0.14	−0.31	−0.24
	(0.11)	(0.09)	(0.09)	(0.14)	(0.11)	(0.13)	(0.12)	(0.11)
Wage and salary	−0.09	−0.19	0.06	0.16	0.12	0.30	0.11	0.14
	(0.19)	(0.17)	(0.17)	(0.26)	(0.21)	(0.24)	(0.24)	(0.20)
% Age (35–59)	−0.00	0.13	0.01	−0.04	−0.06	−0.22	−0.01	−0.11
	(0.04)	(0.05)	(0.03)	(0.05)	(0.04)	(0.05)	(0.05)	(0.04)
Church attendance	−2.04	−1.35	−1.94	0.15	0.05	0.09	0.53	−1.93
	(0.52)	(0.45)	(0.41)	(0.62)	(0.50)	(0.57)	(0.55)	(0.48)
Priests/1,000	−0.49							
	(0.24)							
UD candidate	−0.78	−0.78	−0.78	−0.78	−0.78	−0.78	−0.78	−0.78
	(0.18)	(0.18)	(0.18)	(0.18)	(0.18)	(0.18)	(0.18)	(0.18)
Party candidate	0.68	0.88	0.88					
	(0.19)	(0.20)	(0.21)					
R^2	0.78	0.95	0.62	0.62	0.60	0.75	0.67	0.72

Note: Votes for KLD included in Other category.

7

Liberal Economic Interests and Seat Allocations

The creation of a pro-reform constituency is a necessary but not a sufficient part of choosing a pro-reform government. The method for allocating seats in parliament once votes have been cast is a critical concern. In
any system, but particularly in a parliamentary system with proportional
representation, such as Poland's, the electoral rules creating voting and
parliamentary districts and determining how votes are converted to seats
for these districts have a critical bearing on what influence pro-reform
interests can exert on national policy. At this point the findings about
the clustering of new enterprises and the agglomeration effects identified
in Chapter 3 become very important. The location effects lead to new
businesses being concentrated in certain areas, even beyond what traditional factor prices and resources would predict. A consequence of this
clustering is that the pro-reform voters will also be concentrated rather
than being widely distributed across the country. Thus, how districts are
drawn and how seats are apportioned will affect the representation of
liberal interests.

SEAT ALLOCATION RULES

A critical set of rules was adopted prior to the 1993 election at the urg-
ing of the coalition led by the UD. The political instability experienced
after the 1991 elections was attributed, with some justification, to the
presence of so many small parties in the parliament. Three critical rules
were designed to reduce the representation of smaller parties and to push
consolidation of existing parties: parties had to attain 5 percent and coalitions 8 percent of the national vote in order to hold seats in the new Sejm;
there was a national list of sixty-nine seats allocated to parties with more
than 7 percent of the national vote; and the d'Hondt formula was used

to allocate seats within each voivodship among the eligible parties. (A party's vote share in an individual voivodship is irrelevant so long as its national share surpassed the relevant threshold.) The d'Hondt formula produces one of the least-proportional seat allocations within a proportional representation system and heavily rewards the party or parties with the largest share of the votes within any district. (See Benoit, 2000, for an analysis and discussion of the different allocation rules.) Further, the deviation from proportionality increases as the number of seats to be allocated decreases, which in turn advantages the party or parties with their base in the smaller, rural voivodships, which had fewer seats per district. Because the rural areas were the least successful in stimulating the creation of new firms, this advantage in seat allocations favored the parties opposing reforms, primarily the PSL.

We demonstrate the representational implications of these rules by exploring how seats might have been distributed in 1993 and 1997 under different rules. The two changes examined are increased district magnitudes and a more-proportional, modified Sainte-Laguë seat allocation rule.[1] Both these changes are part of the election reform law passed in spring 2001 to govern the 2001 election, which we discuss in Chapter 8. In 1999 the forty-nine voivodships that formed the basis for allocating seats in 1993 and 1997 were consolidated into sixteen larger voivodships. These were then subdivided into forty-one election districts for 2001. To illustrate the consequences of decreasing the number of districts and thereby increasing the number of seats per district we consider three scenarios. The first aggregates the 1993 and 1997 votes into thirty-eight new districts to match the new districts as closely as possible. In three cases new districts are aggregated to provide the best match with the old districts; hence, we have thirty-eight and not forty-one districts. The second aggregates the votes according to the sixteen new voivodships, further increasing the district magnitudes.[2] Lastly, we treat all seats except

---

1 We are assuming that individuals would have voted for the same parties under these "new" districts and rules as they did under the actual system. This is very likely an appropriate assumption with respect to changing the number and size of the voivodships. With respect to adopting the Sainte-Laguë formula, we have to assume either that there was no strategic voting, which is a difficult assumption given the 5 and 8 percent thresholds, or that there would have been the same amount of strategic voting. The latter assumption is quite plausible, as we have maintained the same thresholds.
2 The boundaries of the new voivodships are not a perfect match to the boundaries of the older ones, but the differences are very small, meaning that our assumption is an excellent approximation, certainly for the expositional purposes of this chapter.

those on the national list as comprising one nationwide district.[3] The seat allocations should become more proportional as we increase the district magnitudes, even using the d'Hondt formula.

The second rule change is the replacement of the d'Hondt rule with a modified Sainte-Laguë method for allocating seats, as was done for the 2001 election.[4] Benoit (2000) concludes that the Sainte-Laguë method is among the most proportional and the least favorable to large parties among all proportional representation formulas. This will not be strictly true with the modified version adopted by the Poles, which for our purposes will be simply referred to as the Sainte-Laguë rule. The use of this seat allocation formula rather than the d'Hondt method should also produce seat allocations that more closely match the vote shares. Both these rule changes should favor the smaller parties relative to the larger parties and bring the distribution of seats closer to the distribution of votes.

The first two columns in Tables 7.1 and 7.2 show the number of seats each party would have received if seats had been allocated proportionally to all votes cast nationally and proportionally to all votes cast nationally for just the eligible parties. Column three shows the actual distribution of seats using the d'Hondt method and the thresholds in place and includes the seats allocated from the national list. The last three columns in Table 7.1 show the seat allocations if these same rules were applied to our set of 2001 districts, to districts defined by the new voivodships, and to a single national district. Table 7.2 shows the seat allocations if the Sainte-Laguë method is used with the larger districts included in Table 7.1. (For this discussion, the votes for the KLD in 1993 are not added to those for the UD so the distributions are comparable with what actually resulted after the 1993 election.)

The actual distribution of seats under the d'Hondt formula with the large number of smaller districts produces the results most skewed in favor of the larger parties. Fewer districts with larger magnitudes produce

3 The electoral reforms enacted in 2001 also eliminated the national list, but we have kept that as part of the 1993 and 1997 scenarios.
4 The modified version of the Sainte-Laguë method adopted in Poland still favors the large parties in small districts. In calculating the highest averages under the pure Sainte-Laguë method, the eligible parties' vote shares are divided by the successive odd integers $1, 3, 5, \ldots, 2^*s + 1$, where s denotes the number of seats already awarded to that party. The party with the highest remaining quotient is awarded the next seat, if one is still open. With the modified rule adopted in Poland, the vote shares of the eligible parties are divided successively by $1.4, 3, 5, \ldots, 2^*s + 1$. This still favors the larger parties in small-magnitude districts, but not to the same degree as the d'Hondt method, which uses the divisors $1, 2, 3, \ldots, s + 1$.

Table 7.1. *Allocations of Seats with d'Hondt Rule and Alternative Districts*

Party	% of All Votes[a]	Majority Vote[b]	Actual Seats	2001 Districts	New Voivodship	National
1993						
SLD	93	144	171	167	154	149
PSL	70	108	132	125	116	112
UD	48	74	74	76	76	77
UP	33	51	41	43	49	52
KPN	26	41	22	24	33	34
BBWR	25	38	16	21	28	32
1997						
AWS	155	178	201	193	184	181
SLD	124	142	164	158	149	144
UW	61	70	60	65	71	71
PSL	33	38	27	29	34	38
ROP	26	29	6	13	20	24

[a] Seats allocated proportionally to vote shares among all parties.

[b] Seats allocated proportionally to vote shares among parties eligible for seats.

Table 7.2. *Allocations of Seats with Sainte-Laguë Rule and Alternative Districts*

Party	All Votes[a]	Majority Vote[b]	Actual Seats[c]	1993/1997 Districts	2001 Districts	New Voivodship	National
1993							
SLD	93	144	171	160	153	149	148
PSL	70	108	132	130	118	114	112
UD	48	74	74	75	79	78	77
UP	33	51	41	45	46	51	53
KPN	26	41	22	28	36	35	34
BBWR	25	38	16	18	24	29	32
1997							
AWS	155	178	201	192	185	180	180
SLD	124	142	164	156	154	146	144
UW	61	70	60	69	72	72	71
PSL	33	38	27	30	31	36	38
ROP	26	29	6	11	16	24	25

[a] Seats allocated proportionally to vote shares among all parties.

[b] Seats allocated proportionally to vote shares among parties eligible for seats.

[c] Seats allocated according to the actual d'Hondt rule.

allocations closer to the actual vote distribution. With a single national district, the seat allocations very closely match the vote shares of the eligible parties. The presence of the national list of sixty-nine seats that are only distributed among parties with more than 7 percent of the vote maintains a small advantage for the larger parties relative to a purely proportional system among the eligible parties even with one large national district. As district magnitudes increase, the SLD and the PSL in 1993 and the AWS and SLD in 1997 consistently lose seats. The UD in 1993 gained a few seats while the UW in 1997 gained a substantial number of seats as the number of districts diminished. The biggest gainers, as expected, as seat allocations become more proportional to vote shares are the minor parties. The KPN and BBWR in 1993 and the ROP in 1997 gain between twelve and eighteen seats when a national district is compared with the set of smaller districts in effect those years.

The Sainte-Laguë formula produces a higher correspondence between the proportions of votes and seats for all district configurations. Applying this formula to the 1993 districts the SLD and PSL combined would have lost thirteen seats, with the UP, KPN, and BBWR gaining most of these. In 1997 the AWS would have lost nine seats and the SLD eight with the UW being the biggest gainer, with nine additional seats. The most dramatic differences occur when the Sainte-Laguë method is combined with larger districts. With this allocation rule the seat allocations approach the vote shares much more rapidly than with the d'Hondt rule. For example, with the d'Hondt rule moving to the 2001 districts reduced the SLD plus PSL seats in 1993 by eleven, the AWS seats in 1997 by eight, and the SLD seats in 1997 by six. With the Sainte-Laguë method and the 2001 districts the corresponding losses relative to the actual numbers of seats are thirty-two for the SLD plus PSL, sixteen for the AWS, and ten for the SLD, respectively. Lastly, and not surprisingly, the larger the district magnitudes the less difference the choice of rule makes. With one national district plus the national list, the two rules give virtually identical seat shares. With the sixteen voivodships as districts there are differences between the two methods, but they are on the order of less than five seats. It is easy to conclude that a different votes to seats rule and larger districts in 1993 and 1997 would have led to a different relationship between the parties' shares of the national votes and their shares of the seats in the two parliaments.

The net effect of these changes would not necessarily have benefited the constituency promoting liberal economic policies. In 1993 the main beneficiary of different rules would have been the UP and the KPN, both of which opposed the liberal policies of the UD coalition. The BBWR, the independent party organized by Wałęsa, might have supported liberal policies, but it only gained sixteen seats under the most advantageous scenario. Offsetting the BBWR gains, the UP and KPN would each have gained twelve seats under the same scenario. These changes would have substantially altered the balance between left and right, as the SLD and PSL coalition would have lost forty-three seats. They would not have stopped the SLD/PSL coalition that formed the government but might have pressured them into a more liberal economic policy. Any changes, however, would not necessarily have been more favorable to new enterprises or less advantageous for state-managed firms given the positions of the UP and KPN leaders.

The possible consequences of the projected 1997 changes are even harder to divine. If we just consider the shift to the Sainte-Laguë formula and the 2001 districts, the AWS would have lost sixteen seats and the SLD ten. With the UW projected to gain twelve seats with this scenario, the AWS and the UW coalition could still govern, though it would be four seats smaller. The UW, however, would comprise a larger bloc within this coalition and might have been more influential. The opposition, however, would have been even more opposed to liberal policies, with the ROP gaining ten seats and the PSL four.

RULES AND JOB CREATION: WHAT MIGHT HAVE BEEN

In this section we analyze how the amount and location of job creation interact with electoral rules to affect the representation of liberal interests. In the course of this discussion, we also begin to explore how the UD/UW's electoral fortunes declined so consistently since 1991, to the point they did not win any seats after the 2001 election (in the next chapter we explore the changes after 1997). Because the UD/UW decline might seem surprising, given the amount of de novo firm and job creation in the Polish economy and our evidence about the contribution of this activity to building a pro-reform constituency and voting group, we review the dynamics of politics following economic and democratic reforms and how reform governments can be more protective of emerging constituencies.

Electoral Rules and Party Coalitions

The electoral rules promoted by the UD and its coalition partners before the 1993 election were explicitly designed to reduce the number of competing parties by providing very strong incentives for their consolidation. The feeling was that the plethora of parties holding seats after the 1991 election had contributed directly to the country's inability to establish a stable coalition government. As it turned out, it was the governing coalition that was least able to consolidate. The main elements in the coalition government that fell in May 1993 were the UD, KLD, and ZChN (Christian National Union). The latter was a church-oriented nationalistic party that had campaigned in 1991 as part of a Catholic coalition party. The Solidarity trade union was a minor and reluctant part of the governing coalition in 1993.

The UD and KLD were virtually identical on all policy questions, particularly regarding the direction of economic reforms. The ZChN was more critical of the Balcerowicz policies, although it remained part of the UD-led coalition. The Solidarity trade union broke with the coalition and was directly responsible for the government's fall. One might think, given the incentives in the electoral rules, that at least the UD and the KLD would coalesce. It is more understandable why the ZChN might not join; it was skeptical of the liberal economic policies and demanded a larger role for church teachings backed by legal force than the UD and KLD were willing to support because both included members with a range of views regarding the role of the church and thus tried to avoid the issue.[5] The Solidarity trade union objected strongly to the liberal economic policies of the incumbent government. It supported privatization but in a form that favored special treatment for the former state-owned enterprises and their workers. The economic views of the trade unionists may have been closer to those of the leaders in the Unia Pracia or the PSL or to some in the SLD. It was the attitudes toward the role of the church and toward former Communist officials that strongly differentiated the Solidarity trade union from the PSL and SLD. It is not surprising, given the leaders' views and behavior, that they would not join a UD- or KLD-led coalition. Lastly, once again Wałęsa split with the UD leadership and promoted his own slate of candidates, the independent BBWR. The BBWR economic platform was possibly closest to that of the economic liberals in the UD and the KLD, but the slate pressed its independence and its ties to the president.

---

5 To illustrate the divisions over the role of the church among UD members, its delegates split on the legislation to prohibit abortions, a major church-supported issue. The SLD was quite explicit and unified in opposing church influence and strongly opposed the limitations on abortions.

Table 7.3. *Seat Allocations for Alternative Coalitions in 1993*

	Actual	UD+ KLD	UD+KLD+ BBWR	Economic Center[a]	AWS93[b]	UD, KLD[c]	AWS93S[d]
SLD	171	161	149	135	131	164	150
PSL	132	128	116	97	98	131	116
UP	41	37	35	28	26	39	35
KPN	22	19	16	14	14	21	15
UD	74						61
BBWR	16	14				15	11
UD+KLD	74	97			81	86	75
UD+KLD+ BBWR	90	111	140			101	86
Economic Center[b]	90	111	140	182		101	130
Catholic+ BBWR+ Solidarity	16	14			106	15	65

[a] Electoral coalition of UD+KLD+BBWR+Catholic parties.
[b] Electoral coalition of BBWR+Catholic+Solidarity trade-union parties.
[c] UD and KLD run as separate parties, and KLD passes threshold for seats.
[d] All parties run separately, and KLD, Catholic, and Solidarity pass thresholds for seats.

All five parties – UD, KLD, ZChN, Solidarity, and BBWR – ran separate campaigns in 1993, even knowing that the rules for allocating seats made these decisions risky. In the end, the KLD received only 4 percent of the vote, less than the necessary 5 percent threshold. The ZChN joined a Catholic coalition, Catholic Electoral Committee "Fatherland," which received 6.4 percent of the vote, but since this was a coalition, its threshold for being seated was 8 percent so it also did not get any seats. The Solidarity trade union also ran separately and received only 4.9 percent of the votes, also not enough to win any seats in the new parliament. The BBWR obtained 5.5 percent of the vote, which was sufficient to be represented in parliament but not sufficient to get any seats from the national list. These splits and the parties' inability to form an effective coalition cost the post-Solidarity and non-Communist parties dearly.

The first set of speculative questions concerns what representation in the new Sejm might have been had these various reform parties, all with origins in the Solidarność movement, formed one or more larger coalitions. The top four entries in the first column in Table 7.3 show the seat proportions observed in the 1993 election for the stable set of parties – the two post-Communist parties plus UP and KPN – that we assume are not part of any coalition-formation effort. Subsequent rows and columns show the seat allocations that would have resulted from a series of different coalitions, assuming no changes in individual vote choices. The last two columns show the possible seat allocations if coalition parties had run separately but received enough votes to be eligible for seats.

The most obvious coalition that "should" have formed is a merger of the UD and the KLD. (This is the first alternative in Table 7.3 and is a combination that is explored in Chapter 6.) If the UD and the KLD had united prior to the 1993 election, as they did in May 1994, it is likely that the coalition would have received the sum of the votes each party won individually given the nearly identical nature of their platforms and past positions. This result would have given them 14.6 percent of the vote, making the coalition a strong third place finisher, only 0.8 percent behind the PSL. Following the d'Hondt formula for allocating seats, the UD+KLD coalition would have received ninety-seven seats, an increase of twenty-three over what the UD won by itself. All other parties would have lost seats, with the SLD losing ten seats and the other parties either three or four seats each, except for the BBWR, which would have lost two seats. This outcome would not have threatened the ability of the SLD and the PSL to form a dominant coalition government, but it would have significantly increased the representation of the liberal economic bloc.

A scenario favorable to the economic liberals, the second alternative in Table 7.3, could have occurred if Wałęsa had not formed the nonaligned BBWR but had supported a UD+KLD coalition. This scenario, if all the BBWR voters had supported a UD+KLD plus BBWR coalition as the advocates assume, would have brought the reform bloc almost even with the SLD and well ahead of the PSL in terms of vote share and number of seats in the new parliament. The liberals would have 140 seats compared with 149 for the SLD and 116 for the PSL.

An even more extreme scenario for the economic liberals, which we call the economic center, assumes the Catholic party joins the UD+KLD+BBWR bloc. This recreates the core of the governing coalition before the 1993 election, minus the Solidarity trade union. Although assuming that all the voters for these individual parties would support the larger coalition is a stretch, it is not totally absurd and offers a good counterfactual exercise. Recall from Chapter 5 that, although voters with confidence in private firms were more likely to vote for the UD+KLD than the BBWR or Catholic parties, the differences are not statistically significant (see Appendix 5B). Further, the results presented in Chapter 6, which are based on the actual election returns, reach the same conclusion.

Table 6.2 shows that additional de novo job creation increased votes for the BBWR and Catholic parties as well as for the UD+KLD. This coalition receives the largest vote share and has the largest bloc of seats in the next parliament, with 182 seats to 135 for the SLD and 97 for the PSL. The interesting speculation were this to occur is whether, and how, this coalition could form a government. It is 48 seats short of a majority, and it is not obvious who would or could be its additional partners. Plus, the SLD and PSL together still hold a tiny majority of the seats.

As appealing as these two scenarios are for the reformers, they are unlikely on several grounds. First, Wałęsa had continually feuded with the leaders of the UD and KLD parties, and the parties posed a challenge to his reelection plans in the 1995 presidential election. Second, in the first scenario some proportion of the BBWR voters would have likely supported a party other than the UD+KLD coalition, such as the Catholic coalition. It is even more likely in the second scenario that some of the Catholic party voters would have voted with the Solidarity party rather than a grand center coalition.

The final alternative expands on this last point and simulates as best one can the coalitions that formed after the 1995 presidential election and that dominated the 1997 election. Marian Krzaklewski, the head of the Solidarity trade union, managed to unite the union, the various Catholic parties, and the organizations that had supported Wałęsa's presidential reelection into a coalition with the name Solidarity Election Action (AWS). The comparable party in 1993, labeled "AWS93" in Table 7.3, would have been a coalition of the Catholic party, the BBWR, and Solidarity trade union. The KPN joined the AWS before the 1997 election, but we consider that very unlikely in 1993 and maintain the KPN as a separate party. If all voters who supported any of these separate slates supported the coalition, the AWS precursor would have garnered 16.7 percent of the vote, making it the second largest bloc of votes, behind the SLD but ahead of a combined UD+KLD. This right-wing alternative would have held 106 seats in the new parliament, second only to the SLD with 131. The UD+KLD bloc would have held 81 seats, an increase of 7 over what the UD had by itself, but 16 less than it might have had without the right-wing coalition. The SLD and PSL would have been 1 seat short of a majority if this scenario had transpired, seriously complicating efforts to create a coalition government. This would have left the UP or the KPN as the pivotal parties in any effort to form a government, neither of which was favorable to the economic liberals.

One explanation for why the different parties did not form coalitions before the election is that each hoped to win enough votes to get seats and planned to form a coalition in parliament, as it had done previously. The d'Hondt rule, because it so heavily favors larger parties, makes coalitions formed after the election smaller than coalitions formed before the election, even if all the parties entered parliament. The last two columns in Table 7.3 nicely illustrate this point. The entries labeled UD, KLD are the seat allocations that might have resulted if the KLD had won enough votes to be eligible for seats. This simulation was done by proportionally reducing the votes for Other parties in each district by enough to give the KLD 5 percent of the vote nationally. The vote shares for all other parties remain the same. The last column, labeled AWS93S, follows the same procedure to give the Catholic coalition and the Solidarity party along with the KLD enough votes to be seated in parliament. Comparing the UD, KLD, and the UD+KLD results and the AWS93 and AWS93S results makes it clear that preelection coalitions hold substantially more seats than coalitions formed after the election. The UD+KLD election coalition had eleven more seats than a UD, KLD coalition formed after the election. An AWS type preelection coalition had forty-one more seats than a parliamentary coalition created after the election among the same parties. These results make it clear there were strong incentives for the various post-Solidarity parties to come together before the election even if they were confident of getting enough votes to enter parliament.

The objective of this short series of alternative histories is to suggest that the actions of the party leaders in not responding to the incentives they inserted into the election reform laws prior to the 1993 election had a substantial impact on the composition of the subsequent parliament. Some of the inability to form the broader coalitions envisioned by the electoral reform can be traced to the clash of personalities and ambitions among the leaders of the post-Solidarność movement. Differences over the direction of economic and social policy, particularly the role of the Catholic Church, and abortion policy, and the inherent conflicts within Solidarność were also major factors in the continuing divisions among the reformers. The net result, however, was a substantial victory, measured in parliamentary seats, for the post-Communists.

Job Creation, Electoral Rules, and the Votes-to-Seats Relationships

Analytically, how does the location of additional job creation interact with decisions about a votes-to-seats rule and district size to affect the seat allocations for economically liberal parties? According to the d'Hondt formula, which is less proportional, as a party gains votes, past some threshold, it will gain seats at a faster rate than with a more proportional rule, such as the Sainte-Laguë formula. The smaller the district magnitude, the greater this advantage conveyed by the d'Hondt formula to the larger parties. (Both formulas become more proportional as the number of seats in a district increases.) These relationships become particularly important because de novo job creation is higher in the urban areas, which have larger districts, so the question is how the different rules affect how increased job creation, and the associated increased voting for the economic liberals, might change the seat allocations.

The formal analysis of the jobs-to-votes-to seats question is done in two parts. The first part is a model of the votes-to-seats implications of the two different allocation rules given the vote shares and district magnitudes in the 1993 and 1997 elections. (Appendix 7A presents the statistical models for the votes-to-seats rules.) The second part combines this model with the estimated relationships between de novo job creation and vote shares to relate seat allocations directly to de novo job creation and the alternative electoral institutions. This discussion uses the parameters and job-creation levels associated with the 1993 rather than the 1997 election. This election is the more pivotal one in terms of the liberal parties and an election where a faster rate of job formation would have had a larger impact.

The votes-to-seats model developed in Appendix 7A has two equations. The first predicts the probability of a party getting any seats, given its vote share, the district magnitude, and whether the d'Hondt or the Sainte-Laguë rule is used. What is particularly notable about the results is the difficulty a smaller party has in getting any seats in districts with a small number of seats. In a district with only four seats a party must have close to 14 percent of the vote among the eligible parties to have an even chance of getting a seat. This threshold drops sharply as the number of seats in the district increases, so that with eight seats in the district about 8.5 percent of the votes is needed for a seat. Close to these thresholds, the relationship between vote share and the probability of getting a seat is very steep, so that small changes in vote shares are associated with very large decreases or increases in this probability. For example, an increase of 1 percent in the vote share can raise the probability of a seat from 0.5 to 0.95. Lastly, the Sainte-Laguë rule lowers this threshold for all size districts but particularly in the smaller districts.

The second equation in the votes-to-seats model estimates the share of the seats allocated to each party getting seats based on its share of the votes, given the district magnitude and the votes-to-seats rule. Again, there is a large distinction between small and large districts. Even with as few as eight seats in a district, the relationship between vote and seat shares is close to being directly proportional. As the number of seats decreases, larger parties get a larger share of the seats than they had votes, and vice-versa for smaller parties. These deviations from proportionality are larger for the d'Hondt than for the Sainte-Laguë rule, as expected, and the deviations from proportionality and the differences between the two rules increase as the district magnitude decreases.

The second part of the analysis of the relationship between job creation and seat allocations is based on the previous analysis relating vote shares to de novo job creation. The coefficients reported in Table 6A.2 for the 1993 election are used to predict how the vote shares for the UD increase with the rate of job creation in an average voivodship. This "average" voivodship has the national mean values for all the variables in the model except de novo job creation and is not the home region for one of the major party's leaders. The vote shares for all parties, including Other, are predicted for increasing levels of job creation, and then the UD's share of the vote among the five parties that got seats after the 1993 election is calculated. This latter vote proportion is then used to predict the probability the UD gets seats and how many seats based on the votes-to-seats model shown in Table 7A.1.

Figure 7.1 plots the seat shares for the UD with different levels of de novo job creation in an otherwise average district.[6] The comparisons are done using the d'Hondt and the Sainte-Laguë rules and districts with four and eight seats, respectively. (To make the number of seats being allocated comparable, one should compare the seat allocations in the eight-seat district with the total number of seats that the UD would have obtained in two four-seat districts.) The curve labeled d'Hondt(4) shows that in a district with four seats, if de novo jobs constituted 4 percent of the work force, the median among voivodships in 1993, and the d'Hondt rule is used, the UD is predicted to get about 5 percent of the seats, or less than half a seat if two districts are combined. If new-job creation is 14 percent of the work force in these districts, the UD would be expected to get a third of the seats, or almost three seats. The remaining curves plot

---

6 The comparisons do not consider the discrete nature of the seat-allocation process but are intended to reflect the statistically expected seat gain aggregated across a large number of comparable districts. A predicted expected seat gain of .5 would imply that among ten such districts, the UD might gain a seat in five of them.

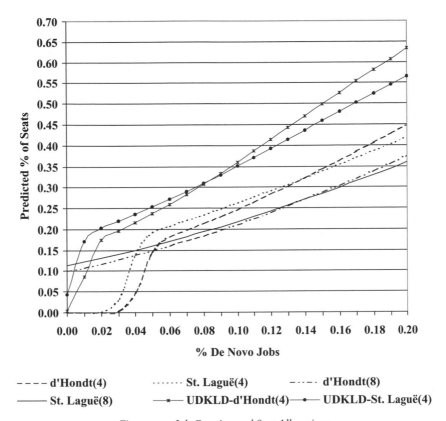

Figure 7.1. Job Creation and Seat Allocations

these expected seat shares for an eight-member district and for both sized districts using the Sainte-Laguë rule.

Figure 7.1 provides a number of important comparisons. Most important, in regions with low levels of de novo job creation, the UD would have been advantaged by having larger districts. Conversely, in areas with high rates of job creation it was in the UD's interest to have smaller districts. With the d'Hondt rule, this tipping point is a job creation rate of 5 percent when comparing four- and eight-seat districts. As the district magnitude increases, this tipping point decreases but at a slow rate. The critical job creation level where small districts are preferred using the Sainte-Laguë rule is about 4 percent, a percentage point lower than with the d'Hondt rule. Second, in all sized districts, given the level of new-firm creation in 1993, the UD would have fared better if the Sainte-Laguë formula had been used to allocate seats. In both sized districts the expected seat allocations for the UD are smaller with the d'Hondt rule when new-job creation is less than 14 percent of the work force, which includes all voivodships. Above that level, the UD is projected to get more seats using the d'Hondt rule.

This formal analysis supports the observation that the choice of political rules has an important bearing on how liberal economic interests are likely to be represented. De novo job creation is concentrated in larger, urban areas, which means that the constituency base for liberal parties is located in these same areas. In 1993 this concentration meant the liberal parties in Poland were systematically disadvantaged by their own rules as well as by their inability to respond to the incentives built into some of the rules. The choice of a more proportional rule, such as a straight Sainte-Laguë rule or even the modified Sainte-Laguë rule adopted for 2001 or the Hare quota system as used in 1991, rather than the d'Hondt rule would have aided the UD.

A second difficulty for the UD is that districts were created that concentrated liberal strength in large districts where seat allocations are more proportional to vote shares and concentrated the opposition's strength, particularly the PSL's, in small districts where it obtained seat proportions well above its vote shares. The liberals, when they designed the 1993 electoral reform, might have opted for larger districts in rural areas and/or created smaller districts within the urban areas. (Konieczny [1996], for one, argues for this option.) For example, combining the rural Ciechanów, Ostrołęka, and Lomża voivodships in northeast Poland into a single district with twelve seats would have netted the UD and the UP an additional seat each and reduced the PSL's allocation by two seats. And, combining the Jelenia Góra, Legnica, and Leszno voivodships in western Poland would have given the UD and the KPN each an additional seat while reducing the SLD's and PSL's allocations by a seat each. On the opposite side of the argument, dividing Poznań's fourteen seats among any combination of smaller districts, such as two four- and two three-seat districts or even two seven-seat districts, would have given the UD six seats rather than the five it got in the one large district. Similarly, dividing Kraków's thirteen seats into three districts with five, five, and three seats, respectively, would also have given the UD an additional seat.[7]

These scenarios only examine the UD's share of the 1993 vote. Had the UD and the KLD merged before the election, as the rules try to promote,

---

7 These projections assume the vote shares in the small districts are the same as in the single large district, as we do not have vote returns on a more local basis that would permit us to construct a set of small districts.

the liberals would have gained a larger share of the votes among those parties eligible for seats, which as we noted, would have increased their seat share by an even larger proportion. A merger would have also produced a much steeper relationship between de novo job creation and seats for the liberal coalition party. Figure 7.1 also plots the predicted relationship between job creation and seat shares for a combined UD+KLD party in 1993 in a four-seat district using both the d'Hondt and the Sainte-Laguë rules. As expected, the combined party gets a larger share of the seats at all levels of job creation.

There are two important, but less obvious, aspects to the jobs-to-seats relationships for the UD+KLD shown in Figure 7.1. First, the liberals' seat share rises more rapidly with job creation with the larger party, meaning it would have taken less additional job creation to add to their parliamentary bloc. Second, the point at which the d'Hondt rule becomes more favorable to the liberals occurs at a lower level of de novo job creation than when the UD enters by itself. With the combined parties in the district with four seats, if job creation exceeds 8 percent of the total work force, the d'Hondt method is likely to give the liberals more seats. Viewed in this context, the choice of the d'Hondt rule does not seem so misguided. Had the two parties merged, which was one of the intentions of the electoral reform, the d'Hondt formula would have been an advantage in more of the districts and would have become more so if there had been more new-job creation. Both of these scenarios could have been in the minds of the liberal reformers.

CONCLUSION

We conclude from these analyses that additional job creation could have made a difference in the balance of power in the parliament, with the pro-reform party, or parties, gaining a larger share of the seats. But the gains, as well as the actual allocations, are dependent upon the rules governing the election and the allocation of seats. From the standpoint of combining economic and political reform, the results indicate there is an important interaction between the success of the economic transformation and the political rules and strategies in affecting how well the economically liberal constituencies that will accompany successful transitions will be represented. Job creation will be geographically concentrated, so that electoral and representation rules that disadvantage these regions will reduce the influence of the pro-reform constituencies. The pro-reform parties must also realize that they are politically vulnerable, particularly at the early stages when the de novo firm creation process is just beginning, and should not adopt strategies that dilute their ability to attract voters and to gain seats.

The important lessons from this comparison are, first, that the advantages conveyed by shifts in electoral rules depend on how those rules change the implicit thresholds for getting seats relative to the parties' vote distributions in the different districts; and, second, that because the location of de novo firm and job creation is both geographically concentrated and greater in larger urban areas, rules that advantage urban areas and majority parties in those districts will increase the representation of pro-reform parties. This, of course, is the opposite of the rules adopted in 1993 and 1997, which advantaged larger parties, but those in more rural areas where there was less de novo job creation.

Appendix 7A: Analysis of Votes-to-Seats Rules

The relationship between a party's share of the votes in a district and its share of the seats awarded will vary systematically with the allocation rule used, the number of seats being allocated, and its share of the votes. A standard work discussing these relationships for proportional representation systems is Taagepera and Shugart (1989), who offer several models for relating seats to votes. King (1990), in a further elaboration on this theme establishes that the proper functional form for the relationship is,

$$\left(\frac{s_j}{1 - s_j} \right) = e^\lambda \left(\frac{v_j}{1 - v_j} \right)^\alpha , \qquad (7A.1)$$

where s_j is party j's share of the seats and v_j is its share of the votes.[8] If $\lambda = 0$ and $\alpha = 1$, the seats-votes relationship is proportional with $s_j = v_j$. Graphically this is represented by a 45 degree line. If $\alpha > 1$, the relationship between s and v has the shape of a cumulative distribution function, with $s_j < v_j$ (below the 45 degree line) for smaller vote shares and $s_j > v_j$ (above the 45 degree line) for larger shares. If $\alpha < 1$, just the opposite holds, with $s_j > v_j$ for smaller vote shares and $s_j < v_j$ for larger shares. The actual inflection point depends on the value for λ, which shifts the relationship up or down, depending on whether it is greater than or less than zero. For $\lambda > 0$, the larger the value for λ, the smaller the value of v_j where

---

8 King (1990) also derives an expression for multiparty elections and seat allocations. With our focus on the UD, and for expositional ease we use a simpler and more tractable single-party formula.

the inflection point occurs and the larger the range of values for v_j where $s_j > v_j$. Conversely for $\lambda < 0$. As the magnitude of λ increases, the inflection point shifts to the right and the range where $s_j > v_j$ decreases. We describe these relationships in some detail as changing the votes-to-seats rule and the number of seats per district changes the magnitude and direction of the deviations from strict proportionality, as reflected in different values for these parameters. For example, the d'Hondt rule is designed to favor the plurality winner in a district, which means that for very low vote shares the votes-to-seats plot for the Sainte-Laguë rule should be above that for the d'Hondt rule, but above some threshold the reverse will be true. The remainder of this appendix describes our estimation of the parameters in Equation 7A.1.

Estimation of the votes-to-seats relationship is done using the vote outcomes and seat allocations for the eligible parties in the fifty-two electoral districts in the 1993 and 1997 elections. The vote outcomes are each party's share of the votes going to parties that were awarded seats, not its share of the total vote. For each election and district there are two sets of observed seat allocations. The first is the one that resulted from the elections in 1993 and 1997 using the d'Hondt rule. The second is the seat allocations that would have resulted from the use of the Sainte-Laguë rule. (The aggregate seat distributions using this rule are shown in Table 7.2.) For a given district in a given election, the vote returns and the number of seats to be allocated are the same. The only factor that varies in this comparison is the seat allocation rule, and thus the number of seats allocated to each of the eligible parties. Vote shares, of course, vary by district, by party, and by election while the seats per district vary by district.[9]

Estimation begins by transforming Equation 7A.1 to its log-log form, which is

$$\log\left(\frac{s_j}{1 - s_j}\right) = \lambda + \alpha\log\left(\frac{v_j}{1 - v_j}\right) + u_j. \tag{7A.2}$$

A stochastic term, u_j, is added because this expression will not fit exactly for every party, district, election, and rule. Equation 7A.2 can be directly estimated as it is linear in the parameters λ and α, which will be functions of the seats-to-votes rule, the number of seats per district, and possibly the particular election. One feature prevents direct estimation of Equation 7A.2. In more than a third of the observations the party did not

---

9 There were four minor changes in the seats allocated to each district between the 1993 and 1997 election.

get any seats in a district, which has two consequences. Most immediate, the left-hand-side variable is undefined so these observations cannot be included in the estimation. But there is a substantive issue as well. There is a possible nonlinearity in Equation 7A.2 such that a party has to surpass some threshold in its vote share to be expected to get any seats, and the relationship in Equation 7A.2 then only holds for parties above that threshold.

We model this possibility using a two-step process. The first equation models the probability that a party will get any seats, that is, the probability that $s_j > 0$. The second equation then estimates Equation 7A.2 directly, using only those cases where the party is allocated seats. There is a catch to this procedure, however, in the form of a selection bias among the latter set of observations. By omitting the cases where a party did not get any seats, the stochastic term in the second equation does not have an expected value of zero. Furthermore, this expected value varies systematically with the right-hand-side variables, which are related to the probability of getting any seats, just as they are related to the proportion of seats.[10] The estimation method used to accommodate this bias is a variation of Heckman's model for selection bias. In this method the selection equation, for example, the probability that a party gets any seats, is estimated as a standard probit model. From this estimation the expected bias in the stochastic term, the inverse Mill's ratio, for the observations selected for the second equation estimation is calculated and included in the estimation of this equation. This equation can be estimated directly using the logit expressions for seat and vote shares as the left- and right-hand-side variables, respectively. Estimation of Equation 7A.2 is done with the generalized linear model, which can accommodate both the logit

---

10 In more formal terms, if an observation draws a large negative value for the stochastic term in Equation 7A.2, this increases the likelihood the party does not get any seats, which means it is more likely to be omitted from the second estimation. This selection means the stochastic terms in the cases in the second estimation represent a truncated distribution. The expected value for such a distribution is not zero but a positive value that varies with the truncation point. We assume that u_j in Equation 7A.2 is drawn from a normal distribution, so that the mean of the truncated distribution can be calculated with the inverse Mill's ratio. (See Greene, 2000, p. 899.) Following the probit format we use, the probability that party j in district k gets any seats is given by $\Pr(u_{jk} > a_{jk})$, where a_{jk} represents the threshold defined by the district magnitude, the rule being used, and the party's share of the vote in that district. All instances where $(u_{jk} \leq a_{jk})$ are omitted from the second step estimation so that in this equation is $E(u_{jk}) = \phi(a_{jk}/\sigma)/[1 - \Phi(a_{jk}/\sigma)]$, where $\phi(a_{jk}/\sigma)$ and $\Phi(a_{jk}/\sigma)$ are the density function and cumulative probability functions for the normal distribution.

form for the seat share variable and the assumption that the observed seat shares are likely to follow a binomial distribution, given the number of seats in the district. The clustering option is used in the estimation, where a cluster is a specific district, election, and rule.

The selection equation includes variables for the log of the number of seats in a district; the logit based on a party's share of the vote in that district, v_{jk}; and the seat allocation rule, denoted by STL for the cases where the Sainte-Laguë rule is used to allocate seats,

$$Pr(s_{jk} > 0) = Pr\{\lambda_{10} + (\lambda_{11} + \lambda_{12}STL)log(Seats_k)$$
$$+ (\alpha_{10} + \alpha_{11}STL)log\left(\frac{v_{jk}}{1 - v_{jk}}\right) + u_{jk} > 0\}. \quad (7A.3)$$

The estimated version of Equation 7A.2 for the seat shares is specified so that both λ and α could, but are not forced to, converge to zero and one, respectively, as the number of seats increases,

$$Log\left(\frac{s_{jk}}{1 - s_{jk}}\right) = \left[\lambda_{20} + \left(\frac{\lambda_{21} + \lambda_{22}STL}{Seats_k}\right)\right]$$
$$+ \left[\alpha_{20} + \left(\frac{\alpha_{21} + \alpha_{22}STL}{Seats_k}\right)\right] Log\left(\frac{v_{jk}}{1 - v_{jk}}\right) + u_{jk}.$$
$$(7A.4)$$

If seat allocations become directly proportional to vote shares as the number of seats get large, then $\lambda_{20} = 0$ and $\alpha_{20} = 1$. The expectation that the Sainte-Laguë rule is more proportional than the d'Hondt formula predicts that λ_{22} and α_{22} are both negative. As discussed in note 9, u_{jk} in Equation 6B.4 does not have an expected value of zero because of the deletion of cases where a party gets no seats. The Heckman-type procedure incorporates this expectation by estimating the mean of the truncated values of u_{jk} from the probit estimation of Equation 7A.3 under the assumption that the u_{jk}'s are normally distributed.

Table 7A.1 shows the statistical results, including the tests for whether the relationships differed among elections and rules. The first column presents the model predicting the probability that a party gets any seats in a district, given the number of seats, its share of the vote, and the particular election and rule in place. The results show very strong positive relationships between a party's vote share and the number of seats in a district and the likelihood of getting seats in that district. In a district with four seats it requires about 14 percent of the vote among eligible parties to have a 0.5 probability of getting at least one seat. This proportion drops

Table 7A.1. *Estimated Votes-to-Seats Rules*

$\text{Prob}(s_{jk} > 0)$		$\text{Log}[s_{jk}/(1 - s_{jk})]$	
Constant $- \lambda_{10}$	17.11	Constant $- \lambda_{20}$	0.002
	(2.82)		(0.04)
Year $= 1997$	-5.32		
	(2.12)		
$\text{Log}\,[v_{jk}/(1 - v_{jk})] - \alpha_{10}$	22.39	$\text{Log}\,[v_{jk}/(1 - v_{jk})] - \alpha_{20}$	1.066
	(3.85)		(0.03)
$\text{Log(seats)} - \lambda_{11}$	17.21	$1/\text{(seats)} - \lambda_{21}$	3.60
	(2.25)		(0.36)
*Sainte-Laguë	0.89	*Sainte-Laguë	-1.43
	(0.25)		(0.25)
*Year $= 1997$	1.71	*Year $= 1997$	-1.13
	(1.04)		(0.25)
*Sainte-Laguë*Year $= 1997$	1.11		
	(0.40)		
		$\text{Log}\,[v_{jk}/(1 - v_{jk})]/\text{Seats} - \alpha_{21}$	1.44
			(0.32)
		*Sainte-Laguë	-1.22
			(0.20)
		*Year $= 1997$	-0.71
			(0.21)
		$E(u_{jk})$	0.53
		(Inverse mills ratio)	(0.07)
Versus saturated model			
χ^2 /degrees of freeedom	6.49/5		0.71/11
Probability of results w/H_o	0.262	Probability of results w/H_o	0.999

to 9 percent with eight seats and to 5 percent if there are sixteen or more seats in the district. To illustrate how rapidly the likelihood of getting a seat increases with vote share, in the smaller districts an additional .4 percent of the vote increases the probability of getting a seat to 0.75 and an additional .9 percent raises the probability to 0.95. In the larger districts the additional shares are about .2 and .4 percent respectively. The probabilities are symmetrical, so that decreases in vote shares of these magnitudes reduce the probabilities of getting seats to 0.25 and to 0.05.

The Sainte-Laguë rule increases the probability of a party getting a seat, but this increase is proportional to the district magnitude and is particularly large in the 1997 election for larger districts. In 1993 use of the Sainte-Laguë rule reduces the proportion of the vote needed to have a fifty-fifty chance at a seat by about .6 percent. In 1997 this difference is nill for a four-seat district and 1 percent for a sixteen-seat district.

The bottom entry in Table 7A.1 reports the results of a test of the hypothesis that the coefficients are different for each election and rule combination, referred to as a saturated model, versus the null hypothesis that the model reported in the table is the correct one. This test incorporates the proposition that the intercept and the coefficients on the log seats and vote logit variables differ by rule and election. If the null hypothesis is correct, the statistical difference in the two models could have occurred by chance a quarter of the time. Given this result and the fact that no combination of rule or year variables is statistically significant when added to the model, we chose the model presented in the table as the best expression for the probability of getting seats.

The right-hand columns in Table 7A.1 show the estimated model for the relationship between seat shares and vote shares, as depicted in Equations 7A.2 and 7A.4. The estimates for λ_{20} and α_{20} indicate that as district magnitudes increase both votes-to-seats rules become virtually proportional, as predicted. (The coefficient of 1.066 for α_{20} indicates a very slight nonlinearity, but one that deviates only barely from a 45 degree line.) These values are quite stable across election and rule changes. The bottom rows again report a statistical test comparing this model with models that had separate coefficient values for each election and rule. The likelihood of the increased fit of the saturated model occurring by chance is more than 0.99, leading us to accept the estimated model shown in the preceding rows in the table.

The most interesting results are those related to how the proportionality of the votes-to-seats relationship changes with the district magnitude. The estimated coefficients for the interaction variables with the reciprocal of the number of seats, labeled λ_{21} and α_{21}, and which adjust the degree of proportionality according to the district magnitude, are positive and statistically significant. These results indicate that for low vote shares and small district magnitudes, the seat share does not rise proportionally with the vote share, and the smaller the magnitude, the further the deviation from strict proportionality. The coefficients for the variables representing allocations with the Sainte-Laguë rule are negative and statistically significant. These results indicate that, as expected, this rule produces more proportional results than the d'Hondt formula for a given district magnitude. The results with the 1997 election variables indicate the votes-to-seats relationship is more proportional in that election than in 1993, although it is still not proportional with the d'Hondt rule.

Table 7A.2. Seats, Vote Shares, and Electoral Rules

% Votes	2 × 4 Seats/District		1 × 8 Seats/District	
	d'Hondt	Sainte-Laguë	d'Hondt	Sainte-Laguë-
0.07	0.00	0.00	0.00	0.00
0.08	0.00	0.00	0.02	0.35
0.09	0.00	0.00	0.56	0.76
0.10	0.00	0.00	0.74	0.85
0.11	0.00	0.00	0.83	0.94
0.12	0.00	0.01	0.93	1.04
0.13	0.06	0.49	1.03	1.13
0.14	0.78	1.38	1.13	1.23
0.15	1.35	1.58	1.23	1.32
0.16	1.50	1.69	1.33	1.41
0.18	1.77	1.92	1.54	1.60
0.20	2.04	2.14	1.75	1.79
0.25	2.72	2.68	2.28	2.27
0.30	3.39	3.20	2.83	2.74
0.40	4.64	4.18	3.89	3.66
0.50	5.69	5.06	4.89	4.54
0.60	6.52	5.85	5.78	5.37
0.70	7.14	6.53	6.55	6.15
0.80	7.57	7.13	7.19	6.85
0.90	7.86	7.62	7.68	7.48
1.00	8.00	8.00	8.00	8.00

Note: Predicted number of seats in two districts with four seats each or one district with eight seats.

Calculating the predicted number of seats party j is likely to receive in district k, given its vote share in the district (v_{jk}), the number of seats to be allocated (s_k), and the votes-to-seats rule, combines both results. We denote the predicted number of seats by $\hat{s}_{jk}$. This value equals the probability of the party getting any seats, $P(s_{jko})$ as given by Equation 7A.3, times the number of seats the party is likely to get given that it gets seats, s_{jk}^* as obtained from Equation 7A.4. More formally, $\hat{s}_{jk} = P(s_{jko}) * s_{jk}^*$. When these two expressions are combined in this manner, the consequences for smaller parties of not getting any seats in districts with small magnitude becomes very apparent. Table 7A.2 shows a party's predicted number of seats for different vote shares in two districts with different magnitudes and with the two votes-to-seats rules. (The 1993 parameter values in Table 7A.1 are used in this table as most of the discussion focuses on that election.)

Several features of these votes-to-seats relationships are important in our discussion of the support for the liberal parties in 1993. It is very apparent that, as a party's vote share increases, it is advantaged by both smaller districts and the d'Hondt formula. A party's preferred votes-to-seats rule depends on its expected vote strength and the district magnitude. In the larger districts, the differences between the two rules is relatively small, never reaching half a seat. In the small districts, by contrast, the differences in predicted seats can vary by as much as one seat between the two rules, and the direction of the difference depends strongly upon the vote share. In the four-seat district if a party expects to get about 13 or 14 percent of the vote, we predict that it will get half a seat more with the Sainte-Laguë rule. If it is likely to get 30 or more percent of the vote, the party is greatly advantaged by the d'Hondt formula, with the difference reaching half a seat if it gets about 50 percent of the vote. This may seem extreme, but the PSL reached that level in some of the smaller rural districts.

8

The Political Economy after 1997

Much transpired in Poland's politics and economy after 1997. Economic growth slowed and unemployment increased dramatically. The rightist coalition of church and trade-union leaders that dominated the 1997 election disintegrated to the point it could not gain enough votes to be seated in the parliament after the 2001 elections. A casual inspection might suggest that these events contradict our previous analysis and conclusions, and this might be true. The detailed economic data that form the basis for the preceding chapters are not available for the years after 1997, preventing a careful analysis of the four years following 1997 and a rigorous testing of the propositions developed earlier. We use what data are available to explore several explanations for what transpired between 1997 and 2001. The goal is to offer some insight into whether the conclusions we reached about the period from 1990 to 1997 are only applicable for that stage of the transition or whether the model we develop is consistent with this later period as well. After a brief summary of the main economic and political events, we examine the economic changes, compare the voting patterns in the 2001 with the votes cast in 1997, and then evaluate the model and its usefulness in understanding the later stages of the Polish transformation.

THE ECONOMY

Table 8.1 shows the level of real GDP relative to 1989, the unemployment rate, and the change in GDP for the period 1989 to 2001. Aggregate growth slowed substantially after 1997 after several years of annual GDP growth exceeding 5 percent. It barely exceeded 1 percent from 2000 to 2001. Concurrently, unemployment increased dramatically, exceeding 18 percent, which put it above the peak level during the early years of the transition.

Table 8.1. *Percent Unemployment and GDP, 1989–2001*

Year	% Unemployment	Real GDP	Real GDP Growth
1989	0.0	100.0	
1990	6.3	92.0	−8.00
1991	8.9	85.6	−7.00
1992	12.9	87.8	2.57
1993	14.9	91.1	3.76
1994	16.5	95.9	5.27
1995	15.2	102.6	6.99
1996	14.3	108.7	5.95
1997	11.5	116.2	6.80
1998	10.0	121.8	4.82
1999	12.0	126.8	4.11
2000	14.0	132.0	4.10
2001	18.2	134.0	1.20

Various external and internal factors likely contributed to this economic performance. One obvious external factor is simply the slowdown in the world economy, which particularly affected Western Europe. Polish exports decreased by 2.3 percent from 1998 to 1999, even in nominal terms. This was the first decrease since 1989. One cost of being more connected to the world economy is reduced immunity to its fluctuations.

A second external factor is the collapse of the Russian economy in 1998. Polish exports to Russia dropped by more than 50 percent between 1998 and 1999. This decline hit the eastern regions particularly hard as firms in these regions still relied heavily on exports to Russia, Ukraine, and Belarus. Poland, however, continued to rely on imports from Russia, particularly natural gas. The trade balance with Russia went from a surplus of U.S. $700 million in 1998 to a deficit of $1.6 billion in 1999. These two external factors themselves could account for some of the economic difficulties.

Important internal factors also contribute to the decline. The restructuring of the Polish economy was not completed by 1997, as evidenced by the large number of enterprises remaining under government ownership or control. How this restructuring proceeded and the same dynamics we examined in Chapter 3 can account for much of the increased unemployment and decreased growth. Table 8.2 shows employment by size category for the smallest and largest enterprises between 1997 and 2001. The employment in the largest group of domestic manufacturing firms is shown separately from that for all large firms. The data on real GDP

Table 8.2. *Small, Large, and New Enterprises, 1997–2001*

	1997	1998	1999	2000	2001
Average employment,[a] 0–50	2.894	3.059	2.941	2.968	3.147
Percentage, 0–50	30.5	31.8	31.3	32.5	35.6
Average employment,[a] > 250	4.302	4.193	3.980	3.693	3.347
Percentage, > 250	45.3	43.6	42.3	40.4	37.8
Domestic manufacturing employ,[a] > 250	1.327	1.217	1.163	1.088	1.063
De novo firms,[b] 0–9		450.8	234.2	203.3	
De novo employ,[b] 0–9		636.8	305.9	267.9	
# Active firms,[b] 0–250	1.580	1.723	1.816	1.763	1.655
% Change in real GDP	6.80	4.82	4.11	4.10	1.20

Note: Data on de novo firms and employment and manufacturing employment are obtained in a special study from the Polish Central Statistical office. Other data are from the Polish Agency for Enterprise Development.

[a] Employment in millions.

[b] Firms and employment in thousands.

growth from Table 8.1 is also included to facilitate comparisons of the timing of the different processes.

The delayed restructuring and privatizing of former state-owned enterprises, principally in the mining, steel, and telecommunications sectors, is an important contributor to the increased unemployment. As seen in Table 8.2, employment in the largest domestic manufacturing firms decreased by about 264,000 workers, or nearly 20 percent of their level in 1997. This is more than 2.5 percent of the nonagricultural work force. Employment in very large enterprises in all sectors declined by more than a million workers between 1997 and 2001. For largely political reasons, these large enterprises had been spared the pressures of hard budget constraints during the early and mid-1990s and were running deficits annually. The privatization act passed in 1996 changed this, and had its fullest impact three, four, and five years later. In most cases the owners of the newly privatized firms were required to maintain the current work force for a specific period of time, as much as three years. After that point they could lay off workers in order to cut costs and raise productivity. These agreements merely delayed the unemployment as the firms could not increase sales sufficiently to maintain the work force. In effect, this is simply a delayed version of the job destruction process expected to accompany the transition to a market economy. This delayed approach to privatization and restructuring and to the downsizing associated with it is simply another form of gradualism in the transition.

The job destruction in the early stages of the transition was eventually offset by a significant amount of job creation in new firms, as shown in Chapters 2 and 3. The rate of de novo job creation lagged the reductions in the large enterprises, leading to a spike in unemployment, but one that was receding by 1997. Could this process be occurring again? Unfortunately, the detailed data on birth, survival, and growth rates used in Chapter 3 are not available after 1997, so we can only infer what is happening in the de novo sector by piecing together fragments of data from a variety of sources. We do have data from the Central Statistical Office on the number of newly registered firms and their employment for the years 1998 to 2000. There are no data on exits and survival and growth rates, so we cannot examine the changes in depth as done in Chapter 3. Despite their limitations, these data may help decipher what is happening in the Polish economy.[1]

Employment in the small-size sector, defined as firms employing fewer than 50 workers, which had risen consistently and significantly before 1997, is essentially flat after that. The number of active enterprises with 0–50 and 51–250 workers peaks in 1999 and declines in 2000 and 2001. What is particularly significant is that the rate of entry of new firms and new jobs, defined as starting enterprises with fewer than 10 employees, declines by more than 50 percent between 1998 and 2000. (If we examine the larger initial-size categories of those with 10–50 or even 50–250 workers, the proportional decline is the same.) Our speculation then is that a significant contributor to the increased unemployment by 2000 and 2001 is a decline in the job creation process in the de novo sector so that job creation is not offsetting the job destruction in the larger enterprises.

The slowing of the transition and the decline of the whole economy is having serious distributional consequences. The increases in regional unemployment since 1997 have been very uneven, just as we saw in the beginning of the transformation (Chapter 4), and the reverse of the trend in the mid-1990s when the unemployment gap was decreasing (see Table 4.1). In 2001, unemployment ranged from a low of 7.5 percent in the Warsaw subregion to more than 25 percent in some of the more rural areas in the northeast and west central subregions. There is considerable concern

---

1 The obstacle with these data is that in contrast to the longitudinal data used earlier, we do not know what dynamics took place in terms of firms exiting a given size category because they grew, declined, or failed all together. Thus, changes in employment in any given category can arise for a number of reasons.

about this growing regional inequality and the pressures it places on social and political structures.

The period 1997 to 2001, both in the aggregate and in its regional variations, mirrors the early stage of the transition when job destruction in large enterprises dominated the transition and de novo firm creation had yet to accelerate. This job destruction is having similar political consequences to what we observed in the early 1990s. The question is whether new-firm creation can be stimulated to offset the job destruction, as occurred between 1993 and 1997, and to expand the liberal political constituency.

Two changes in the Polish political economy beginning in 1997 and 1998 may help explain why de novo job creation has fallen since 1997 and 1998. These changes also raise questions about the likelihood of de novo firm creation expanding sufficiently to raise the job creation level to what is needed to bring down the unemployment rate. One of these is a substantial increase in the subsidization of the large enterprises, even those that had been privatized, effectively softening the budget constraints for inefficient firms. The second is a rise in the perceived amount of corruption in the public and private economies. We discuss both of these factors in comparison with other transitional countries in Chapter 9, but these trends are significant enough to warrant discussion here to help explain why the firm creation process may be lagging and why confidence in private firms has declined markedly since 1997.

The imminent accession to the European Union, and its rules about enterprise subsidies, is requiring the Polish government to report publicly the value of its subsidies, which the Office for Competition and Consumer Protection has begun doing. Their report shows that the amount of state aid to business increased by 2.2 million złotys between 1997 and 2001. Tax exemptions are reported to have decreased by 2 million złotys, but this was more than offset by increases in grants (1.1 million), preferential loans (0.9 million), credit guarantees (1.7 million), and other programs (0.8 million). The vast proportion of this aid went to very large enterprises and firms under state control.

There are many incentives and means for underreporting, and Polish law is only slowly forcing the government to follow EU standards. Thus the data for the late 1990s likely understate the true level of subsidization. A study done by two Polish economists (Neneman and Sowa, 2001) estimates the actual level of tax arrears increased from 7.6 million złotys in 1996 and 1997 to 15.5 million in 1998. The official figures actually report a decrease from 5.2 million to 4.8 million złotys for these years. The reversion to subsidies and soft budgets is a marked contrast to the policies under the reform governments that backed the Balcerowicz Plan in the early 1990s despite the fact that there was relatively little privatization. Kornai, for one, contends that it is the hardness of the budget constraints rather than privatization per se that is important (Kornai, 2000). We discuss this point in more detail in Chapter 9.

The second worrisome trend is an increase in corruption, or at least the perception and reporting of corruption. Numerous studies report a negative relationship between corruption and economic growth. (See Brunetti, Kisunko, and Weder, 1997; Katchanovski, 2000; and Tanzi, 1998, for brief reviews of the literature.) Although entrepreneurial activity is not examined specifically, we think these results apply even more so to the latent de novo sector. In the early and mid-1990s Poland's rating on several international organizations' corruption scales indicated relatively lower levels of corruption. For example, Hellman, Jones, and Kaufman (2000) develop a corruption measure based on what participants in a survey of firms report paying in bribes. Poland ranks among the least corrupt of the transitional countries on this measure. Freedom House in its report *Nations in Transition* (Karatnycky, Motyl, and Schnetzer, 2001) also rates corruption in Poland as being very low. (See Table 9.5 for these figures.)

These favorable ratings began to change, however, in 1997 and 1998. Transparency International reports a marked decrease in its Corruption Perception Index beginning in those years. (Higher values indicate the absence of corruption in its index.) The index is 5.6 in 1996, which is higher than both Hungary and the Czech Republic, the only other Central European transitional countries included. The Polish index then decreased monotonically to a level of 3.6 in 2003, indicating a substantial increase in the amount of perceived corruption. These indices always contain noise and are not precise indicators, but systematic changes of this magnitude clearly indicate a significant trend. Comparisons with trends in other countries provide additional insight into what is occurring in Poland. The corruption perception index values for the Czech Republic are comparable with Poland's, decreasing from 5.4 to 3.8. By contrast, the values for Estonia and Hungary begin and stay about 5.6 and 5.0, respectively. Russia and Ukraine provide alternative examples of more corrupt economies, with perception scores between 2.0 and 2.5 for the entire period.

Official figures, which themselves are not necessarily reliable given reporting difficulties, show a similar trend. Palacz, Wojtkowski, and Woźnicki (2001) report that in 2000 the number of proven corruption cases was 61 percent higher and that the value of proven bribes was ten times higher than in 1992. Even accounting for inflation, these data indicate an increase in the proven corruption cases. One can only speculate about the number of cases that are not reported, let alone successfully prosecuted, and whether the amount of underreporting is also increasing. This lack of transparency and clean transactions distorts the allocation of resources against de novo firms and raises the level of suspicion and cynicism about the private sector and the whole transition.

Chapter 9 has a discussion of how Poland compared with other transitional countries during the early and mid-1990s on various measures of reform, including the quality of government, the degree of financial reform, and lack of corruption. The focus of this discussion is that Poland was a leading country on almost all measures during this period. This is also the period when the Polish economy was performing the best, both in the aggregate and in stimulating the creation and growth of new firms. We contend that hard budget constraints and a lack of corruption are among the critical and even necessary elements for a successful transition. The increase in subsidies to large state enterprises and the growing amount, or perception, of corruption beginning in 1997 and 1998 likely contribute to the decline in the entry of and job creation by de novo firms during the 1997 to 2001 period, which is a major factor in the poor macroeconomic performance and the slowing of the transition.

STATISTICAL ANALYSIS OF UNEMPLOYMENT CHANGES

We now want to use what data are available to examine whether the unemployment increase after 1997 is consistent with the model and conclusions developed in Chapter 3. The variations in regional unemployment increases are used to examine several propositions about the economic decline. These propositions follow the creative destruction theme. Areas with a higher concentration of state industries are likely to experience larger unemployment increases, whereas those with more de novo firms will have smaller increases. As we do not have longitudinal data on the entry, exit, growth, and decline of firms for the 1997 to 2001 period, we base our tests on the structure of the regional economy in 1997. The key explanatory variables for estimating the unemployment changes are the concentration of 1997 employment in state-owned firms facing restructuring, the proportion of the 1997 work force employed in de novo firms, and the proportion of the workers in restructured and in fully privatized firms. The data for these measures come from the longitudinal data analyzed in Chapter 3.

Relating Creative Destruction and Unemployment Changes

If the proposition that part of the unemployment problem stems from the restructuring and privatization of firms still in the state sector, the proportion of the work force employed in these enterprises in 1997 should account for a significant increase in the unemployment. We consider a general version and two very specific versions of this variable. The broadest measure is the log of the proportion of the 1997 work force in all enterprises still owned by the state. The first specific measure is the log of the proportion of the 1997 work force in state-managed mining, basic metal, and transportation manufacturing other than cars and trucks. These are the sectors that had most effectively avoided privatization during the early transition. The transportation sector is included because it includes ship and locomotive production, which are classic old state industries faced with restructuring and extensive downsizing. The second specific variable omits the employment in mining from the previous measure. The state subsidies described earlier went predominately to the mining industry, which may have forestalled layoffs in that industry.

The log of the proportion of the 1997 work force employed in de novo firms captures two different, but related, propositions. One is that the new private firms are likely to be more efficient and adaptive, and thus better equipped to cope with an economic recession, than older inefficient firms. (See Caballero and Hammour, 1994, on the cleansing effect of recessions.) The second proposition, based on the evidence about agglomeration effects, is that regions with a growing de novo economy between 1990 and 1997 are likely to continue to have higher rates of firm creation. We also include the variable measuring the number of local development agencies as a further proxy that the region probably continued to create new firms. Chapter 3 shows that this variable was strongly associated with the birthrate of new firms, which again we assume is likely to continue. If the size of the de novo economy in 1997 and the local area's effort to stimulate economic growth, as reflected in the number of development agencies, are negatively related to the increase in unemployment, it suggests that a second part of the explanation for the variations in regional economic performance, and ultimately for the downturn as a whole, is too little growth in the de novo economy. Evidence for this explanation offers important support for the creative destruction premise.

The proportion of the 1997 work force employed in restructured and fully privatized firms is included to test whether the concentration of these firms contributed to the unemployment problem in any ways that differed from state-managed firms or from the de novo private firms. The evidence presented in Chapter 3 and the evidence that Jurjada and Terrell (2001) present about job creation and destruction in fully privatized firms suggest that they destroy jobs at the same rate as state-managed firms if both face hard budget constraints. This observation would suggest that regions with a large proportion of restructured and of fully privatized firms should see unemployment increases comparable with regions with a similar concentration of state-managed firms. If, however, the restructured and privatized firms had completed their reductions and begun to function as market-based firms, then there should be a smaller or even a negative relationship between the concentration of these firms and the increase in local unemployment.

Lastly, we include two additional variables to represent additional explanations for the increases in unemployment. The variable measuring the percentage employed in farming is included because farming is less sensitive to the business cycles, plus many Poles use farming as a second job and are less likely to be formally unemployed than those in urban areas who do not have this alternative.[2] A dummy variable for whether the subregion was on the eastern border is included as a proxy for whether being closer to the Russian market, and thus more likely to be dependent on trade with Russia and the former Soviet state, left the region more susceptible to the collapse of the Russian economy.

One difficulty in testing these propositions, in addition to the inability to construct the type of longitudinal data used in Chapter 3, is that the regional districts were reorganized and consolidated beginning in 1999. The original forty-nine voivodships are consolidated to sixteen new voivodships, which in turn were divided into employment subregions. This means one must match new to old districts in order to have meaningful comparisons. We matched combinations of the old voivodships that best constitute the new subregions.[3] Using this configuration, we could measure the 1997 conditions and subsequent unemployment increases for each new subregion.

---

2 Jackson and Mach (2002), report that between 1988 and 1998 Polish farmers were much less likely to experience spells of unemployment than were industrial workers despite the transition.

3 There is a fairly good correspondence between boundaries for the old voivodships and the new subregions. In some cases a good match requires aggregation of current subregions to match aggregations of the old voivodships. For example, several major cities are now treated as subregions, but we aggregated their unemployment with that of the surrounding subregion to approximate the older voivodships.

Table 8.3. *Estimated Unemployment Change Models*

Variable	1	2	3
Log(% de novo jobs)	−2.52	−2.09	−2.52
	(1.31)	(1.22)	(1.17)
Log(% privatized)	−1.76	−1.92	−1.89
	(0.73)	(0.69)	(0.69)
Log(% restructured)	−0.03	0.10	−0.01
	(0.63)	(0.56)	(0.55)
Log(% SOE)	0.23		
	(0.57)		
Log(% mining+metal+trans)		0.23	
		(0.14)	
Log(% metal+trans)			0.26
			(0.14)
Development agencies	−0.22	−0.23	−0.20
	(0.12)	(0.11)	(0.11)
% Farm	−0.22	−0.20	−0.22
	(0.05)	(0.05)	(0.04)
Russian border	−1.59	−1.28	−1.54
	(0.91)	(0.85)	(0.81)
Constant	19.79	19.06	20.50
	(4.52)	(3.87)	(3.72)
R^2	0.639	0.671	0.676

Note: Model for the change in unemployment between 1997 and 2001. Standard errors in parentheses.

Statistical Results

The statistical results are shown in Table 8.3. The three columns are for the different measures of employment in the state sector. Most of the results are what we expect, though not all are statistically significant. The variables measuring the size of the de novo economy and the number of development agencies are negatively related to the increase in the unemployment rate. The magnitudes of the coefficients indicate that each additional 10 percent of the work force in de novo firms is associated with 0.2 to 0.25 percent less unemployment in 2001, and each additional development agency is associated with about a .2 percent decrease in unemployment, though the agency coefficient is generally not statistically significant at the 0.05 level.

The associations between unemployment changes and the concentration of different types of older firms provide some interesting, and unexpected, results. The concentration of employment in privatized firms is strongly and negatively associated with the 2001 unemployment level. Each additional 10 percent of the work force in fully privatized firms is associated with about a 0.18 percent lower unemployment rate. There is no relationship between the concentration of restructured but not fully privatized firms and the change in unemployment. The coefficients estimating this relationship are both small and statistically insignificant. The relationship between the proportion of the work force in state-owned firms and unemployment becomes clearer and more statistically significant as the scope of the variable is narrowed. The weakest association is with the variable measuring state-sector employment in all sectors. The magnitude and statistical significance increase when the definition is restricted to employment in the primary metal and transportation sectors. This variable has a slightly better fit and slightly larger coefficient than when mining employment is included. These sectors had been the most protected from restructuring in previous years, which meant they faced the greatest need to reduce employment. Mining, as we said, was likely protected from this downsizing given its political connections.

The proportion of farmers is negatively related to the increases in unemployment, as expected, while being on the eastern border is negatively related to unemployment, contrary to expectations. The latter relationship was not statistically significant, although the coefficient is important in magnitude. This result casts doubt on the argument that the higher unemployment in the eastern regions is attributable to the collapse of the Russian economy.

These results offer further support for our basic proposition about the relationship between job destruction and job creation and the speed of transition and aggregate economic performance. Regions with large concentrations of state-managed firms in sectors that had not restructured, which eventually faced strong pressures to restructure and shed employment, had larger increases in unemployment between 1997 and 2001. By contrast, regions that have a larger proportion of their work force in de novo and privatized firms in 1997 and that are likely to have continued to have higher rates of new-firm creation had smaller increases in unemployment in this same period. These relationships do not explain the entire increase in national unemployment, given the external factors, but we think they account for a significant proportion of the increase. How much of the increase in national unemployment is accounted for by the job destruction and job creation process depends upon the actual rates of firm creation, survival, and growth, for which we have no data, but which we estimate to have declined during this period. The same prescription given for how to speed up the pace and success of the transition in the beginning period still applies during the later years as the economy is still faced with the need to restructure and raise efficiency.

POLITICAL TRANSITIONS

The transformations in the political structure after 1997 have been at least as dramatic as the economic changes. The dominant party after the 1997 election, the AWS, and its coalition partner, the UW, failed to win enough votes in the 2001 election to even hold a seat in the new parliament. This event made international headlines as it marked the political end of the Solidarność movement that so heroically initiated the transformation twenty years earlier. The headlines also noted that the election marked the return with nearly a majority of the seats of the former post-Communist SLD party. Why these changes occurred and how they relate to the job creation and destruction processes and to our proposition about the relationship between the development of the de novo economy and the evolution of parties supporting liberal economic policies pose an intriguing puzzle that we hope to assemble in the remainder of this chapter.

Despite their considerable differences over economic policy, the AWS and the UW formed a coalition government following the 1997 elections. The strains over economic policy were evident fairly quickly thereafter. The UW leadership with Balcerowicz at the head favored far more liberal policies with respect to the pace of privatization, government spending and tax rates, and subsidies for old firms than did the AWS leadership. The AWS, nominally led by Jerzy Buzek but dominated by Marian Krzaklewski, the head of the Solidarity trade union, took a far more corporatist approach hoping to protect jobs and wages in the larger and older industrial sectors while simultaneously pursuing privatization. The bickering over economic policy finally came to a head, and the UW left the government in August 2000. The AWS then continued as a minority government until the elections in September 2001.

Aleksander Kwaśniewski, the former leader of the SLD, was reelected president in 2000, soundly defeating Marian Krzaklewski and others without even a runoff. The surprising second place finisher, ahead of Krzaklewski, was Andrzej Olechowski, who ran without any party affiliation. Olechowski's success combined with the poor showing of the candidates from the right parties was followed by serious internal conflicts among the leaders of both the UW and the AWS. A division always existed within the UW (and, before it, the UD) between more social-welfare-oriented leaders who were less enthusiastic about the rigorous economic reforms and the economic liberals, including those who were formerly in the KLD, who promoted the reforms. This disagreement finally split the party in late 2000, with the social reformers taking control.

The AWS further disintegrated, with the Solidarity trade union deciding to leave the party and several new parties forming to compete on the right wing. The social action group within the AWS continued as a party and contested the 2001 election under the name AWSP. The conservative Catholic groups under the leadership of Roman Giertych formed the League of Polish Families (LPR). This party adopted very conservative and nationalistic views, such as limited roles for women outside the home, restricted foreign investment and ownership, and opposition to participation in the European Union. Another right-wing party ran under the name Law and Justice (PiS) and was led by the Kaczyńscy brothers, who had been among the Solidarność leaders in the early 1990s and held posts in the first reform government. The PiS platform was an unusual amalgamation of positions. Some parts, such as a managerial approach to public administration, controls on government spending, and strict interpretation of the legal code, particularly regarding corruption among government leaders, were close to those advocated by the liberal parties. Other parts, such as limits on foreign investment and economic integration, were more nationalistic and resembled the positions of the ROP in the 1997 election. The most right-wing party, Samoobrona (SRP), was the creation of a dissident and perpetual radical Andrzej Lepper. This party opposed all the liberal reforms, foreign investments, and integration and promoted extensive state subsidies for workers and farmers. Samobroona's appeals were directed at individuals and regions most disadvantaged by the transition and fearful about future cooperation with the European Union.

The most interesting, and successful, of the new parties on the right is the Civic Platform (PO). The leaders of this new party are Andrzej Olechowski, the independent candidate for president; Donald Tusk, deputy Senate speaker and former KLD and UW leader; and Maciej Płażyński, Sejm speaker and one of the AWS leaders. The PO's central theme is an economic development policy based on the encouragement of de novo firm and job creation. In an interview in the *Warsaw Voice* (January 28, 2001) Olechowski said, "Certainly, we target the middle class and those aspiring toward membership in this class.... [O]ur approach to the economy is the most compatible with entrepreneurs' needs." With a leadership drawn from former liberal members of several parties and with the demise of the UW, the PO became the most prominent liberal and centrist party.

The major change among the left-wing parties was the merger of the UP and the SLD to form a unified social democratic coalition party, the SLD/UP. This is not a totally surprising development given the UP's failure to gain any seats after the 1997 election and the relative similarity of their economic platforms, with the former UP being somewhat more to the left of most but not all of the SLD leaders. Perhaps the only remarkable feature of this coalition is that it marks the end, for most voters at least, of the post-Communist, non-Communist division. As noted in Chapters 2 and 5, the UP had its early roots in the Solidarność movement and in 1993 had campaigned vigorously as a non-Communist alternative to the liberal economic reforms. The joining of the UP and SLD leadership establishes economic issues as paramount.

In Chapters 5 and 6 we propose that the growth of new enterprises creates a constituency that both supports economically liberal parties and constrains other parties from undermining these reforms. The Civic Platform's economic plan nicely fits our proposition. Our second contention, that this economic constituency would constrain the actions of other parties, is evidenced in the platform of the SLD/UP proposed at a March 2001 party conference: the SLD/UP hoped to attract entrepreneurs and business leaders by promising to reduce red tape and taxes and follow other policies to promote the private sector. Its statements about economic policy in the party platform issued before the election specifically mention the need to stimulate small and medium-sized enterprises and to reduce tax and regulatory barriers to their growth. These are campaign statements, but they come from the party that only a decade earlier was advocating government support for heavy industry and, when it controlled the government between 1993 and 1997, was slow to promote privatization and supported wage increases for workers in state-managed firms that went beyond productivity increases and exceeded wage increases in the private sector.

The election outcome was no surprise. Table 8.4 shows the vote and seat distributions. The SLD/UP took 41.0 percent of the votes and 216 seats. The Civic Platform (PO) was second with 12.7 percent of the vote and 65 seats. The shares of the AWSP and the UW, 5.6 and 3.1 percent, respectively, are below the thresholds required to obtain seats, which marks the end for both parties and for what remained of the Solidarność movement from the 1980s. The other surprise is the success of Samoobrona, the PiS, and the LPR, which received 10.2, 9.5, and

Table 8.4. *Distribution of Votes, Seats, and Responses in PGSS Survey*

Party	Vote (%)	No. of Seats	PGSS Share
SLD/UP	41.0	216	45.0
PO	12.7	65	9.8
SRP	10.2	53	9.3
PiS	9.5	44	9.2
PSL	9.0	42	10.3
LPR	7.9	38	5.5
AWSP	5.6	0	4.4
UW	3.1	0	5.7
Other	1.1	2[a]	0.9

[a] Two seats went to German ethnic parties, which received 0.4 percent of the vote.

7.8 percent of the votes, respectively. The SLD/UP finished 15 seats short of a majority and was forced to partner with the PSL, with 42 seats, to form a coalition government, despite the tension created by the vast differences between the two on economic issues.[4]

ANALYSIS OF INDIVIDUAL VOTING IN THE 2001 ELECTION

We examine data for the 2001 election to see if the electoral model that fits the 1993 to 1997 elections helps us understand the 2001 election, despite all the economic and political changes. The analysis examines whether the attitudes, and cleavages, that were strongly related to vote choices in the 1993 to 1997 elections continued to define the electorate. If the variations in the same attitudes continue to be associated with vote choices in 2001, it suggests a continuity in the divisions within the electorate and in how the electorate is aligning itself with the different parties, even though the party structure changed substantially. To modify the metaphor about politicians

4 None of the SLD's options received much enthusiasm, given that they did not win an outright majority. Everyone agreed that the PO was closest to the SLD on many policy issues and that there were serious differences between the SLD and the PSL and the right-wing parties. Some hoped the SLD and the PO would create a grand coalition and govern from the center. The PO felt it was better positioned to remain as the main opposition party. There was also discussion that the SLD might form a minority government and that the PO would refrain from calling for a vote that might topple the government and lead to new elections. In the end the SLD leaders opted for a return to the coalition with the PSL that governed between 1993 and 1997.

dancing before a blind audience (Aldrich, Sullivan, and Borgida, 1989), stability in the vote choice equations suggests the audience is not blind and is using the same criteria to discriminate among the dancers even though the cast changes continually. Given the longevity and continuity among the leading politicians, we might suggest, however, that the dancers remain the same but appear in different costumes.

The analysis of the 2001 election is again based on PGSS data. PGSS interviewed several thousand Poles in early 2002, asking people to re-call their votes in the fall's parliamentary election. The distribution of votes among those who reported their votes matches the actual distribu-tion quite closely, with the SLD getting a larger share among the respon-dents than among the electorate by 4 percent and the others falling within 2.5 percent or less of the actual returns. (See the left column in Table 8.4.) These distributions are sufficiently similar that we are comfortable using the 2002 PGSS data to examine individual choices in the 2001 election.

The variables used to discriminate among the vote choices are the same ones used in the analysis of the 1997 election in Chapter 5: respondents' confidence in private relative to state-supported enterprises, their retro-spective assessments of their personal and the country's economic situa-tion, their views of communism as a form of government, their opinion of whether the Catholic Church had too much influence, and whether they lived in a village or on a private farm. Unfortunately the questions about confidence in private and state enterprises were asked only in half the sample, limiting the analysis to 677 cases. The statistical results reported in Table 8.5 are based on this half sample. (This table omits the results for the Other category as there were only five respondents that reported voting for one of the very minor parties, rendering the results meaning-less.) The base party for this model is the PO, so the coefficients indicate how the log of the odds of voting for one of the parties relative to voting for the PO changes with variations in each explanatory variable.

The structure observed for the previous elections replicates itself very strongly in these results. Table 8.6 shows how the vote shares for each party are expected to differ between two groups of average respondents whose attitudes equal 0.5 and 0.667, respectively.[5] (This difference, for example compares those with more confidence in private enterprises with those with equal confidence in state and private firms.) Confidence in

---

5 The entries in Table 8.6 must be compared with a party's share of the vote, shown in Table 8.4. A 1 percent change in the SLD share of the vote is proportionally equivalent to about a .1 percent shift in the vote share for the AWS or UW.

Table 8.5. *Model of Voting Choices in the 2001 Election*

Attitude	SLD/UP	AWSP	UW	SRP	PiS	PSL	LPR
Confidence in	−3.10	−2.76	−0.87	−4.35	−2.04	−1.55	−1.65
private firms	(0.76)	(1.22)	(1.14)	(1.04)	(1.02)	(0.88)	(1.34)
Retro personal	−0.05	−0.85	−0.20	0.49	0.68	0.01	0.21
	(0.40)	(0.77)	(0.59)	(0.58)	(0.55)	(0.58)	(0.78)
Retro collective	0.45	0.65	0.23	2.74	0.04	1.28	2.73
	(0.54)	(0.93)	(1.05)	(0.97)	(0.97)	(0.78)	(1.00)
Communism	2.67	0.97	0.77	2.60	0.40	1.78	0.61
	(0.80)	(1.03)	(1.10)	(0.85)	(0.89)	(0.87)	(0.88)
Church power	3.79	−4.50	1.27	1.01	0.22	1.24	−2.04
	(0.58)	(1.06)	(0.78)	(0.95)	(0.83)	(0.86)	(1.27)
Private farmer	−1.57	−0.27	−0.38	−0.55	−35.10	1.46	−0.39
	(0.90)	(1.08)	(1.51)	(0.87)	(0.92)	(0.88)	(1.15)
Village	−0.16	0.24	−0.68	1.08	−1.19	1.44	0.32
	(0.42)	(0.64)	(0.64)	(0.50)	(0.58)	(0.54)	(0.59)
PO leaders	−1.79	−1.79	−1.79	−1.79	−1.79	−1.79	−1.79
	(0.17)	(0.17)	(0.17)	(0.17)	(0.17)	(0.17)	(0.17)
Party leader	0.22	1.21	0.55	0.38	0.88	0.92	0.37
	(0.13)	(0.19)	(0.29)	(0.18)	(0.20)	(0.20)	(0.24)
Constant	−0.69	2.60	−0.87	−2.55	0.49	−2.51	−1.03
	(0.68)	(0.76)	(1.31)	(0.96)	(0.79)	(1.01)	(1.35)

Note: Equations for log odds of voting for each party relative to voting for the PO. Standard errors in parentheses.

Table 8.6. *Attitudes and Vote Shares, 2001 Election*

Party	Confidence in Private Firms	Communism a Good Government	Church Too Influential	Retrospective Personal	Evaluations Collective
PO	4.6	−1.5	−2.3	−0.1	−0.7
SLD/UP	−6.8	5.9	16.0	−1.0	−1.1
AWSP	−0.2	−0.4	−4.5	−0.4	0.0
UW	2.3	−1.2	−0.7	−0.3	−0.4
SRP	−1.4	0.6	−1.0	0.5	1.9
PiS	0.5	−2.5	−3.8	1.2	−1.1
PSL	0.6	−0.2	−0.4	−0.0	0.4
LPR	0.5	−0.7	−3.4	0.1	1.0

Note: Expected difference in vote shares among average Poles whose attitudes differ by 0.167.

private enterprises strongly differentiated those voting for the Civic Platform, the UW, and to some extent the PiS from support for other parties, particularly Samoobrona, the SLD/UP, and the AWSP. Voters with the greatest confidence in private enterprises, who presumably favor the most liberal policies, do not seem to have accepted the SLD's efforts to associate itself with some policies that might aid small and medium-sized enterprises.

Assessments about the church's political influence is very important to the choice between the SLD/UP, the most secular party, and the AWSP and the LPR, both of which were aligned with the Catholic Church. Finally, views about communism as a form of government clearly distinguished between votes for the SLD/UP, PSL, and Samoobrona and the former Solidarity parties, particularly the PO, the PiS, the UW, and the LPR. These results indicate that religious and ideological differences continue to be major electoral issues in Poland, along with views about the direction of economic policies. Furthermore, the choices voters make given their positions on these issues continue to track closely with the configuration of the parties, despite the fluidity in the composition of and alliances among the party leaders.

Respondents' retrospective assessments of their own finances and of the Polish economy played at best a small role in the choices among the parties, once these more prospective policy issues are considered. The largest difference for those who say their personal situation has gotten worse is a smaller likelihood of voting for the AWSP and the SLD/UP and a higher probability of voting for Samoobrona and the PiS. These differences are at best weakly consistent with the retrospective model. One would have expected both larger defections from the AWSP and more movement toward the SLD/UP, the major opposition party. Collective retrospective evaluations are more strongly associated with votes, but not necessarily in the manner the traditional model might predict. Among those who assess the Polish economy as having worsened, there is a higher probability of voting for the far-right parties, Samoobrona and the LPR, but at the expense of the PO, the UW, and the PiS and not the AWSP. The latter was the incumbent party one might associate with the economic difficulties that began in 1999, whereas both the PO and the PiS are parties formed a relatively short time before the election and, except for one individual who left the AWS for the PO, would not be associated with the economic situation. These associations are more likely an expression of policy voting, with those with the most negative assessments of the Polish economy choosing to vote for the proscriptions offered by Samoobrona and the LPR and rejecting the more liberal policies of the other parties.[6]

The basis for the SLD/UP success in the 2001 election can be easily developed from these results. People's confidence in private enterprises, which had been increasing through the 1990s, declined substantially between 1999 and 2002. Mean confidence fell to 0.34, compared with 0.38 in 1999, and the proportion with more positive ratings of state enterprises exceeded those with positive ratings of private firms by 49 percent, compared with 38 percent in 1999. (Among voters the mean was marginally higher and the gap between negative and positive confidence levels was smaller.) Similarly, those saying that communism is a good form of government or good for some countries, likely indicating nostalgia for the old regime, increased from just less than 25 percent in 1997 and 1999 to 34 percent in 2002. The poor economic performance, the high unemployment rate, the increasingly corrupt reputation of the AWS government, and the evidence of scandals among the privatized firms surely all contributed to this decline in confidence in the private sector and the increased positive assessments of communism. In all the elections analyzed, the coefficients in the voting models and the illustrations of voting differences among those with different opinions clearly indicate that decreasing confidence in private firms and increasing positive opinions of communism translate directly into more votes for the SLD and fewer votes for the liberal parties, such as the UW and the PO. (See Tables 5.6 and 8.6.) This is precisely what we observe in 2002. The only new event is the emergence of Samoobrona and the LPR to capture a share of the votes of those with little confidence in private enterprise and who are angry with the economic situation.

ANALYSIS OF PARTY SHIFTS

Analysis of the choices of individual voters is only part of the story of electoral politics between 1997 and 2001. The second part is the disintegration and restructuring of the parties across the political spectrum and the ultimate allocation of seats given the party vote shares. This discussion examines the stability and shifts of the parties' vote shares. We

---

6 Personal economic evaluations contribute to one's confidence in private versus state firms, but only as one among many factors. The simple correlations between the confidence and communism variables and personal evaluations are −0.15 and 0.11, respectively. The correlations with retrospective collective evaluations are both −0.01.

have just seen that voter choices were still made on the basis of preferences about policies related to the economy, to views on communism as a form of government, and to opinions about the political influence of the Catholic Church, as they were in previous elections. To continue the previous metaphor about the Polish electorate being an observing audience watching and interpreting the political theater being played out by costumed dancers on stage, we should see predictable shifts in party support. Unfortunately, data on the distribution of de novo firm and job creation are not available for 2001 so we cannot undertake the analysis of regional voting patterns done in Chapter 6. Our best, and only, alternative is to compare the regional patterns of party support in 2001 with those observed in 1997. The consistency among individual voters should produce predictable and systematic relationships between which parties did well or poorly in 1997 and their counterparts in 2001.

One expectation is stability in the votes for the continuing parties, such as the SLD/UP and the PSL. The other expectations are about which parties likely gained votes at the expense of the AWS and the UW. Given that the platforms of the PO in particular and the PiS to a lesser extent had elements of liberal economic policies and that the leaders of both parties had been active in the early reform governments, we could expect these parties to gain votes at the expense of the UW. The disintegration of the AWS suggests that its support is likely to be divided among several parties. Some voters can be expected to follow Płażyński's lead and go to the PO. The strongly Catholic elements are likely to move to the right-wing LPR Catholic party. The trade-union elements have the choice of staying with the remaining elements of the AWS; overcoming their aversions to a post-Communist party and vote for the SLD or PSL, which are closer to their economic positions; or not voting at all. Finally, Samoobrona is likely to split some of the previous PSL vote by virtue of its even more-radical arguments for subsidies and opposition to reforms. Samoobrona may also attract nonvoters in 1997 who felt alienated from all of the parties seriously contending in that election. What is important for our model is that these moves should be consistent and predictable rather than being purely random, as one would expect from an inattentive or blind audience.

We analyze these interparty movements by relating each contending party's share of the 2001 vote, including nonvoting, in each district to the shares received by each party competing in the 1997 election. This approach enables us to examine statistically if the support for each of the parties in the 1997 election is systematically related to parties' support in the 2001 election and how consistent these relationships are across districts. This method contains the well-known ecological regression fallacy so we are careful not to claim that these results represent the pattern of switching of individual voters. (See Achen and Shively, 1995, for an excellent and fairly recent discussion of these difficulties.) What we hope to infer from these results is whether regional variables that were strongly related to 1997 votes, as we found in Chapter 6, might also be related to 2001 votes. For example, in 1997 the UW vote share was larger in areas with high levels of de novo job creation. If these areas are also likely to continue to have a higher proportion of employment in new firms, as we suggest in the previous section, then the economically liberal parties such as the UW and the PO should do well in these districts in 2001. And, conversely, for regions with low levels of de novo economic activity, they would be more likely to vote for the SLD/UP or the AWSP. These are only inferences, however, and possibly weak ones at that.

We model the vote returns for each of the 2001 parties, as well as the proportion not voting, as functions of the vote shares for each party in 1997, and the proportion not voting. Let V_{ij} denote the vote share for party j in district i in 2001 and V_{ik} the votes for party k in that district in 1997. The 2001 parties represented by index j are SLD/UP, AWSP, UW, PO, PiS, LPR, PSL, SRP, and Other plus No Vote.[7] The 1997 parties indexed by k are SLD+UP, AWS, UW, PSL, ROP, Other (OTR), and No Vote. (Because the SLD and the UP merged before the 2001 election, we combine their votes in the 1997 election to create a comparable "party.") Dropping the i subscript for convenience, the basic statistical model for V_j is,

$$V_j = B_{j,SLD+UP} V_{SLD+UP} + B_{j,AWS} V_{AWS} + B_{j,UW} V_{UW}$$
$$+ B_{j,PSL} V_{PSL} + B_{j,ROP} V_{ROP} + B_{j,OTR} + B_{No\ Vote} V_{No\ Vote} + U_j.$$

$$(8.1)$$

The coefficient B_{jk} indicates the relationship between party j's share of the vote in 2001 and party k's share in 1997. If j and k are the same party, the coefficient indicates how well the party did at holding onto its share

7 We omit the votes for the two German ethnic parties in both 1997 and 2001. In 2001 these votes are concentrated in three districts and constitute 0.42 percent of the national vote. Their inclusion would overstate the stability of voting in the Other category given the composition and concentration of these two parties. With these omissions in 2001 the Other category received only .6 percent of the vote nationally while in 1997 7.5 percent of the voters chose one of the Other parties.

of the vote. A value of 0.2, for example, would indicate the party held onto only a fifth of its previous share while a value of 1.0 would indicate that its 2002 share maintained its 1997 share. If j and k refer to different parties, the coefficient indicates what proportion of k's vote share went to party j. The individual coefficients are constrained in two ways. First, they must be positive. Party j cannot get a negative proportion of party k's vote share. Second, when the coefficients for party k are summed across all J equations, the sum must equal 1 as we have an exhaustive list of possible parties and shares must sum to 1. The U_j indicates how the actual share for party j deviates from that predicted on the basis of the party shares in 1997. The U_j's are not independent across equations as the vote shares sum to 1. To accommodate this fact, estimation of Equation 8.1 is done using a seemingly unrelated regression model. Lastly, a dummy variable denoting if the district is the home district of a party's leader is included in the equation for that party. The results in Table 8.5 show that voters in these districts are more likely to vote for that party than the systematic part of the model predicts, and this pattern is likely to be evident in the aggregate data as well.

The analysis is a bit complicated as the 2001 election districts differ from the ones in 1997. In most cases the new districts are combinations of previous districts so it is possible to aggregate the 1997 votes to measure accurately the party shares in the 1997 election, which are the explanatory variables in equations interpreting the 2001 vote shares.[8] In one case we had to combine 2001 districts in order to obtain a proper match to 1997 districts. The net result is that there are thirty-eight districts to use in this analysis.

The results are presented in Table 8.7. The blank cells indicate where we infer there is no relationship between the 1997 and 2001 votes, either because the coefficient does not satisfy the nonnegativity constraint or because the coefficient is smaller than its standard error. The estimated equations are shown in the columns and can be interpreted as indicating where a 2001 party picked up votes. For example, the SLD/UP kept virtually its share of the 1997 vote and drew voters who had voted for the AWS and nonvoters in 1997. The R^2 values in the last row indicate that

---

8 It is not possible to disaggregate the 2001 districts to match the 1997 districts, although this method is preferable for statistical purposes. This procedure leaves errors associated with mismatches among districts on the left-hand side and keeps the right-hand-side variables without error. Our procedure introduces these errors into the right-hand-side variables, the consequence of which is attenuated coefficients, the classic errors-in-variables problem.

Table 8.7. *Transition of Vote Shares for the 1997 to 2001 Elections*

1997 Parties	2001 Parties								
	SLD/UP	AWSP	UW	PO	PiS	LPR	PSL	SRP	N Vote
SLD/UP	0.99		0.01						
	(0.01)		(0.01)						
AWS	0.07	0.13	0.01	0.08	0.07	0.17	0.08		0.38
	(0.02)	(0.02)	(0.01)	(0.02)	(0.02)	(0.01)	(0.01)		(0.03)
UW			0.17	0.55	0.28				
			(0.01)	(0.03)	(0.03)				
ROP					0.55	0.45			
					(0.07)	(0.07)			
PSL							0.81	0.19	
							(0.03)	(0.03)	
Other		0.12		0.25				0.22	0.41
		(0.08)		(0.12)				(0.15)	(0.21)
N Vote	0.05							0.06	0.89
	(0.01)							(0.01)	(0.01)
Leader's district	0.92	2.14	0.72	4.88	1.95	−1.50	1.85	4.15	
	(0.76)	(0.37)	(0.20)	(0.41)	(0.40)	(0.51)	(0.69)	(0.61)	
R^2	0.91	0.65	0.89	0.90	0.78	0.67	0.88	0.63	0.82

Note: Small sample standard errors in parentheses below coefficients.

the 1997 vote shares do a good job of predicting the 2001 vote shares, suggesting that the transition rates are consistent across voting districts.

The row entries are of particular interest as they indicate how a party's share of the 1997 vote is expected to be distributed in 2001. The two post-Communist parties, particularly the SLD, do an excellent job of holding onto their voters. Ninety-nine percent of the SLD plus UP share in 1997 remains with the combined SLD/UP party in 2001. A statistically significant but meager 1 percent is predicted to become part of the UW share.[9] No other party exhibits that level of stability. For the PSL, over 80 percent of its 1997 share remains in 2001.

The AWS and UW collapses are very evident in these results, although the UW share contributes strongly to the liberal bloc in 2001. In an average district, the UW is expected to keep 16.8 percent of its 1997 vote, with 55.2 percent going to the PO and 27.9 percent to the PiS, meaning that districts that voted strongly for the UW in 1997 also voted overwhelmingly for a liberal party in 2001. The PiS also shared some of the UW's

---

9 The estimated coefficient is 0.013 with a standard error of 0.006, which rounds to the values shown in Table 8.7.

views about government management and spending, though it disagreed about international economic policy. The interesting speculation is what the liberal share would have been if these parties, and particularly the UW and the PO, had not competed against each other, reminiscent of the division between the UD and the KLD in 1993.

The splintering of the AWS shares among almost all parties shows its fragile composition. Its 2001 share was only 13 percent of its 1997 share in an average district. The largest fraction of its share, 38.4 percent, contributed to the nonvoting bloc. Otherwise, as one might expect from a party that was a weak coalition of very disparate groups in the first place, its 1997 share is very widely distributed among the other parties. The LPR got an even larger share of the 1997 AWS vote than did the remaining AWS faction. Smaller fractions are distributed equally between the SLD/UP, PiS, PO, and PSL. Most of these distributions reflect the elements that constituted the 1997 AWS coalition – the church, trade unions, and a small set of the Solidarność liberals, such as Płażyński, who had originally stayed with the AWS rather than the UD/UW but then moved to the PO.

Lastly, we can see the base for the rise of the far right-wing parties, the LPR and Samoobrona. The LPR inherited a large bloc of voters from the AWS, presumably the set of conservative Catholic voters who wanted a government with closer ties to the Catholic Church. The LPR also gained a significant share of the ROP vote, which was also a very conservative party. Samoobrona attracted about 19 percent of the PSL share from 1997. This outcome is expected, given Lepper's efforts to attract the most radical and angry individuals who feel excluded and threatened by the continuing reforms, a group that includes many farmers. Samoobrona's other systematic source of votes was from the nonvoters in 1997 and those who had voted for one of the fringe parties in that election, both of which likely include many of the people angriest about the reforms and most alienated from mainstream parties.

The results suggest a high level of cohesion in the support given to each party, despite the chaotic nature of the party leadership. There is great consistency across regions in how the 1997 votes divided among the parties contesting the 2001 election, as evidenced by the good statistical fits. This consistency along with the previous results supports two important conclusions. First, Polish voters' choices are based on the same set of issues and concerns that we first saw in the 1993 election. Furthermore, despite the instability among the post-Solidarity parties and their leaders, the voters are quite consistent in their ordering of the parties relative to their own preferences. Those who support economically liberal policies are very likely to vote for the same party, even though the particular party changes from election to election. They are not Aldrich et al.'s blind audience. Second, the regional consistency in economic conditions shown in Table 8.3 and the voting consistency seen in Table 8.7 suggest that areas that maintained their base of de novo employment continued to vote for liberal parties, and conversely that those areas not benefiting from this activity voted against them. The difficulty facing the liberal parties is the slowing of the rate of entry and survival of new firms relative to the mid-1990s.

VOTES AND SEAT ALLOCATIONS

The last question is how the vote distributions in the 2001 election translated into seat shares in the new parliament. In spring 2001, barely six months before the parliamentary election and with the polls showing the lack of support for the AWS, the AWS managed to pass an election law reform that dramatically altered the rules for allocating seats following the 2001 election. As discussed in Chapter 7, the rules in place in 1993 and 1997 favored the larger parties and parties doing well in small districts, which at the time primarily meant the PSL. The reforms passed by the AWS with the support of the smaller parties in the Sejm changed both the districts and the allocation formula. Instead of fifty-two districts ranging in magnitude from three to seventeen seats as in 1997, in the 2001 election there were forty-one districts with a range of seats from seven to nineteen. The reforms also eliminated the national list of sixty-nine seats allocated to parties with more than 7 percent of the vote. Lastly, the seat allocation rule was changed from the d'Hondt formula to the Sainte-Laguë formula. As discussed in Chapter 7 the former is one of the least proportional ways to allocate seats, whereas the latter is one of the most proportional, though the modified form adopted by the parliament is not as proportional as the pure Sainte-Laguë rule. An obvious consequence of moving to larger districts and use of the Sainte-Laguë rule is to benefit the smaller parties at the expense of the larger parties. Elimination of the national list again was expected to favor the smaller parties who in the past did not reach the 7 percent threshold even if they passed the 5 percent threshold required to receive any seats.[10] The consolidation of

10 This distinction between the 5 and 7 percent thresholds and the ability to get seats from the national list did not affect coalitions, as distinguished from parties, as coalitions were required to get more than 8 percent of the national vote to obtain any seats.

Table 8.8. *Alternative Seat Allocations, 2001*

	Sainte-Laguë	d'Hondt	Gain/Loss
SLD/UP	216	243	+27
PO	65	63	−2
SRP	53	46	−7
PiS	44	41	−3
PSL	42	36	−6
LPR	38	29	−9
German ethnic	2	2	0
Total	460	460	

the small rural districts would presumably disadvantage the PSL. The SLD/UP vociferously opposed the reforms but was not able to prevent their passage, and President Kwaśniewski presumably could have vetoed the bill but chose not to.

The question is how might the seat allocations differ had there been no electoral reform. It is straightforward to use the d'Hondt formula to allocate the seats in each district given the actual vote returns. Even allowing for strategic voting it is hard to see how changing the seat allocation formula would have altered the individual vote choices. We can then compare the seat allocations under the two allocation formulas. The critical question is whether the SLD/UP might have won an outright majority using the d'Hondt rule, whereas they fell fifteen seats short of a majority with the current rules. We cannot explore the consequence of creating fewer and larger districts because we do not have vote returns according to the previous districts. We also do not explore the consequences of eliminating the national list by trying to simulate seat distributions if the list had remained as we do not try to ascertain what the district magnitudes would have been with sixty-nine fewer seats to be allocated among the districts.

Table 8.8 shows the seat allocations under the different allocation rules. The first column is the actual allocation using the Sainte-Laguë formula. This method left the SLD/UP fifteen seats short of a majority and led to including the PSL in a coalition government. Use of the d'Hondt formula with the same districts would have given the SLD/UP an outright majority by twelve seats and eliminated the need for a coalition government. The SLD/UP gains would have reduced the seat shares of all the other parties but especially the two far-right parties, Samoobrona and LPR, who collectively would have sixteen fewer seats.

As we concluded at the end of Chapter 7, the institutional rules used to determine the seat allocations, given the vote distributions, are critical. In the 2001 election the choice of a formula was far more important than in 1993 and 1997. Use of the d'Hondt rule would have given the SLD/UP a pure majority and avoided the need for a coalition with the PSL. In terms of representation of a middle-class, economically liberal constituency, this difference is important. The SLD/UP's policies, as articulated before the election, are oriented more toward new and small firms than is the case for most other parties (PO and the UW are exceptions). The SLD/UP also has its electoral strength in the urban areas where the de novo economy is clustered. The 2001 election presents the opposite conclusion from 1993. In 1993 a more-proportional seat allocation rule would have benefited the economically liberal UD, given its relatively small size and concentration in the larger districts. In 2001 the less proportional d'Hondt rule would have benefited the neoliberal SLD/UP, given its size and geographic concentration.

SUMMARY

This chapter examines the events and changes occurring after 1997, which show a sharply different direction to Poland's development, to examine whether the conclusions reached in earlier chapters are limited to the early phase of the transition. The answer to this question is, we believe, that the changes after 1997 are consistent with the model. This answer is justified on two grounds, despite the far more limited data. The direct response follows from the analysis in this chapter. The increase in Polish unemployment and the decrease in the rate of GDP growth after 1998 can be attributed at least partially to the deferral of restructuring and the slowing of de novo firm creation. Besides the aggregate data on restructuring and new-firm creation, the evidence of the relatively better performance of regional economies where firm creation had been strong previously and where there were fewer remaining state-owned firms also supports this view. Thus, the conclusions reached in Chapter 3 that de novo firm creation is a critical factor in determining the speed and success of transition applies to the succeeding period as well.

A second reason for a no answer to the question of whether the model is limited to transitional economies is found in the evidence from mature market economies. These economies continually face challenges that require restructuring and transitions. In those economies as well, the Schumpeterian view of economic development as an evolutionary process of creative destruction is very evident. Caballero and Hammour (1994 and 2000) make this point. There is also detailed evidence from the

United States and particularly the state of Michigan that de novo firm creation plays a critical role in the development and transition in these economies. (On the Michigan and Polish comparison, see Jackson et al., 1999, and on the Michigan case, Jackson, 1998.) The Polish case then continues to be an example, albeit an extreme one, of the how market economies evolve and how our model helps us to understand this evolutionary process.

There is also continuity in the political model. The evidence offered by the 2001 election offers further evidence for our contention that a successful economic transition, built on de novo firm creation, creates the basis for and is closely tied to the successful political transition. The evidence from the 1991 to 1997 elections is that the growth of this de novo economy stimulated a liberal political constituency that voted strongly for centrist, liberal parties. Despite the very fluid nature of Polish parties, voters continued to sort out the various parties and to vote for ones that are consistent with their assessments on the direction that reforms should take. After 1998 elites abandoned the UW and the AWS to form new parties, and the consistency of voting patterns between the 1997 and the 2001 elections suggests the voters followed the ideological positions of these new parties, just as they had in deciding how to vote for their predecessors.

The policies and statements of the SLD in its evolution from 1991 to 1997, in its 2001 campaign as the SLD/UP, and as the lead party in the post-2001 government provide support for the broader proposition in our electoral model. This party has moved substantially away from its anti-market, prosubsidy positions of the early 1990s to openly and strongly embrace market principles and the need to stimulate de novo firm creation. As suggested earlier, this may well be a rational response to the empirical evidence and economic arguments about the sources of job creation and growth in the Polish economy. We contend that this policy shift is facilitated, if not stimulated, by the growth of the economically liberal constituency created by the de novo economy. As this constituency expands, which it clearly has in Poland, competing parties will need to adopt policies that attract these voters, and the expansion of this constituency makes it easy for one or more of the competing parties to offer liberal policies to compete with the traditional liberal parties. This political evolution in historically antireform parties is an important prediction of our model as well as a key element in how countries can pursue economic and political reforms simultaneously.

9

The Political Economy of Transition

Why Poland?

We began with the question, Why Poland? The answer in Chapter 1 was based on comparing the pace and early success of the Polish reforms, both economic and political, with those of other transitional countries. The comparisons suggested that Poland was a relative success, at least in the initial years, and that we could learn important lessons about transitions from studying the Polish transformation in detail. This chapter addresses the same question, but with a different meaning. We can now interpret the question in terms of what factors explain Poland's relative success. We have observed and analyzed in great detail the more and less successful aspects and consequences of Poland's transition. According to this interpretation, the answers are unique in some respects but broadly general in others. The challenge is to examine factors contributing to the Polish transition in the context of other political economies in Central and Eastern Europe.

LESSONS FROM THE POLITICAL ECONOMY OF TRANSITION

The answer begins with the two main lessons from our study. Our analysis suggests that Schumpeter's model of economic development, though nearly a century old, is applicable in a broad range of settings. Successful development and transitions depend on what he called the creative destruction process in which firms with outdated technologies, organizational structures, or products are replaced by new enterprises embodying new forms. The presence and growth of these new enterprises stimulates a political constituency that supports liberal policies and continued economic reform. This constituency influences policy both directly by voting for parties likely to pursue liberal policies and indirectly by constraining the actions of other parties who might otherwise be less favorable to liberal policies. The Polish case, during the early parts of the transition in the early and mid-1990s and in its later phases since 1997, illustrates both parts and their interconnections.

The Economics of Transition

Models of transition rely on the creation of a new private sector that is presumed to be more efficient, productive, and consumer-oriented than the old state sector. A major distinction is in the assumptions about the origins of this private sector. In one version it is created by the privatization of state firms. In the second the private sector arises from the entrance of new enterprises. Kornai (2000) refers to these as the accelerated privatization and organic methods, respectively. The emphasis in the latter is on the entrance of de novo enterprises, with state firms being sold outright when possible and closed when not. In reality, transitions entail both processes, but countries can be characterized by the relative emphasis on and the amount of de novo firm creation. Accelerated privatization, characterized by mass privatization plans and management takeovers, was followed most notably in the Czech Republic and Russia.[1] Kornai offers Poland and Hungary as examples of organic transitions. Other transitional countries, such as Slovenia, the Baltic countries, Slovakia, and parts of the former Soviet Union provide examples of varying mixes of these two methods. The evidence suggests that in all these countries, regardless of the strategy, de novo firm creation is the major source of job creation and thus is the major determinant of the speed and success of the transition. When de novo job creation, as a proportion of the work force is low, as apparently is true in Russia and Ukraine, the speed and eventual success of the transition is in doubt. Even the Czech Republic, noted for its accelerated mass privatization, had a relatively high level of de novo firm and job creation, as noted in Tables 1.3 and 1.4.

The faster jobs can be created in the de novo sector, the faster labor being shed in the less-productive state sector can be absorbed into more-productive jobs in the private sector. (See Johnson and Loveman, 1995, and Winiecki, 2000, for similar arguments also using the Polish case.) Simply privatizing the old sector is not a sufficient strategy. Those firms lose jobs and sales as rapidly as the state firms, do not necessarily become more productive, and thus are not a source of job and income creation. Laid-off

---

1 Poland eventually had its mass privatization program; however, Table 1.2 shows that the rate of privatization in Poland lagged that in other transitional countries.

workers must be absorbed by new enterprises, or become unemployed. We believe the evidence is very strong that to be successful in a transition, there must be high rates of creation, survival, and growth of de novo firms.

The Electoral Politics of Transition

The second part of our argument is that the creation of the de novo sector stimulates a liberal constituency that favors economic and political reforms and that votes for centrist, liberal parties. This centrist bloc reduces support for both left-wing and far-right parties, as we saw in Chapters 5 and 6, as Fidrmuc (2000a and 2000b) shows for other Central European countries and as Frye (2002) shows for Russia. Several important implications follow from this observation. Debates about the speed of transition and whether it can or should proceed rapidly or slowly often include a political argument about how much opposition and support there will be for continuing the reforms. This opposition and support derives from the employment and unemployment levels in the various sectors. We argue that in both its economic and political dimensions the speed of transition must take into account the rate with which new firms can be created and can grow into healthy enterprises. The faster this de novo sector can be created, the faster the economy will grow and the larger the bloc of centrist, liberal voters who will provide support for the reforming incumbent party or parties.

There is a second, and possibly more important, way the growth of the new economic sector and its associated political activities pressures the government to maintain more liberal policies. The larger this centrist bloc of liberal voters, the more constrained other parties will be in how far they can move from the center and still be politically viable. Electoral politics in all of the transforming countries are more complicated than described by a simple spatial model because the issue space is multidimensional and because there are more than two competing parties. Thus, bold predictions that parties will be forced to move to the center are too strong, particularly as the leaders and activists in these parties often have ideological views that are expressed in party platforms. Nonetheless, even with multiple dimensions and multiple parties there remain penalties for parties that move too far from the center. This will be particularly true for the larger, more pragmatic parties that hope to win a large bloc of seats in the parliament.[2]

---

2 See Cox, 1990, and Merrill and Adams, 2002, for models that predict that as the density of voters in the center increases, parties will move toward this center, even in multiparty elections.

One of the surprising aspects of the democratic reforms in the region has been the resurgence of the post-Communist parties. These parties have been effective political organizations in Poland, Hungary, the Slovak Republic, Russia, and other former Soviet states. In some of these countries they have constituted the largest parliamentary bloc at times and have been the lead party in the governing coalition on several occasions. Several have also become more liberal in their economic policies, proposing to support new and small enterprises and, in the case of the Hungarian MSzP and SLD in Poland, have even discussed reducing the capital-gains taxes as a way to stimulate economic growth. In the SLD party congress of June 2003 Leszek Miller, the head of the SLD government, explicitly referred to the liberal roots of the SLD economic program. These post-Communist parties are not your mothers', or your grandmothers', Marxists. Such transformations of the former Communist parties have not occurred in countries such as Russia and Ukraine, for example.

There are numerous explanations for why some of these post-Communist parties become more liberal economically, but at the core of these explanations is that their leaders forced the parties to become more pragmatic and to appeal to a broader set of voters. (For an excellent description of this resurgence in Poland and Hungary but not in the Czech Republic, see Grzymała-Busse, 2002.) A large part of the pressure on these parties was to maintain the political liberalizations, which were broadened to include economic liberalization. The pressures to produce economic growth and to reduce unemployment and the incentives and pressures from international institutions such as the International Monetary Fund, World Bank, and the EBRD surely contributed to this pragmatism as well. (On the role of the IMF, see Stone, 2002.) We contend, however, that an important contributor to this pragmatism is the development of the liberal economic constituency. In transitional countries such as Ukraine and Russia, where there is relatively little de novo firm creation, these constituencies did not reach a sufficient size to constrain the nonliberal parties. The Communist parties in Russia and other former Soviet states remain both ideologically intact and electorally viable.

The Czech Republic offers an important contrast to the Polish and Hungarian cases and to the Russian case. The Czech post-Communist party remains weak and uncompetitive in contrast to those in the other countries. Grzymała-Busse explains these differences by showing that the Czech Communist Party has retained its ideological orientation, not choosing to adapt to the new economic and political circumstances, as did the parties in Poland and Hungary. But, because of the success of the transition, this ideological orientation has not attracted Czech voters as has the Russian Communist Party. These four countries, Poland, Hungary, the Czech Republic, and Russia, succinctly illustrate our claims about the critical role played by de novo firms in successful economic and political transitions.

FACTORS IN A SUCCESSFUL TRANSITION

Successful transitions both economically and politically, as observed in Poland during the 1990s, require the entry of new enterprises. These new enterprises provide everything from more consumer-oriented products, to new organizational structures and cultures, higher productivity, and employment for those in the labor force who can adapt to the new organizations and technologies. The new enterprises and the economic development associated with them stimulate centrist political constituencies that vote for liberal parties and that constrain the platforms and policies of other parties that need to compete for votes. It was when this entry of new firms slowed after 1998 that the Polish transition began to falter, with rising unemployment and growing support for nonliberal parties. This discussion and explanation for Poland's success during the 1990s and difficulties in the 2000s narrow the focus on Poland's sucess to the more specific queries of why Poland had such success in stimulating and growing new enterprises and what we can learn from its experience.

Numerous factors are part of Poland's success and offer instructive lessons for transitions in other countries, not just for Central and Eastern Europe and the former Soviet Union. The factors can be grouped into several broad categories – policies, institutions, and attitudes – going from the most proximate and relatively easiest to alter to the most distant and difficult to change.

Economic Policies

The so-called Washington Consensus, characterized by the phrase stabilize, liberalize, and privatize, guided much of the initial policy making in the transitional countries and was used to justify the arguments for rapid transitions, or the so-called shock therapy. Although grouped together as if this is a single proscription, it actually consists of many different policies, both macroeconomic and microeconomic. This is not the place to try to contribute one more piece to what is now an extensive literature debating the appropriateness of these policies (see Kołodko, 2000, and

Table 9.1. *Annual and Cumulative Inflation*

	Country						
Year	Czech Republic	Estonia	Hungary	Poland	Russia	Slovak Republic	Ukraine
0	9.5	1,069.0	28.6	585.8	1,353.0	10.0	1,210.0
1	56.5	89.0	34.8	70.3	895.9	61.2	4,734.9
2	11.1	47.7	22.8	43.0	302.0	10.0	891.2
3	20.8	28.9	22.4	35.3	190.1	23.0	376.4
4	10.0	23.1	18.8	32.2	47.8	13.4	80.2
5	9.1	11.3	28.3	27.9	14.7	9.9	15.9
6	8.8	8.2	23.5	19.9	27.7	5.8	10.6
7	8.4	3.3	18.3	15.1	85.7	6.1	22.7
8	10.7	4.0	14.4	11.7	20.8	6.7	28.2
Cumulative[a]	3.29	5.73	5.16	8.59	563.83	3.26	8,287.57

[a] Year 1 = 1.00.

Roland, 2000), but we want to add a few observations drawn from our analysis. Poland is cited as having pursued the most vigorous form of shock therapy, and some use its success as justification for the approach, so it is fitting that we relate our findings to this set of policies.

Stabilization. Getting control of the macroeconomy was a central aspect of the reforms in Poland and in other transitional countries. Reducing the budget deficit to a few percentage points of GDP and controlling the money supply were seen as necessary to control inflation and create positive real interest rates. It worked in the Polish case and in several other countries, such as the Czech Republic, Hungary, and Estonia. Inflation declined monotonically, leading to a much more certain price regime in these countries. Stone (2002) claims, by contrast, that the Russian government never met the budget and monetary targets, which led to high levels and fluctuations in inflation. Table 9.1 shows the CPI inflation rates for these transitional countries, beginning with their first year after the transition. (This is 1990 for Hungary, Poland, the Czech and Slovak republics and 1992 for Estonia, Russia, and Ukraine.) The last line shows the price index in the eighth year of the transition, with year one as the base.

Hungary and the Czech and Slovak republics inherited stable price regimes at the beginning of the transition, which they maintained. The other countries, by contrast, started the transition with very high inflation levels, largely due to efforts by previous regimes to maintain artificially low prices for basic commodities. These countries also inherited much larger foreign debts from the Communist regimes, which further limited their policy options and flexibility. Poland and Estonia, in contrast to Russia and Ukraine, by virtue of very stringent fiscal and monetary policies got inflation under control, leading to workable levels, with the expectation that inflation would continue to decline. There are many advantages to stable, not just predictable, price levels in a transitional economy. One, however, has to be its effect on people's ability to obtain credit and their willingness to make the financial investments to begin new firms.

Liberalization. Another of the fundamentals in all the transitions is liberalization. It applied directly to freeing prices, so that they became a true measure of the values of goods and services and to setting exchange rates, so that the price of the domestic currency relative to foreign currencies reflected the true differences in the respective economies. Liberalizing exchange rates also introduced effective and fairly immediate foreign competition for domestic producers, which produced the predictable political criticisms. Once prices reflect actual values and are the result of market-clearing forces, they can operate as a signaling mechanism, inducing investments in activities where there is a shortage of supply and reducing investments and resource allocation to activities not in demand. Table 9.2 shows EBRD price and trade and currency liberalization ratings of several transitional countries. In the most successful transitions, such as Poland, Hungary, Estonia, and the Czech Republic, price and currency liberalization took place quite rapidly and effectively. In parts of the former Soviet Union, Ukraine, and the Slovak Republic, this was less often the case, with governments continuing to try to set some prices, particularly in basic commodities such as energy. As with stabilization, it is hard to picture a successful entrepreneurial economy where prices are distorted and do not function as signals for investors and those starting businesses.

Table 9.2. *EBRD Indices of Price and Trade and Currency Liberalization*

	Country						
Index[a]	Czech Republic	Estonia	Hungary	Poland	Russia	Slovak Republic	Ukraine
Prices[a]	0.76	0.86	0.86	0.78	0.63	0.55	0.49
Trade and currency	0.94	0.94	0.96	0.96	0.74	0.92	0.45

[a] Index normalized to 0 = poorest and 1 = strongest performance.
Source: European Bank for Reconstruction and Development, 1999.

Privatization. In the third leg of the early reform triad, the idea was that rapid privatization of the existing state-owned industries would create an immediate private sector. These enterprises would then be subject to the discipline of the market, particularly if prices were liberalized, forcing them to adapt to new conditions and to become more efficient and consumer-oriented. In most instances, this meant laying off large numbers of workers, as these organizations were badly overstaffed.

Rates of privatization varied greatly among the transitional countries, with Poland lagging most others (see Table 1.2). On net, this delay may be only a small problem as it helps avoid some of the serious problems associated with privatization. These are problems of monopolization, partial reform, and insider manipulations. (See Alexeev, 1999, for a theoretical discussion on this point, and Kornai, 2000, for a more policy-oriented discussion.) Much of Hellman's partial reform trap is associated with the behavior of the managers and owners of the privatized firms, who then act to protect the rents obtained because the privatized firms often are effective monopolies. Insider manipulations and associated fraudulent behavior are found in all the privatization programs and particularly in those that depend on manager and worker ownership and control. Both partial reform and fraudulent insider manipulations are very evident in Russia and some of the former Soviet states. The Czech Republic, with its heavy dependence on privatization through existing management suffered from extensive insider activity and poor corporate governance as well. Hungary avoided some of these problems as its privatization strategy depended more heavily on selling the former state firms to outsiders, particularly foreign buyers. Poland had its instances of alleged fraud associated with privatization; the privatization of the Bank Slaski was a well-publicized case, though given the smaller amount of privatization, the total amount of fraudulent behavior was less. The evidence in Table 1.2 and Kornai's discussion suggest that privatization is not necessarily required, nor is it by itself a path to a successful transition.

What is more important than privatization per se is the ending of implicit and explicit subsidies to the state firms and forcing either adaptation or closure. To quote Kornai (2000, p. 7), "The budget constraint on companies has to be hardened.... the 'trinity' of privatizaton, liberalization, and stabilization will not suffice for a successful transition. Hardening the budget constraint has equal priority with these." As we noted in Chapter 8, part of Poland's current economic crisis is the result of having continued and then expanded the subsidies for certain sectors with large state enterprises and delaying the necessary restructuring and even closures. Restructuring and privatizing the financial sector pose a special set of problems, which we discuss subsequently.

Tax Policy. There is no consensus about how tax policy affects entrepreneurial activity. (See Bruce and Mohsin, 2003, and Gentry and Hubbard, 2002, for summaries of the evidence.) There are very strongly held views on this relationship, often both ideological and heavily tinged with self-interest. Issues such as the capital-gains tax and marginal tax rates have received considerable attention, and we will not delve into them here. Two critical points should be noted: the effect of wage taxes on job creation, and the horizontal equity and administration of the tax system itself. Employment taxes raise the effective wage rate paid by a firm and may seriously restrict labor flexibility and be particularly hard on new enterprises. For example, Poland currently imposes a variety of taxes that amount to close to a 50 percent tax on all wages. These taxes significantly reduce the incentives for and ability of new and smaller firms to take on additional workers.[3]

Not surprisingly hiring by de novo firms is sensitive to the total labor cost. In Jackson's (2003) simulation model of the speed of transition, increases in total labor costs sharply reduced the employment in new firms and the speed of transition. Tichit (2003) shows a significant negative relationship between the unemployment level early in the transition and the speed and success of the transition. An important part of the dynamics is that with a competitive labor market, higher unemployment drives down wages and labor costs. These lower costs make new firms more profitable, which in the long run enables them to grow and to hire more workers, which ultimately drives the wage rate up. The results shown in Figure 3.5 and Tables 3A.8 to 3A.9 show that wages are initially low in all cohorts of new firms, but among the surviving and growing firms and particularly among those with high productivity and rising sales, wages increase at a sufficient rate to catch up to wages in older and larger firms.

We could not find comprehensive data on payroll taxes among the transitional countries, so it is hard to know how to compare them. Carey and Tchilinguirian (2000) estimate taxes on labor for the period 1991 to 1997 for a set of OECD countries following a methodology proposed by Mendoza, Razin, and Tesar (1994). The Czech Republic, Hungary, and

---

3 In Poland, at least, this is a contributing factor to a gray labor market where people work but are not officially employed. It also raises the amount of self-employment as firms will contract out various tasks, particularly professional services, to individuals on a temporary and piecework basis.

Poland were all estimated to have an average effective tax rate on labor of about 0.42. This compares with the OECD average of 0.37, a European Union average of 0.43, and rates in the United States and Japan of about 0.27. The transitional countries' rates match those of the European Union, which is known for its labor market rigidity, but are higher than other industrialized countries.

A second critical aspect of tax policy is that it must be horizontally equitable, fully and fairly administered, and compliance must be very high with no exceptions for arrears and nonpayment. We talk subsequently about the need for an effective government and various public services. None of this is possible without adequate revenue. Horizontal equity, effective administration, and compliance are obvious needs on normative grounds and have been standard in the public-finance literature for a long time. They are also necessary to avoid serious distortions in the economy that arise when economic decisions become geared to tax avoidance rather than to market incentives. We do not have data on tax arrears, for example, but they have become substantial in many of the transitional countries, Russia most notably. These arrears, most heavily concentrated in the current and former state-owned firms, are simply a continuation of soft budget constraints and retard the transition. They also effectively rob the government of revenues needed to provide public goods, such as education, physical infrastructure, and a legal system.

What is missing from the so-called Washington Consensus model is any recognition of the dynamics of transition economies. The policies grouped under this theme take the economic structure as given and focus solely on transforming this structure, with most of the attention paid to macroeconomic variables, such as deficits and the money supply. There is no reference in these policies to the need or methods for stimulating new-firm creation. (See Murrell, 1992, for a strong critique of the shock-therapy approach on these grounds.) Yet, one of the important lessons from the transitional economies is the dynamic nature of the process, with old firms being replaced by new, more productive firms following the Schumpeterian process.

Institutional Factors

A common refrain among some writers during discussions of transitions was that it was important to get the institutions right. There are three institutions that are critical to "get right." At the top of the list is a legal system that can insure property rights and provide legitimate protection for emerging businesses. A second set of institutions is the finance sector. Access to financing is critical to new enterprises, and how financial institutions are structured and administered will have considerable effects on this access. Lastly, legitimate, well-functioning, noncorrupt governments at both the national and local levels are necessary for a successful transition. Legitimate and effective governments are central parts of the first two institutions, and they are important in their own right as they are the primary providers of vital public goods.

Property Rights and Legal Institutions. The existence and enforcement of property rights is central to the development of a market economy (Johnson, McMillan, and Woodruff, 2000), and writers early in the transition process made this point very strongly (Litwack, 1991, and Riker and Weimer, 1993). But it is easier to make these arguments than to implement them, as many transitional countries discovered. Some of the problems are historical, as countries may lack the foundation for the type of property rights and legal structures best suited for a market economy. (See Sachs and Pistor, 1997, for an explanation for Russia's difficulties on this score.)

The EBRD and other organizations have produced a number of ordinal measures ranking transitional countries on their legal environments. Johnson et al. (2000), for example, cite data presented in the *Central European Economic Review* (1998) based on rankings by a group of investment professionals. Table 9.3 shows ratings on the rule of law, as measured by Freedom House and the *Central European Economic*

Table 9.3. *Indices of Rule of Law and Legal Institutions*

Index	Country						
	Czech Republic	Estonia	Hungary	Poland	Russia	Slovak Republic	Ukraine
Rule of law[a]	0.92	0.79	0.88	0.92	0.46	0.50	0.50
Rule of law[b]	0.87	0.78	0.93	0.90	0.54	0.62	0.39
Legal institution[c]	1.00	0.96	0.93	0.93	0.47	0.58	0.28
Mean	0.93	0.84	0.91	0.92	0.49	0.57	0.39
Uphold contracts[d]	0.46	0.21	0.23	0.22	0.55	0.32	0.59

[a] Freedom House Index for rule of law (Karatnycky et al., 2001).
[b] *Central European Economic Review* (1998) rule of law index.
[c] EBRD factor score index on legal institutions.
[d] Percent disagree or strongly disagree that courts would uphold contract (EBRD, 1999).

Review, and an assessment of the strength of legal institutions, as evaluated by the EBRD. We also include EBRD data showing what proportion of managers in private firms strongly disagree or disagree that the legal system would uphold their contract and property rights in a dispute. Estonia, Hungary, and Poland rank close to the top on all measures. The Czech Republic shows more variation than Hungary and Poland on the first three measures and does not fare so well with regard to perceptions about upholding contracts. Nearly half the Czech respondents, compared with less than a quarter of those in the former three countries, disagree that courts would uphold a contract. There is a large gap between the first four countries and the Slovak Republic, whereas Ukraine gets uniformly low scores and is ranked at or very near the bottom among these countries. (To complete the comparison, the Asian republics in the former Soviet Union fare worse, with scores close to zero on all indices.) The not-so-surprising conclusion is that the pace and success of the transition are highly correlated with the commitment to the rule of law and with the integrity of the legal institutions.

Financial Reforms. Access to financing is routinely recognized as critical to the development of new businesses. (See Pissarides et al., 2003, though Johnson et al., 2000, see bank finance as important but less so than property rights.) The literature and evidence cited in Chapter 3 argue that access to financing for new firms is strongly related to the existence of locally based financial organizations. The word private must be added to this description. It is very important to privatize the financial sector, despite earlier claims that it is possibly better to avoid some of the problems of privatization. Governments' objective functions and information bases for learning about and evaluating de novo business investments are likely to be very different from those of private organizations, such as banks and investment firms. The Czech Republic is a good example of the consequences of not privatizing and decentralizing the banking sector. The Czech banks remained largely intact and continued to loan to the old state enterprises after privatization, incurring increasingly high levels of nonperforming loans. But, because the banks were still under state control, the state continued to fund the banks rather than let them fail. What this accomplished was simply the continuation of soft budget constraints for the privatized firms, with the funds now routed through the banks rather than coming directly from the government. This ultimately produced a banking crisis that was a large factor in the country's economic difficulties in the late 1990s.

Table 9.4. *EBRD Indices of Financial Reform*

Index	Country						
	Czech Republic	Estonia	Hungary	Poland	Russia	Slovak Republic	Ukraine
Banking	0.6	0.7	0.9	0.7	0.3	0.5	0.3
Nonbanking	0.6	0.6	0.7	0.7	0.2	0.4	0.3

Source: European Bank for Reconstruction and Development, 2002.

Rankings of the amount of bank and nonbank financial reform and liberalization in the transitional countries are produced by the EBRD, which are shown in Table 9.4. These indices consider bank solvency and privatization, amount of prudential regulation, and interest rate liberalization. Unfortunately, they do not evaluate the amount of geographic decentralization in the banking system, so we cannot assess how effective the financial system is likely to be at providing access to financing for new and emerging enterprises. But, to the extent that this index offers some insight into the restructuring of the financial sector, we see which countries have done well and others less so. Hungary ranks the highest, followed by Poland. The Czech Republic scores below these two countries and Estonia, which is consistent with its slowness to privatize and liberalize the banking sector. As with the other measures, Russia and Ukraine rate quite poorly.

Another important factor is how the banking industry is structured and regulated. The problem of bank failures and subsequent crises are well known in market economies, and all engage in some form of deposit insurance, bank auditing, supervision, and governance. The U.S. experience during the depression of the 1930s and Russia's experience in 1998 are good examples of how bank crises can precipitate even larger economic crises. In the 1990s Russia allowed a proliferation of independent banks, most of which were seriously undercapitalized and which eventually failed, contributing to the severity of the 1998 collapse and crisis. The need for deposit insurance and oversight does not mean the government should be bailing out banks or other financial institutions that make bad decisions. But there must be careful and honest auditing, publicly available information about the banks' performance, and security and insurance for depositors, all of which requires some form of public regulation and supervision.

Legitimate and Effective Governments. At the center of effective policies and institutions is an effective, legitimate, and transparent government.

Kaufman and Kraay (2002) report a strong positive correlation between per capita incomes and quality of governance. They further argue that the relationship from governance to incomes is much stronger than the reciprocal relationship from incomes to governance. This causal argument (independent of the second claim) should not be a surprise. An effective legal system and property rights, supervision of markets to prevent monopolization, the enforcement of contracts, the proper supervision of financial institutions to prevent securities fraud, and agencies to provide depository insurance all require a properly functioning government. In addition, governments must provide important public goods, such as physical infrastructure, education, and public conditions that meet basic standards.

The transitional countries have varied substantially in the quality, fairness, and openness of their governments. Table 9.5 shows the distribution of values on a number of indices measuring the quality of governmental services and administration. On the World Bank (1997) measures of overall efficiency in providing services and average efficiency ratings on four specific services (customs, roads, mail, and health services), Poland ranks among or at the top, with Ukraine holding a distant last place. On

Table 9.5. *Indices of Government Performance, Corruption, and Capture*

	Country						
Index	Czech Republic	Estonia	Hungary	Poland	Russia	Slovak Republic	Ukraine
Quality of services and administration							
World Bank[a]	0.43	0.45	0.44	0.44	0.38	0.36	0.30
Mean[b]	0.46	0.47	0.46	0.84	0.43	0.43	0.16
Administration[c]	0.67	0.63	0.71	0.71	0.29	0.38	0.23
Mean[d]	0.52	0.52	0.54	0.66	0.37	0.39	0.23
Corruption and quality of governance							
Corruption[e]	0.58	0.67	0.71	0.79	0.13	0.54	0.17
Corruption[f]	2.5	1.6	1.7	1.6	2.8	2.5	4.4
Capture[g]	0.11	0.10	0.07	0.12	0.32	0.24	0.32

[a] World Bank (1997) assessment of overall efficiency in providing services, 1996–97.
[b] Mean of World Bank (1997) assessments of efficiency in customs, roads, mail, health care.
[c] Freedom House (Karatnycky et al., 2001) assessment of government and public administration.
[d] Mean of a, b, and c.
[e] Inverted corruption index from Karatnycky et al. (2001).
[f] Percentage of revenues paid in bribes among sampled firms (Hellman et al., 2000).
[g] Hellman et al. (2000) rating of capture.

the Freedom House assessment of the quality of government and public administration, Poland and Hungary rate at the top with Russia and Ukraine at the bottom.

Quality and transparency of governance is a second important dimension. On a corruption index, Poland, Hungary, and Estonia receive the highest scores, Russia and Ukraine the lowest, with the Czech and Slovak Republics in the middle. Hellman et al. (2000) report a corruption index based on a survey of firms in transitional countries where managers estimated what proportion of revenues in firms like theirs were paid in unofficial payments to "get things done." Their ranking matches the Freedom House ranking fairly well, although the Czech Republic is closer to Russia and Slovakia, and Ukraine is ranked even lower. Russia and Ukraine rate uniformly poorly on all the quality of government scales done throughout the transitional period.

The comparative data as well as the temporal data for Poland support our argument about the importance of a noncorrupt and transparent government. Cross-sectionally there is a strong correlation between low levels of corruption and the success of the transition. The Polish government through the 1990s gets high ratings for efficiency and for a lack of corruption. This is the period when Poland was most successful at generating new firms and for the success of its transition generally. Beginning in 1998, however, the Transparency International ratings cited in Chapter 8 show a marked decline in the perception of corruption, both in absolute terms and compared with Hungary and Estonia. This is also the beginning of the decline in the entry of new firms and in overall growth and of rising unemployment.

Transitional countries face an ironical dilemma here. Governments must be strong enough to collect taxes, enforce laws, execute contracts, and fulfill other public duties. Successful execution of these functions requires a considerable amount of governmental power and influence and the ability to coerce the appropriate citizens. The government must also be strong enough to resist being captured by corporate economic interests. Hellman, Jones, and Kaufman have a series of papers documenting through survey data the amount of capture of governments in transitional countries. (See Hellman et al., 2000, for a good summary.) In high-capture states, economic interests exert a high degree of influence on the government and use their influence to maintain and/or create rents through the government's ability to restrict entry, to provide favorable contracts, and to do other favors. The last line in Table 9.5 shows the Hellman et al. ratings of our set of countries on their capture scale. Again, the rapidly transforming countries rank low (meaning low capture), whereas Russia and Ukraine are rated fairly high. The dilemma, of course, is that governments can become too powerful, to the point that they become the criminals and the economic predators. Frye and Schleifer (1997) nicely frame this as the contrast between invisible-hand and grabbing-hand governments. They illustrate the difference by contrasting the experiences of shopkeepers in Warsaw, the invisible hand, with those in Moscow, the grabbing hand, in dealing with their respective governments. Warsaw shopkeepers report fewer inspections and fines and less need to bribe officials and to pay for private protection than do Moscow shopkeepers. Frye and Zhuravskaya (2000) expand the findings to include shopkeepers in a set of Russian cities. A very significant aspect of mature democratic governments is the ability to solve this dilemma by having checks and balances, both within the government itself and between governmental and civil organizations.

Necessary Attitudes and Norms

The development of an entrepreneurial economy requires a climate and set of individual attitudes that support this activity. These attitudes must exist among the mass public as well as among those who may become entrepreneurs. It is necessary that the former see entrepreneurship as an important activity and be willing to insure financial and social rewards for those who become successful entrepreneurs. The limited data we have on this point from mass surveys indicate substantial variation among the transitional countries. Jackson and Marcinkowski (1996) report the results of a study of a set of entrepreneurial attitudes in the United States in 1985 and in Poland and Ukraine in 1995. We also have access to responses from surveys in European Russia in 1993 and 1996 that asked some of the same questions. Table 9.6 reports the marginal distributions for a set of these questions.

The overall picture is that the Polish public has a far stronger orientation toward entrepreneurs and entrepreneurial behavior than do Russians and Ukrainians, and in some instances Poles appear to be more entrepreneurially oriented than Americans, at least in 1995 and 1985 respectively.[4] Polish respondents were the most likely to strongly agree

---

4 It would be very enlightening to see a current comparison, as the United States has become far more attentive to the role of entrepreneurship since 1985, while Polish citizens seem to have become less so.

Table 9.6. *Entrepreneurial Attitudes in Four Countries*

Question	United States	Poland	Russia	Ukraine
Risk failure[a]	16	26	18	13
Use savings[b]	48	37	21	21
Entrepreneurs get wealthy[c]	–	35	18	25
Importance of new firms[d]	−0.53	1.06	−2.06	−1.90

[a] Percent strongly agreeing that one should start a business even though it might fail.
[b] Percent saying they would be very likely to use their savings to start a business.
[c] Percent strongly agreeing that those who start a successful business can become richer than other people. Not asked in the U.S. survey.
[d] Importance of new firms in creating jobs minus importance of state-owned firms in creating jobs, both measured on a ten-point scale. U.S. survey asked about entrepreneurs relative to large firms.

with the statement that one should start a new business even though it might fail and rated new private firms as a more important source of jobs than large or state firms. They were also more likely than Russian and Ukrainian respondents to strongly agree that entrepreneurs whose firms created new jobs could become wealthier than other citizens. (This question, unfortunately, was not asked in the U.S. survey.) Only on the question of using savings to start a business did U.S. respondents appear more entrepreneurial than Poles, who were still much more likely to say they would use their savings to start a firm than were the Russians and Ukrainians. Unfortunately we do not have similar data from other transitional countries, but among this set, Poles in 1995 appear to be far more oriented toward and supportive of entrepreneurial behavior than Russians and Ukranians.

THE NECESSITY VERSUS THE SUFFICIENCY OF THESE FACTORS

All the factors just discussed are much more likely to be necessary conditions rather than sufficient conditions. It is not a question of whether it is more important to get the policies or the institutions right or which factor is "most important" – both the policies and the institutions need to be right, along with other factors. We contend after examining the Polish case in detail and briefly comparing Poland with other transitional countries that each factor is likely to be a necessary, but not a sufficient, condition for a successful transition. If we think about these elements in quantitative terms, a very low amount of any one factor is likely to lead to a very low level of success in the transition, regardless of the amounts of other factors. Metaphorically, a transition is like a production function with the output, or success (however measured), given by the quantity of each input, or factor, with relatively little elasticity of substitution between inputs.

Stabilizing the macroeconomy and liberalizing prices and exchange rates in order to stimulate entrepreneurial activity is surely important. But without property rights, effective government and tax policies, and well-functioning institutions, including financial institutions, the reforms are unlikely to succeed, and one is left only with the pain created by the stringent macropolicies. Conversely, we see countries with well-functioning institutions but with the wrong prices or bad macroeconomic policies become economic basket cases. Poland, Estonia, and Hungary by the later 1990s, in contrast to other transitional countries such as Russia and Ukraine and to some extent the Slovak Republic, illustrate these points well. The three successful countries rarely do poorly on any of the factors, except possibly privatization in Poland, but succeeded admirably on almost all of them, and certainly on the important ones. (Privatization is likely not as important a factor as some thought initially. That is our view after looking at the rates of de novo firm creation and also seems to be Kornai's view.) Again, the discussion in Chapter 8 of Poland after 1997 further illustrates our point. The macroeconomic policies remained favorable but some of the institutional factors became problematic, which was followed by a declining rate of new-firm creation, a significant slowing of the aggregate growth rate, rising unemployment, and increasing income inequality.

The argument for the necessity, rather than the sufficiency, of these many factors will certainly be disappointing to some but unsurprising to others. Many in the former group hope to find a small set of tractable solutions for transitional problems, which if implemented will produce the desired results. We believe this hope is naive. For those who view the world in more complex and highly interconnected ways, the challenge is to find ways to recognize this complexity and connectedness while also developing strategies that are likely to move societies toward well-functioning market economies and democratic polities.

THE NEXT CHALLENGE

Poland and several of the countries we have included in these comparisons face another imminent significant economic shock, which will occur as they join the European Union. The basic lessons drawn from the analysis of the transition to a market economy will apply to this transition as well. The issue is not simply whether accession will create or destroy jobs, but how it will transform the economies in the joining countries (and the economies of the existing members, we might add). Any transition, or transformation, will destroy jobs as some enterprises will not be well structured for the new environment, and few economic enterprises have proved to be very adaptive.

At this point the evidence from the transition in the state of Michigan in the United States becomes relevant, not just as an example of the basic Schumpeterian logic, but as an example of an economy forced to adjust to more open markets and wider international competition. (See Jackson et al., 1999, for an explicit comparison of the structures and transitions in the Polish and Michigan economies.) The various economic shocks of the 1970s left the state's major manufacturing enterprises at a serious competitive disadvantage. Their response, as we saw among the former state-owned firms in Poland and the other transitional countries, was to lay off massive numbers of workers as revenues dropped and in an effort to become competitive. The amount of job destruction that occurred in Michigan in the ensuing years is shown in Table 1.3, which as a proportion of the labor force matched that of the transitional countries. The subsequent job creation and recovery in the Michigan economy during the 1980s and 1990s was accomplished through the entry of new enterprises and the expansion of existing small firms, just as we saw in Poland.

Opening the economies of Eastern and Central Europe will be different in that they currently have lower wages so they are likely to attract foreign firms that will want to be a low-cost producer for the European market. But this is likely to create both opportunities and challenges for the existing firms, and opportunities for new firms. How successful these countries are at stimulating the new firms will determine how successfully they manage the transition.

The ability of these economies to stimulate new firms will also affect how these countries adapt to the political pressures that will emerge as a consequence of accession. Some groups in these countries already feel marginalized by the transition to the market economy and often vote for extreme parties in protest. Samoobrona's success in Poland is just one example. The evidence from Poland is that success in creating new enterprises creates a centrist political constituency that inhibits the growth of the more extreme parties.

THE NECESSITY OF SIMULTANEOUS ECONOMIC
AND POLITICAL REFORM

The book started with the puzzle of how to explain the presence of simultaneous economic and political reform, as observed in Poland and some of the other transitional countries. We cited writings published near the beginning of the transition that are pessimistic about this possibility. The hardships of the economic reform would generate an antireform constituency, which if given open access to the political process via the democratic reforms would elect parties that would halt or seriously slow the reforms by returning to soft budget constraints, abandoning fiscal and monetary discipline, and limiting the expansion of the private sector. And that has clearly happened in some countries, but not all. Hence our use of the word "puzzle."

We contend that the answer to this puzzle is the rate of de novo firm and job creation. The narrow version of the pessimistic scenario focused primarily on the privatization process, and the subsequent downsizing of these firms as they struggled with hard budget constraints, foreign competition, and the need to become efficient and profitable. It did not foresee the indigenous de novo sector, its potential for job creation, and its political implications. In a more theoretical piece modeling economic transitions with an endogenous political sector, Jackson (2003) shows that the rate of expansion of the de novo sector is the key to a successful transition. When the rate of formation of new firms is too slow, one gets the pessimistic scenario – unemployment rises and voters support regimes that will continue the subsidies for state firms, hoping to maintain their viability. With a high rate of firm creation the liberal constituency grows at a sufficient rate to provide leverage for the liberal parties, the reforms are maintained, and resources are shifted to the more efficient private sector. The keys to a successful transition in this model are the rate of new firm creation, the degree to which the liberal parties can attract voters from this de novo economy, and how well these parties convert electoral support at the ballot box into seats in parliament, where they can enter the government or at least exert pressure on the governing coalition to maintain the reforms. Under this optimistic scenario the compromises between the various parties, as reflected in the parliamentary coalitions, may slow the reforms, but not to the point where they lead to economic collapse, as has occurred in some of the states of the former Soviet Union.

A rapidly growing de novo sector also decreases the likelihood of falling into the partial reform trap described by Hellman (1998). In this view of the difficulty of reform, insiders capture key positions in the privatized firms, the banks, and the government and then exploit this capture to enrich themselves while simultaneously restricting the entry of enterprises that might reduce their monopoly position and stimulate growth. This model is often associated with Kornai's top-down privatization approach to reform because such privatization does not introduce competition to the large, concentrated enterprises. One possible way to avoid this situation is to break up the large state enterprises, creating smaller and competing firms, although there is still the real possibility of collusion between the managers of the new enterprises, who were formerly part of the state enterprise. A second possible escape route is strong democratic reforms and rapid de novo firm creation. These two actions reinforce each other, with the de novo firms decentralizing the economy; stimulating a liberal, centrist political constituency; and pressuring for a more open government. The EBRD (1999, ch. 6) presents statistics showing a strong negative association between the quality of the governance in transitional countries and the degree of capture by narrow economic interests. This report does not present data that would associate the size and growth of the de novo sector with the quality of governance. The associations we see in Poland and that Frye (2003) reports for Russia on the political views of those working and managing in the de novo sector clearly suggest that the de novo firms create a constituency that desires political and economic reforms, which is likely to lead to a more-open and higher-quality government.

Many of the transitional countries, including Poland, Hungary, the Czech and Slovak republics, Estonia, and Slovenia, demonstrate that it is possible to have simultaneous economic and political reform. These successes can be associated with many historical and cultural factors, such as better experiences with democracy and market economies between the two world wars, closer ties to Western Europe, the presence of stronger religious and other civic organizations, and earlier and more-effective efforts at economic reform within the socialist system. One thread that runs through all these cases, however, is the importance of entrepreneurial activity that generates new entrants to the economy. These new firms are the primary, if not perhaps the only, source of job creation. They are also the stimulus for the development of an economic and political middle class that supports liberal, centrist political parties.

Poland, particularly during the first seven or eight years of the transition, was able to generate a high rate of de novo firm entry, survival, and growth. This propelled the transition to a market economy and built the political constituency that helped pressure parties to maintain the reforms. Why Poland was able to accomplish this feat appears to be the result of the convergence of a number of important factors – good policies, effective institutions, and appropriate norms and behaviors – each of which is necessary and none of which are sufficient to raise significantly the likelihood of success.

Appendix A

Assessing Measures of New and Small Firms in Poland

Obtaining reliable measures of firm creation, survival, and growth is a challenge in any setting but is particularly important and problematic in the transitional countries in East Central Europe. The research reported here is based on a unique dataset prepared jointly with the Research Center for Economic and Statistical Studies of the Polish Central Statistical Office. These data constitute a longitudinal file on the employment, payroll, and sales of firms existing in Poland between 1990 and 1997. This longitudinal dataset is based on the information that firms are required to report to the Central Statistical Office on an annual basis. They have an obvious limitation, however, in that they exclude information on firms that chose not to report or that were not required to report. The first category, those who chose not to report information, covers the so-called gray economy, which was very much in evidence in these countries, although it may be shrinking, in Poland at least (Dzierżanowski, 1999, p. 31). The second category constitutes a more serious concern for this research. In Poland, firms employing five or fewer workers are exempt from filing annual reports with the statistical office. The consequences of this omission could be substantial, as this sector is large, possibly employing as many as 2 million people, and constitutes the critical early stage of the entrepreneurial process. In this extended appendix we want to explore the possible statistical consequences of this omitted information.

There are two considerations in assessing biases introduced by the omission of the very small firms in our data. Obviously, any effort to use these data to estimate the aggregate number of jobs created by new private enterprises will be seriously underestimated. One cannot, therefore, use our data to support statements such as, "the creation of new enterprises was not sufficient to offset the job loss among present and former state-managed enterprises." One must, at least, have some means for extrapolating from the present data to the actual aggregate number of firms and jobs, including the firms with five and fewer employees.

The second type of possible bias is harder to identify though it may be easier to overcome. These are biases introduced into the statistical analysis by having erroneous measures of the size of the new private sector. The magnitude and direction of any bias depend on how our measure correlates with the actual number of firms and jobs in this new sector. In other words, how well do our variables serve as a proxy for the true size of this sector? Obviously we do not have alternative data that measure the number, size, and growth of new firms, particularly those with five or fewer employees, or we would be using them. We do have, however, annual estimates of the number of small and medium-sized enterprises prepared by the Central Statistical Office and published by the Polish Foundation for Small and Medium-Sized Enterprise Promotion and Development. These data are collected from the registry of firms, referred to as the REGON data. Theoretically, firms must register when they are formed. The statistical office uses the registration information to estimate the size of the small and medium enterprise sector, including very small enterprises, defined as firms with five and fewer employees.

The REGON data are reported in different employment size categories: firms with 0 employees, 0–5 employees, 0–50 employees, 51–250 employees, and more than 250 employees. The firms with 0 employees are self-employed individuals who choose to register as a firm. We expect data on this group to be very unreliable given the likelihood of not reporting either at the time of formation or when activity ceases. The latter point, obviously, is difficult to define for self-employed persons, particularly if they have a primary job paying a salary. We group these data into three categories: firms with 0 employees (REGON0), with 1–5 employees (REGON5), 6–250 employees (REGON250), and with more than 250 employees (REGON>250). We will compare statistically the REGON estimates of the number of firms in each size category with the number of firms identified in our data, referred to as GUS>5. These comparisons should offer an idea about how well our data serve as a proxy for the whole sector.

Before we begin this comparison, it is important to acknowledge explicitly the limitations of the REGON data. Obviously firms that choose not to register are not counted, just as they are omitted from our data. Second, and more important, firms that cease doing business are not purged from the data. In theory, firms are supposed to deregister if they cease doing business. In practice, this does not happen. These data, then, could

Table A.1. *Firms per 1,000 Population*

	1991	1992	1993	1994	1995
REGON0	0.58	0.48	0.63	0.83	1.39
REGON5	8.38	18.80	43.32	45.73	43.84
REGON250	2.99	3.70	3.95	4.07	3.97
REGON>250	0.19	0.19	0.17	0.16	0.14
GUS>5	0.49	0.65	0.79	0.87	1.22

not be used for the type of cohort analysis of survival and growth that is at the core of our project. As mentioned earlier, these factors make the data on self-employed enterprises particularly problematic. The REGON data also overstate the number of firms because the data include firms that no longer exist. Lastly, these data do not stratify firms by ownership. This means the REGON data include state-owned firms, which will be a particular problem for the category of firms with more than 250 employees where the foundation report for 1996 estimates that about half the firms in this category are state-owned.[1] Our data, on the other hand, only count firms in the private sector regardless of size.

The first comparisons, shown in Table A.1, are the mean number of firms per 1,000 population from each dataset for the years 1991 to 1995, which is the period for which we have the REGON data.[2] As expected given the basis for the REGON data, the number of firms, even for the category of firms with 6–250 employees, is much larger than with the GUS data. These differences in numbers of firms reinforce the point that our data understate the size of the new private sector. They do not necessary invalidate our data as adequate proxies for the size of this sector, which is based more on how they correlate with each other and what, if any, systematic biases may exist in the data.

Table A.2 shows pairwise correlations across voivodships among the number of firms per 1,000 population. The first set of correlations is between the REGON variable measuring the number of firms in the 6–250 category and the other REGON variables. These correlations provide an idea of how well the REGON variable that is most comparable with the GUS variable correlates with the other REGON size variables. Thus, for a given methodology we can see how well the number of firms of one size correlates with the number of firms of a different size. For our GUS

---

1 The actual proportion estimated to be private was 47.0 percent (Kubisz, 1998).
2 The table shows the mean number of firms per 1,000 population among the forty-nine voivodships.

Table A.2. *Correlations in Firms per Population among Data Measures*

	1991	1992	1993	1994	1995
REGON250 and REGON0	−0.08	−0.06	0.09	0.12	0.19
REGON250 and REGON5	0.78	0.67	0.77	0.77	0.80
REGON250 and REGON>250	0.52	0.71	0.72	0.71	0.76
GUS>5 and REGON0	0.23	0.12	0.14	0.12	0.18
GUS>5 and REGON5	0.68	0.61	0.75	0.79	0.83
GUS>5 and REGON250	0.66	0.80	0.87	0.90	0.91
GUS>5 and REGON>250	0.61	0.77	0.75	0.73	0.77

Note: Variables in log form.

variable to do a good job of serving as a proxy for the full size of the new private sector, the variable for one size category must be highly correlated with the variables for other size categories. The higher these correlations, the more confidence we may have that a measure based on firms with 6–250 employees is related to the number of very small firms, REGON5, which is by far the largest omitted category in the GUS data. These results show a very high correlation between the number of these two different sets of firms, particularly beginning in 1993 when the correlations are consistently above 0.75. Thus, regions with a large, or small, number of medium-sized firms (6–250 employees) are also very likely to have a large, or small, number of very small firms (1–5 employees). The REGON data for medium-sized firms are largely uncorrelated with the number of firms with no employees, except possibly by 1995 when the correlation is 0.19. Lastly, the REGON measure of medium-sized firms correlates well with the measure of large firms (more than 250 employees).

When the GUS and REGON data are compared, there is a very high correlation between our measure of the number of firms with more than 5 employees and the REGON measures of the numbers of firms with between 6 and 250 workers, the most comparable category to the GUS data. From 1993 on, these correlations are about 0.9. This indicates a high intermeasure reliability. Second, the GUS variable's correlations with the REGON measure of very small firms (1–5) are about the same as the correlations between the two REGON variables, particularly in the 1993 to 1995 period. As a proxy for all firms in the REGON data in the 1–250 range, the GUS data perform well.

The last concern is whether there are systematic differences in the variables or whether they are measuring the same phenomena, albeit with purely random error. If we find the latter case, then the GUS variable would be an adequate proxy for the phenomena, and might even be a better measure, depending upon the proportion of measurement error in each variable. We examine the amount of systematic and random error in the measures using a traditional latent variable covariance model. The latent term in this case is the actual number of firms in the new private sector in voivodship i in each year t, which we denote by Y_{it}. We do not observe this variable but instead observe the five different measures of the number of firms – the REGON estimate of the self-employed, the REGON estimate of the firms with 1–5 employees, the REGON estimate of the firms with 6–250 employees, the REGON measure of firms with more than 250 workers, and our GUS estimate of the number of private firms with more than 5 employees. We denote these variables by F_0, F_5, F_{250}, $F_{>250}$, and F_G, respectively. This model has two components. The first is a very simple equation that relates Y_{it} to a set of observed exogenous variables for each voivodship, denoted by X_i. We write this equation in linear form as $Y_{it} = X_i B + U_{it}$. The coefficients denoted by B indicate how the true number of firms is associated with each of the exogenous variables. The variables describing each voivodship are selected to represent a reduced form model of firm creation and survival and are taken from the analysis in Chapter 3. The variables are:

% Farm   percentage of the work force engaged in farming
Density   log of population per square kilometer
% SOE   percentage of the work force employed in large state-owned enterprises (defined as those employing more than 100 workers) in 1990
West   dummy variable indicating voivodships that bordered Germany or the Baltic, and thus had better access to Western markets and foreign firms
Ln(Pop) log of population
Educ   average years of schooling of population older than eighteen
Unemp   percent unemployment in the voivodship

The second part of the model, often referred to as the measurement equations, relates each of the observed variables to Y_{it}, $F_j = Y_{it} A_{jt} + e_{ijt}$. There is one of these equations for each measure in each year. The critical elements of the part of the model are the magnitudes of the coefficients denoted by A and the variances and covariances of the e_{jt}'s. The A's indicate how strongly each measure is related to the true number of firms. The larger the value of A_{jt}, the more F_j varies when Y_t varies. A value of $A_{jt} = 0$ clearly indicates that F_j is not related to the number of firms in

Appendix A

Table A.3. *Fits for Alternative Measurement Models*

Model	Years Included	Chi-Squared	Degrees of Freedom	Probability
1	1991–95	408.72	217	0.000
2	1991–95	219.11	199	0.156
3	1992–95	133.61	159	0.929
4	1991–95	35.59	62	0.997

year t. We denote the variances and covariances of the e_{jt}'s by Σ_e. The larger the variances, the greater the proportion of the measured variable that is error and not related to the true variable. The covariances will be zero if the e_{jt}'s are pure random measurement error and it is unlikely there is some unmodeled systematic factor related to more than one measure.

The estimation strategy is to fit the model for each year (1991–95) with a strong set of constraints. These constraints are that the values for B and the variance of U are identical for all five years and that Σ_{et} is diagonal. These constraints can then be relaxed depending on the fit. The constraints that must be relaxed along with the estimated coefficients will indicate how much of the differences in the variables is likely to be random measurement errors, how close each comes to being an adequate proxy for the unobserved true number of new firms, and finally how much reliance we can put on the GUS data as measures of the new economy. One more factor is included in the basic model to accommodate the fact that the REGON variables include state-owned and state-managed firms as well as private enterprises. If the latent variable does represent the number of private-sector firms, as we hope and assume, then the REGON variables and particularly the REGON>250 variable will contain some systematic bias based on the number of nonprivate firms in a voivodship. To accommodate this bias a variable measuring the number of large nonprivate firms in each voivodship in each year is constructed from the GUS data. (Given the definitions in the GUS data, large here refers to more than 500 employees.) This variable is then included in the measurement part of the model for REGON>250.

Table A.3 shows the summary statistics for each of the models estimated. The table shows the value of the chi-squared statistic measuring the fit of the model relative to the perfect fit of a saturated model, the degrees of freedom of the estimated model, and the probability of obtaining this or a worse fit by chance if the specified model were the true model. For a given number of degrees of freedom, the lower the value of the chi-squared statistic, the better the fit and the higher the probability of getting a worse fit by chance. The actual specification of the different models is presented in the following discussions.

Model 1. This model, covering all five years, with the most stringent constraints, did not conform to the observed data. The probability level indicates there is virtually no possibility of obtaining a worse fit by chance. Clearly, the five observed variables for all years are not consistent with the strict model of only random measurement error and a single latent component representing the number of private firms. Examination of the estimated structure revealed two consistent areas where the model did not fit the data. The variations in the REGON variables measuring the number of self-employed, F_0, and the number of firms with more than 250 employees, $F_{>250}$, were inconsistent with the proposed structure, suggesting that there are likely systematic factors that explain the variations in these variables that are specific to these variables and which differ from the single latent variable measuring the number of firms. The model was altered to include separate components for these two variables, with the constraints that the relationships between these factors and the exogenous variables describing each voivodship are constant over time.

Model 2. This model, with separate factors to explain the observed variations in F_0 and $F_{>250}$, provided a better fit to the observed variables. The statistics suggest we could get a worse fit by chance about 16 percent of the time if the estimated model were the true structure. Even this fit, however much better it is than the fit for model 1, suggests there are some observed outcomes that are inconsistent with the model. Once again examining the model's fit made it clear that the inconsistency was associated with the data for 1991, for all variables. This should not be too surprising, given that this is only two years after the beginning of the transformation. The evidence in Table A.1 indicates that the number of enterprises is still small, so that the distribution of firms among voivodships in 1991 might be quite different from what it becomes in later years as the process proceeds. In addition, one might suspect difficulties both with firms registering and with the data collection and reporting, which would make 1991 a less reliable year to observe this process than later years. The model was reestimated one more time but only for the years 1992–95.[3]

3 This procedure is equivalent statistically to estimating a fully saturated model for 1991.

Table A.4. *Estimated Measurement Model*

Parameter	1992	1993	1994	1995
Coefficients on unobserved # firms				
A_t – REGON0	–	–	–	–
A_t – REGON5	0.854	0.588	0.589	0.678
	(0.163)	(0.067)	(0.064)	(0.066)
A_t – REGON250	0.572	0.675	0.684	0.696
	(0.051)	(0.045)	(0.046)	(0.045)
A_t – REGON>250	0.282	0.076	0.067	0.100
	(0.122)	(0.129)	(0.133)	(0.135)
A_t – GUS>5[a]	1	1	1	1
Variance of random component				
σ_e^2 – REGON0	0.504	0.154	0.218	0.337
	(0.103)	(0.031)	(0.044)	(0.069)
σ_e^2 – REGON5	0.130	0.021	0.019	0.021
	(0.027)	(0.005)	(0.004)	(0.005)
σ_e^2 – REGON250	0.010	0.006	0.007	0.007
	(0.003)	(0.002)	(0.002)	(0.002)
σ_e^2 – REGON>250	0.015	0.014	0.015	0.015
	(0.003)	(0.003)	(0.003)	(0.003)
σ_e^2 – GUS>5	0.021	0.016	0.011	0.009
	(0.006)	(0.005)	(0.004)	(0.003)
Reliability: Random variance as % of observed variance				
REGON0	0.866	0.844	0.740	0.772
REGON5	0.610	0.344	0.324	0.280
REGON250	0.210	0.107	0.122	0.117
REGON>250	0.162	0.152	0.147	0.136
GUS>5	0.154	0.122	0.084	0.069

[a] Coefficient set to 1 to scale the equations.

Model 3. This model had an exceptionally good fit to the observed data. One would expect to obtain a worse fit about 93 percent of the time if this were the correct model. Table A.4 shows the estimated coefficients and standard errors for the measurement part of this model. The two most relevant REGON measures, for firms with 1–5 employees and with 6–250 employees are strongly and consistently related to the unobserved variable that we assume to be the true number of firms.[4] For each unit increase in the unobserved variable, the log of the number of firms with

4 The coefficient relating the GUS measure to the unobserved variable is set to 1 to provide a scale for the model and the unobserved variable. This scaling is arbitrary and does not alter the relative magnitude of the other coefficients.

1–5 employees per capita increases by .6 to .7 while the log of the number of firms with 6–250 workers increases by .7. The number of self-employed per capita and the number of firms with more than 250 workers per capita are not related to this unobserved variable.

The second important part of the results is the estimates of the variance of the measurement error in the key variables and the reliability of the measures, defined as the error term's variance as a proportion of its total variance. These variances indicate that the quality of the measures is increasing over time, as the variances for REGON5, REGON250, and GUS decrease significantly between 1992 and 1995, with the biggest improvements coming between 1992 and 1993. The reliability of these measures also improved over the four years. Lastly, and most important, the GUS variable has the smallest proportion of error in its variations among voivodships, suggesting that it is a better proxy for the size of the new private sector in each voivodship than either of the two key REGON variables.

The second part of the model is the relationship between the exogenous variables describing each voivodship and the unobserved variable and the two variables that were not related to this latent term. The important part of this model is not so much the substantive interpretation of the coefficients, but the question of whether these relationships are stable over time and significantly related to our conceptual variables. These relationships are shown in Table A.5.

The most important aspect of these relationships is only implicit in Table A.5. With the exception of 1991, the same equations fit the data for all four years, indicating that the relationships are very stable over time and that our unobserved variable is very likely representing the same concept each year. The second important result is that most of the standard errors are small relative to the size of the coefficients. This result means that the stable relationships we find are based on coefficients with relatively small sampling variances, lending further credibility to the argument that there is a single underlying stable component to the three primary measures of the private economy.

One last estimation was done and reported as model 4 in Table A.3. The number of firms with 1–5 employees and those with 6–250 employees were combined to create a single variable measuring the number of small and medium-sized firms per capita (defined as firms with 1–250 employees). This variable ought to be the closest possible estimate for the number of firms in the new private sector using the REGON data. The question

Table A.5. *Estimated Models for Number of Firms per Capita*

Variable	# Firms[a]	Log(Self-Employed)	Log(Employment>250)
% Farm	−1.278	2.041	−0.953
	(0.138)	(0.780)	(0.221)
Log(pop/km²)	0.109	−0.101	−0.086
	(0.033)	(0.154)	(0.036)
% Emp in SOEs	−1.116	1.993	1.155
	(0.156)	(0.849)	(0.226)
West	0.122	0.152	−0.025
	(0.037)	(0.173)	(0.039)
Log(pop)	0.032	0.207	−0.019
	(0.037)	(0.177)	(0.037)
Years schooling	0.205	0.424	0.067
	(0.026)	(0.151)	(0.036)
% Unemployment	−0.825	−1.541	−1.216
	(0.263)	(1.272)	(0.296)
Log(large firms/pop)	–	–	0.203
			(0.057)

[a] Latent measure for true number of firms, F_s.

was how these two basic measures compare and how well each might do as proxies for the new private sector. The results indicate that the only difference between the two variables is a small amount of measurement error in each that is uncorrelated with any other components. Even including the year 1991, the fit of the model was excellent. The chi-squared statistic indicated the probability of getting a worse fit by chance was greater than 0.99. All the estimated coefficients were nearly identical to those reported in Tables A.4 and A.5.

The original question was whether and how well the data developed in the project with the Polish Central Statistical Office to build a longitudinal database on firm creation, survival, and growth serve as proxies for the size of the new private sector, despite the fact that firms with 5 or fewer employees are omitted from the data. The only way to test the ability of these data to serve as proxies for the size of the emerging private sector is to compare the distributions of variables developed in the GUS data with the distributions of data measuring the same factor, but from a different data source. We were able to develop several measures of the number of firms in the Polish economy using data collected through the REGON system, which is a registry of firms. These data are collected from a different source and are broken into different sized components, creating a set of variables to compare with the GUS data. The correlations and statistical results presented here offer strong evidence that even though the GUS data exclude the very small firms, they do a very acceptable job of providing a proxy for the total size of the new private sector in each voivodship. In fact, the more closely the REGON data are constructed to measure private firms with employment, the more comparable the two different measures become. The most direct comparison, the differences between the GUS variable measuring the number of firms with more than 5 employees that are privately owned and the REGON variable for the number of firms with 1–250 employees are pure random errors that are uncorrelated with each other and with all other parts of the model. Finally, the GUS measure contains a smaller proportion of these measurement errors and thus should be a more reliable estimate of the size of the new private sector.

We do not have independent estimates of the employment in these different-sized firms so we cannot do a comparison of size and employment. On the critical question of the number of firms, even disaggregated by employment, the GUS variable performs very well, suggesting that these data are likely to be reliable proxies for other aspects of the emerging economy. Consequently, our statistical results analyzing how the growth of the new private sector relates to various factors describing each voivodship and relating election outcomes to the size of the new sector should be reliable. Also any projections of scenarios conditioned by a different level of firm and job creation should be reliable because the high consistency of the statistical results over several years, and particularly in the years 1993 to 1995, suggests that the underlying relationships between the GUS variable and the REGON variables and between these variables and the unobserved variable are very consistent.

References

Achen, Christopher H., and W. Phillips Shively. 1995. *Cross-Level Inference.* Chicago: University of Chicago Press.

Aghion, Philippe, and Olivier-Jean Blanchard. 1994. "On the Speed of Transition in Central and Eastern Europe." *NBER Macroeconomics Annual* 9:283–320.

Aitken, Brian J., and Anne Harrison. 1999. "Do Domestic Firms Benefit from Direct Foreign Investment: Evidence from Venuzuela." *American Economic Review* 89(3):605–14.

Aldrich, John H., John L. Sullivan, and Eugene Borgida. 1989. "Foreign Affairs and Issue Voting: Do Presidential Candidates 'Waltz before a Blind Audience'?" *American Political Science Review* 83(1):123–42.

Alexeev, Michael. 1999. "The Effect of Privatization on Wealth Distribution in Russia." *Economics of Transition* 7(2):449–65.

Amburgey, Terry, and Rao Hayagreeva. 1996. "Organizational Ecology: Past, Present and Future Directions." *Academy of Management Journal* 39(5):1265–86.

Arthur, W. Brian. 1990. "'Silicon Valley' Locational Clusters: When Do Increasing Returns Imply Monopoly?" *Mathematical Social Sciences* 19:235–51.

Arthur, W. Brian, Y. M. Ermoliev, and Y. M. Kaniovski. 1987. "Path-Dependent Processes and the Emergence of Macro-Structure." *European Journal of Operational Research* 30:294–303.

Audretsch, David B. 1995. "Innovation, Growth and Survival." *International Journal of Industrial Organization* 13:441–57.

Balcerowicz, Leszek, Barbara Błaszczyk, and Marek Dąbrowski. 1997. "The Polish Way to the Market Economy, 1989–1995." In Wing Thye Woo, Stephen Parker, and Jeffrey D. Sachs (eds.), *Economies in Transition: Comparing Asia and Eastern Europe*, pp. 131–60. Cambridge, MA: MIT Press.

Benoit, Kenneth. 2000. "Which Electoral Formula Is the Most Proportional? A New Look with New Evidence." *Political Analysis* 8:381–88.

Berkowitz, Daniel, and David N. DeJong. 2001. "Entrepreneurship and Post-Socialist Growth." William Davidson Institute Discussion Paper, University of Michigan, Ann Arbor.

Birch, David L. 1981. "Who Creates Jobs?" *Public Interest* 65 (fall):3–14.

References

Bonaccorsi di Patti, Emilia, and Giovanni Dell'Ariccia. 2004. "Bank Competition and Firm Creation." *Journal of Money, Credit and Banking* 36(2):225–51.

Brainerd, Elizabeth. 2001. "Unraveling the New Russian Enigma: A Study of Age and Cause Specific Mortality across Russia's Regions, 1989–1999." Paper presented at the WDI/CEPR annual conference on Transitional Economies, Portoroz, Slovenia, June 23–26.

Bruce, Donald, and Mohammed Mohsin. 2003. "Tax Policy and Entrepreneurship: New Time Series Evidence." Department of Economics, University of Tennessee, Knoxville.

Brunetti, A., G. Kisunko, and B. Weder. 1997. "Institutions in Transition: Reliability of Rules and Economic Performance in the Former Socialist Countries." World Bank Working Paper. Washington, DC.

Buchtíková, Alena. 1995. *Privatization in the Czech Republic.* Center for Social and Economic Research, Studies and Analyses no. 53. Warsaw.

Caballero, Ricardo J., and Mohamad L. Hammour. 1994. "The Cleansing Effect of Recessions." *American Economic Review* 84:1350–68.

——— 2000. "Creative Destruction in Development: Institutions, Crises, and Restructuring." Paper prepared for the World Bank annual bank conference on Development Economics, Washington, DC, April 18–20.

Carey, David, and Harry Tchilinguirian. 2000. "Average Effective Tax Rates on Capital, Labor and Consumption." OECD Economics Dept., Working Paper 258. Paris.

Carroll, G. R. 1988. *Ecological Models of Organizations.* Cambridge, MA: Ballinger.

Castanheira, M., and Gérard Roland. 2000. "The Optimal Speed of Transition: A General Equilibrium Analysis." *International Economic Review* 41(1):219–39.

Caves, Richard E. 1998. "Industrial Organization and New Findings on the Turnover and Mobility of Firms." *Journal of Economic Literature* 36(4):1947–82.

Central European Economic Review. 1998. "Welcome to the World." 5(10):15–21.

Chan, Kenneth Ka-Lok. 1995. "Poland at the Crossroads: The 1993 General Election." *Europe-Asia Studies* 47:123–45.

Cichomski, Bogdan, and Paweł Morawski. 1999. *Polish General Social Surveys: Machine Readable Data File, 1992–7.* Warsaw: Institute for Social Studies, University of Warsaw.

Cox, Gary. 1990. "Centripetal and Centrifugal Incentives in Electoral Systems." *American Journal of Political Science* 34:905–35.

Davis, Steven J., John C. Haltiwanger, and Scott Schuh. 1996. *Job Creation and Destruction.* Cambridge, MA: MIT Press.

Dewatripont, M., and Gérard Roland. 1992. "Economic Reform and Dynamic Political Constraints." *Review of Economic Studies* 59(4):703–30.

Diewald, Martin, and Bogdan W. Mach. 1999. "Market Transition, Institutions, and the Restructuring of Earnings: East Germany and Poland during the First Five Years of the Transformation Process." Max-Planck-Institut für Bildungsforschung, Berlin.

References

Dzierżanowski, Włodzimierz (ed.). 1999. *Report on the Condition of the Small and Medium-Sized Enterprise Sector in Poland for the Years 1997–1998.* Warsaw: Polish Foundation for Small and Medium Enterprise Promotion and Development.

Elster, Jon. 1993. "The Necessity and Impossibility of Simultaneous Economic and Political Reform." In Douglas Greenberg, Stanley N. Katz, Melanie Beth Oliviero, and Steven C. Wheatley (eds.), *Constitutionalism and Democracy,* pp. 267–74. New York: Oxford University Press.

European Bank for Reconstruction and Development (ERBD). 1999. *Transition Report, 1999.* London.

———. 2002. *Transition Report, 2002.* London.

Fidrmuc, Jan. 1998. "Political Sustainability of Economic Reforms: Dynamics and Analysis of Regional Economic Factors." *Journal of Policy Reforms* 3(2):139–56.

———. 2000a. "Political Support for Reforms: Economics of Voting in Transition Countries." *European Economic Review* 44:1491–1513.

———. 2000b. "Economics of Voting in Post-Communist Countries." *Electoral Studies* 19:197–217.

Fiorina, Morris. 1981. *Retrospective Voting in American National Elections.* New Haven: Yale University Press.

Frydman, Roman, Cheryl Gray, Marek Hessel, and Andrzej Rapaczynski. 1997. "Private Ownership and Corporate Performance: Evidence from Transition Economies." World Bank Working Paper 26. Washington, DC.

Frydman, Roman, Andrzej Rapaczynski, and Joel Turkewitz. 1997. "Transition to a Private Property Regime in the Czech Republic and Hungary." In Wing Thye Woo, Stephen Parker, and Jeffrey D. Sachs (eds.), *Economies in Transition: Comparing Asia and Eastern Europe,* pp. 41–101. Cambridge, MA: MIT Press.

Frye, Timothy. 2002. "Markets, Democracy and New Private Business in Russia." Discussion paper, Department of Political Science, Ohio State University, Columbus.

———. 2003. "Ownership, Voting and Job Creation in Russia." Paper presented at the joint Williiam Davidson Institue and the Center for European Integration conference on the Political Economy of Transition: Job Creation and Job Destruction, Bonn, Aug. 14–17.

Frye, Timothy, and Andrzej Schleifer. 1997. "The Invisible Hand and the Grabbing Hand: Private Shops in Moscow and Warsaw." *American Economic Review Papers and Proceedings* 87(2):354–58.

Frye, Timothy, and Ekaterina Zhuravskaya. 2000. "Rackets, Regulation and the Rule of Law." *Journal of Law, Economics and Organization* 16(2):478–502.

Gentry, William M., and R. Glenn Hubbard. 2002. "Tax Policy and Entry into Entrepreneurship." Graduate School of Business, Columbia University, New York.

Geroski, P. A. 1991. *Market Dynamics and Entry.* Oxford: Blackwell.

Greene, William H. 2000. *Econometric Analysis.* 4th ed. Upper Saddle River, NJ: Prentice-Hall.

References

Grzymała-Busse, Anna M. 2002. *Redeeming the Communist Past*. Cambridge: Cambridge University Press.

Hannan, M. T., and J. H. Freeman. 1977. "The Population Ecology of Organizations." *American Journal of Sociology* 82:929–64.

1989. *Organizational Ecology*. Cambridge, MA: Harvard University Press.

Harper, Marcus A. G. 2000. "Economic Voting in Post-Communist Europe." *Comparative Political Studies* 33(9):1191–1227.

Hellman, Joel S. 1998. "Winners Take All: The Politics of Partial Reforms in Postcommunist Transitions." *World Politics* 50(2):203–34.

Hellman, Joel, S., Geraint Jones, and Daniel Kaufman. 2000. "Seize the State, Seize the Day." Policy Research Working Paper 2444. World Bank, Washington, DC.

House, James, S., Debra Umberson, and Karl R. Landis. 1988. "Structures and Processes of Social Support." *Annual Review of Sociology* 14:293–318.

Jackson, John E. 1998. "Firm Size and the Dynamics in a Market Economy." Paper prepared for the White House Conference on Small Business, Washington, DC. Reprinted in D. Brophy (ed.), *Public Policy and Entrepreneurial and Small Businesses* (forthcoming).

2002. "A Seemingly Unrelated Regression Model for Multiparty Election Data." *Political Analysis* 10(1):49–65.

2003. "A Computational Political Economy Model of Transition." In Jan Fidrmuc and Nauro Campos (eds.), *The Political Economy of Transition: Politics, Institutions and Policies*, pp. 117–38. Boston and Dordrecht: Kluwer Academic Publishers.

Jackson, John, E., Jacek Klich, and Krystyna Poznańska. 1999. "Firm Creation and Economic Transitions." *Journal of Business Venturing* 14(5–6):427–50.

2003a. "Democratic Institutions and Economic Reform: The Polish Case." *British Journal of Political Science* 33(1):85–108.

2003b. "Economic Transition and Elections in Poland." *Economics of Transition* 11(1):41–66.

Jackson, John, E., Jacek Klich, Krystyna Poznańska, and Jósef Chmiel. 1997. "Economic Change in Poland: 1990–94." *Research Bulletin*, Polish Central Statistical Office and the Polish Academy of Sciences, Warsaw, 6(1):7–20. Reprinted in Polish as "Przemiany Gospodarcze w Polsce: 1990–1994," *Studia i Prace*, Zprac Zakladu Badan Statystyczno–Ekonomicznych, Polish Central Statistical Office; and "Rozowój Sektora Prywatnego w Polsce w Latach 1990–1994," *Gospodarka Norodowa* 8(fall):75–82.

Jackson, John E., and Bogdan W. Mach. 2002. "Job Creation, Destruction and Transition in Poland, 1988–1998: Panel Evidence." Paper presented at the annual WDI/CEPR international conference on Transitional Economies, June 20–23, Riga, Latvia.

Jackson, John E., and Aleksander S. Marcinkowski. 1996. "An Analysis of Entrepreneurial Attitudes in Poland" (in Polish). In Krzysztofa Frysztackiego (ed.), *Z Zagadnien Socjologii Stosowanej*. Cracow: Universitas. Reprinted in English in Ewa Hauser and Jacek Wasilewski (eds.), *Lessons in Democracy* (Rochester, NY: University of Rochester Press, and Cracow: Jagiellonian University Press, 1999), pp. 171–200.

References

Jackson, John E., and Ann Thomas. 1995. "Bank Structure and New Business Creation: Lessons from an Earlier Time." *Regional Science and Urban Economics* 25:323–53.

Johnson, Simon, and Gary G. Loveman. 1995. *Starting Over in Eastern Europe: Entrepreneurship and Economic Renewal.* Boston: Harvard Business School Press.

Johnson, Simon, John McMillan, and Christopher Woodruff. 2000. "Entrepreneurs and the Ordering of Institutional Reform." *Economics of Transition* 8(1):1–36.

Jovanovic, B. 1982. "Selection and the Evolution of Industries." *Econometrica* 50(3):649–70.

Jurjada, Štěpán, and Katherine Terrell. 2001. "What Drives the Speed of Job Reallocation during Episodes of Massive Adjustment?" William Davidson Institute Working Paper no. 432. Ann Arbor, MI.

Karatnycky, Adrian, Alexander Motyl, and Amanda Schnetzer. 2001. *Nations in Transit.* New York: Freedom House.

Katchanovski, I. 2000. Divergence in Growth in Post-Communist Countries. *Journal of Public Policy* 20(1):55–81.

Kaufman, Daniel, and Aart Kraay. 2002. "Growth without Governance" *Economia* 3(1):169–229.

King, Gary. 1990. "Electoral Responsiveness and Partisan Bias in Multiparty Democracies." *Legislative Studies Quarterly* (2):159–81.

Kołodko, Grzegorz. 2000. *From Shock to Therapy.* Oxford: Oxford University Press.

Konieczny, Robert. 1996. "Mechanizmy, Ciekawostki i Felery: Ordynacje Wyborcze do Semju i Senatu" (Mechanisms, Curiosities and Failures: Voting Rules for Sejm and Senate). *Rzeczpospolita*, April 3, p. 5.

Konings, Jozef, and Patrick Paul Walsh. 1999. "Employment Dynamics of Newly Established and Traditional Firms: A Comparison of Russia and the Ukraine." LICOS Discussion Paper no. 81. Katholieke Universiteit Leuven, Leuven, Belgium.

Kornai, János. 1990. *The Road to a Free Economy.* New York: W. W. Norton.

———. 1995. *Highways and Byways: Studies on Reform and Post-Communist Transition.* Cambridge, MA: MIT Press.

———. 2000. "Ten Years after 'The Road to a Free Economy': The Author's Self-Evaluation." Paper prepared for the World Bank annual bank conference on Development Economics, Washington, DC, April 18–20.

Krugman, P. 1991. *Geography and Trade.* Cambridge, MA: MIT Press.

Kubisz, Michel. 1998. *Report on the Condition of the Small and Medium-Size Enterprise Sector in Poland for the Years 1996–1997.* Warsaw: Polish Foundation for Small and Medium Enterprise Promotion and Development.

Kwast, Myron L., Martha Starr-McCluer, and John D. Wolken. 1997. "Market Definition and the Analysis of Antitrust in Banking." *Antitrust Bulletin* 42:973–95.

Lewis-Beck, Michael. 1988. *Economics and Elections.* Ann Arbor: University of Michigan Press.

References

Litwack, John M. 1991. "Legality and Market Reforms in Societ Type Economies." *Journal of Economic Perspectives* 5(4):77–89.

Mach, Bogdan W., and John E. Jackson. 2003. "Job Creation/Job Destruction and Voting during Poland's Transiton: Longitudinal Evidence from 1988 to 1998." Paper presented at the joint Williiam Davidson Institue and the Center for European Integration conference on the Political Economy of Transition: Job Creation and Job Destruction, Bonn, Aug. 14–17.

Mendoza, Enrique G., Assaf Razin, and Linda L. Tesar. 1994. "Effective Tax Rates in Macroeconomics: Cross Country Estimates of Tax Rates on Factor Incomes and Consumption." NBER Working Paper 4864. Boston.

Merrill, Samuel, III, and James Adams. 2002. "Centrifugal Incentives in Multi-candidate Elections." *Journal of Theoretical Politics* 14(3):275–300.

Murrell, Peter. 1992. "Evolution in Economics and the Economic Reform of the Centrally Planned Economies." In C. Clague and G. Rausser (eds.), *The Emergence of Market Economies in Eastern Europe*, pp. 35–53. Cambridge, MA: Blackwell.

Nelson, Joan M. 1993. "The Politics of Economic Transformation: Is Third World Experience Relevant in Eastern Europe?" *World Politics* 45(3):431–63.

Neneman, Jarek, and Marcin Sowa. 2001. "Miękki Budżet." *Rzeczpospolita*, Nov. 24.

Nowak, Andrzej, Jakub Urbaniak, and Leszek Zienkowski. 1994. "Clustering Processes in Economic Transition." *Research Bulletin*, Polish Central Statistical Office and the Polish Academy of Sciences, Warsaw, 3(3):43–61.

Pakes Ariel, and Richard Erikson. 1995. "Markov-Perfect Industry Dynamics: A Framework for Empirical Work." *Review of Economic Studies* 10:53–82.

Palacz, Daniel, Andrzej Wojtkowski, and Darius Woźnicki. 2001. "Korupcja i Mechanizmy jej Zwalczania." Stephan Batory Foundation, Warsaw.

Pissarides, Francesca, Miroslav Singer, and Jan Svejnar. 2003. "Objectives and Constraints on Entrepreneurs: Evidence from Small and Medium Enterprises in Russia and Bulgaria." *Journal of Comparative Economics* 31:503–31.

Powers, Denise V., and James H. Cox. 1997. "Echoes from the Past: The Relationship between Satisfaction with Economic Reforms and Voting Behavior in Poland." *American Political Science Review* 91(3):617–33.

Przeworski, Adam. 2001. "Public Support for Economic Reforms in Poland." In Susan C. Stokes (ed.), *Public Support for Market Reforms in New Democracies*, pp. 103–27. Cambridge: Cambridge University Press.

Riker, William H., and David L. Weimer. 1993. The Economic and Political Liberalization of Socialism: The Fundamental Problem of Property Rights. *Social Philosophy and Policy* 10(2):79–102.

Rodrik, Dani. 1995. "The Dynamics of Political Support for Reforms in Economies in Transition." *Journal of Japanese and International Economics* 9(4):403–25.

Roland, Gérard. 1994. "On the Speed and Sequencing of Privatisation and Restructuring." *Economic Journal* 104:1158–68.

2000. Politics, Markets, and Firms: Transition and Economics. Cambridge, MA: MIT Press.

Sachs, Jeffrey. 1992. "Building a Market Economy in Poland." *Scientific American* 265(3):34–40.

Sachs, Jeffrey, and Katharina Pistor. 1997. *The Rule of Law and Economic Reform in Russia.* Boulder, CO: Westview Press.

Schumpeter, Joseph. 1934. *The Theory of Economic Development.* 1911. Cambridge, MA: Harvard University Press. Reprint, Oxford: Oxford University Press Paperback, 1980.

Singh, Jitendra. 1990. *Organizational Evolution: New Directions.* Newbury Park, CA: Sage.

Singh, Jitendra V., and Charles J. Lumsden. 1990. "Theory and Research in Organizational Ecology." *Annual Review of Sociology* 16:161–95.

Slay, Ben. 1994. *The Polish Economy: Crisis, Reform and Transformation.* Princeton, NJ: Princeton University Press.

Stansfeld, Stephen A. 1999. "Social Support and Social Cohesion." In Michael Marmot and Richard G. Wilkinson (eds.), *Social Determinants of Health*, pp. 155–78. Oxford: Oxford University Press.

Stokes, Susan C. 2001. "Introduction: Public Opinion of Market Reforms: A Framework." In Susan C. Stokes (ed.), *Public Support for Market Reforms in New Democracies*, pp. 1–32. Cambridge: Cambridge University Press.

Stone, Randall. 2002. *Lending Credibility.* Princeton, NJ: Princeton University Press.

Taagepera, Rein, and Matthew S. Shugart. 1989. *Seats and Votes: The Effects and Determinants of Electoral Systems.* New Haven: Yale University Press.

Tanzi, V. 1998. "The Corruption around the World: Causes, Consequences, Scope, and Cures." IMF Working Paper no. 63. Washington, DC.

Tichit, Ariane. 2003. "The Optimal Speed of Transition Revisited." Paper presented at the WDI-ZEI conference on the Political Economy of Transition: Job Creation and Job Destruction, Bonn, Aug. 15–17.

Tworzecki, Hubert. 1996. *Parties and Politics in Post-1989 Poland.* Boulder, CO: Westview Press.

Večerník, Jiří. 1999. "The Middle Class in the Czech Reforms: The Interplay between Policies and Social Stratification." *Communist and Post-Communist Studies* 32(4):397–416.

Weigel, George. 1992. *The Final Revolution: The Resistance Church and the Collapse of Communism.* Oxford: Oxford University Press.

Winiecki, Jan. 2000. "Crucial Relationship between the Privatized Sector and the Generic Private Sector in Post Communist Privatization: Determinants of Economic Performance." *Communist and Post-Communist Studies* 33(4):505–15.

World Bank. 1997. *World Development Report, 1997.* Washington, DC.

Zimmerman, William. 2002. *The Russian People and Foreign Policy.* Princeton, NJ: Princeton University Press.

Index

Index

Index

Alastair Smith, *Election Timing*
David Stasavage, *Public Debt and the Birth of the Democratic State: France and Great Britain, 1688–1789*
Charles Stewart III, *Budget Reform Politics: The Design of the Appropriations Process in the House of Representatives, 1865–1921*
George Tsebelis and Jeannette Money, *Bicameralism*
John Waterbury, *Exposed to Innumerable Delusions: Public Enterprise and State Power in Egypt, India, Mexico, and Turkey*
David L. Weimer, ed., *The Political Economy of Property Rights*